1 MONTH OF
FREE
READING

at

www.ForgottenBooks.com

By purchasing this book you are eligible for one month membership to ForgottenBooks.com, giving you unlimited access to our entire collection of over 1,000,000 titles via our web site and mobile apps.

To claim your free month visit:

www.forgottenbooks.com/free596814

ISBN 978-0-483-03103-6
PIBN 10596814

This book is a reproduction of an important historical work. Forgotten Books uses
state-of-the-art technology to digitally reconstruct the work, preserving the original format
whilst repairing imperfections present in the aged copy. In rare cases, an imperfection in
the original, such as a blemish or missing page, may be replicated in our edition. We do,
however, repair the vast majority of imperfections successfully; any imperfections that
remain are intentionally left to preserve the state of such historical works.

(DEDICATED BY PERMISSION TO THE KING.)

CONSTABLE'S MISCELLANY,

VOL. LII.

On the 6th March will appear,

HISTORY OF MUSIC,

ANCIENT AND MODERN.

BY

WILLIAM COOKE STAFFORD, Esq.

EDINBURGH:

CONSTABLE AND CO., 19, WATERLOO PLACE;

AND HURST, CHANCE, AND CO., LONDON.

ORIGINAL WORKS

PREPARING FOR

CONSTABLE'S MISCELLANY.

———————

I. LIFE of SIR WILLIAM WALLACE of ELDERSLIE, with the History of his Struggle for the Independence of Scotland, including Biographical Notices of contemporary English and Scottish Warriors. By John D. Carrick, Esq. 2 vols.

II. LIFE of KING JAMES the FIRST. By Robert Chambers, Author of "The Rebellions in Scotland," &c. 2 vols.

III. The ACHIEVEMENTS of the KNIGHTS of MALTA, from the Institution of the Hospitallers of St John, in 1099, till the Political Extinction of the Order, by Napoleon, in 1800. By Alex. Sutherland, Esq. 2 vols.

IV. LIFE of FRANCIS PIZZARO, and an ACCOUNT of the CONQUEST of PERU, &c. By the Author of the "Life of Hernan Cortes." 1 vol.

V. HISTORY of MODERN GREECE, and the Ionian Islands; including a detailed Account of the late Revolutionary War. By Thomas Keightley, Esq., Author of "Fairy Mythology," &c. 2 vols.

VI. A TOUR in SICILY, &c. By J. S. Memes, Esq. LL.D., Author of the "History of Sculpture, Painting, and Architecture," &c. 1 vol.

VII. MEMOIRS of the IRISH REBELLIONS; including the History of Ireland, from its First Invasion by the English, till the Union with Great Britain in 1800, By John M'Caul, Esq. M.A. of Trinity College, Dublin. 2 vols.

VIII. HISTORY of FRANCE, from the earliest authentic era till the present time. By William Fraser, Esq.; Editor of "The Foreign Review." 3 vols.

IX. A JOURNEY through the SOUTHERN PROVINCES of FRANCE, the PYRENEES, and SWITZERLAND. By Derwent Conway, Author of "A Tour through Norway, Sweden, and Denmark," &c. 2 vols.

LIST OF WORKS ALREADY PUBLISHED.

Price 3s. 6d. each Volume, cloth boards; or on fine paper, 5s.

Vols. 1. 2. 3. CAPT. BASIL HALL'S VOYAGES.

4. ADVENTURES of BRITISH SEAMEN. By HUGH MURRAY, Esq. F.R.S.E.

5. MEMOIRS of LA ROCHE JAQUELEIN. With a Preface and Notes, by SIR WALTER SCOTT, Bart.

6. & 7. CONVERTS from INFIDELITY. By ANDREW CRICHTON.

8. & 9. SYMES' EMBASSY to the KINGDOM of AVA. With a Narrative of the late Military and Political Operations in the Birman Empire.

10. TABLE-TALK; or, SELECTIONS from the ANA.

11. PERILS and CAPTIVITY.

12. SELECTIONS of the MOST REMARKABLE PHENOMENA of NATURE.

13. & 14. MARINER'S ACCOUNT of the NATIVES of the TONGA ISLANDS, in the South Pacific Ocean.

15. & 16. HISTORY of the REBELLIONS in SCOTLAND in 1745, 1746. By ROBERT CHAMBERS.

17. VOYAGES and EXCURSIONS in CENTRAL AMERICA. By ORLANDO W. ROBERTS, many years a resident Trader.

18. & 19. The HISTORICAL WORKS of FREDERICK SCHILLER, from the German, by GEORGE MOIR, Esq. Translator of "Wallenstein."

20. & 21. An HISTORICAL VIEW of the Manners, Customs, Literature, &c. of Great Britain, from the Time of the Saxons, down to the 18th Century. By R. THOMSON, Author of "Chronicles of London Bridge."

22. The GENERAL REGISTER of Politics, Science, and Literature, for 1827.

23. LIFE of ROBERT BURNS. By J. G. LOCKHART, LL. B.

24. & 25. LIFE of MARY, QUEEN of SCOTS. By HENRY GLASSFORD BELL, Esq.

26. EVIDENCES of CHRISTIANITY. By the Venerable Archdeacon WRANGHAM.

27. & 28. MEMORIALS of the LATE WAR.

THE

ISTORY OF CHIVALRY

AND

THE CRUSADES.

BY THE

EV. HENRY STEBBING, M.A. M.R.S.L.

IN TWO VOLUMES.

VOL. II

EDINBURGH:

PRINTED FOR CONSTABLE AND CO.;
AND HURST, CHANCE, AND CO., LONDON.

1830.

CONTENTS.

CHAP. VII.

CHAP. VII. *

CHAP. VIII.

CHAP. IX.

CHAP. X.

CHAP. XI.

CONSTABLE'S MISCELLANY

OF

Original and Selected Publications

IN THE VARIOUS DEPARTMENTS

— OF —

LITERATURE, SCIENCE & THE ARTS

VOL. LI.

CHIVALRY AND THE CRUSADES VOL. II.

EDINBURGH:

**PRINTED FOR CONSTABLE & C? EDINBURGH:
AND HURST, CHANCE & C? LONDON.
1830.**

HISTORY

OF

CHIVALRY AND THE CRUSADES.

CHAPTER I.

DEATH OF GODFREY.—HIS IMMEDIATE SUCCESSORS — ESTA-
BLISHMENT OF THE HOSPITALLERS, THE TEMPLARS, AND THE
ASSASSINS.

A.D. 1099. THE feelings of the Christians in the
West were powerfully wrought upon by the accounts which the crusaders gave of the sufferings
they had undergone, and of the conquests which
had attended their sacred arms. Thousands were
roused by these narratives to seek the means of
proceeding at once to the Holy City ; and several
noblemen were induced, either out of devotion or
a dread of shame, to raise the standard of the cross,
and offer themselves as their leaders. The losses
and sufferings, the desperation and fanaticism, of
these fresh armaments, were as great as those which

had marked the proceedings of the earlier crusaders; and we should derive neither profit nor pleasure from a particular recital of their misfortunes.

Godfrey, having taken the means which have been described to establish order and justice in his dominions, turned his eyes towards the petty states by which they were surrounded, and which still harboured bands of hostile Moslems. Tancred obtained possession of Tiberias; and Godfrey was equally successful in his attacks on Ptolemais, Cæsarea, and Ascalon. Arsur was besieged with less good fortune; and in the assault of this place, the anxious chief coolly devoted to destruction one of his bravest knights, who had been lately left in the town as a hostage. Exposed by the enemy to the fiercest assault of the besiegers, this knight implored them not to commence or continue an attack which must cause his instant death; but Godfrey represented the necessity which compelled him to make the attempt, and added, that he would not desist from the assault to save his own brother. The unfortunate man could say nothing to this, and only begged that his horse might be offered in sacrifice at the Holy Sepulchre. The conflict was then immediately begun, and the besiegers supposed that their fellow-soldier was pierced through and through by their darts; but the Moslem, with a noble generosity which ought to be forever commemorated, removed the Christian from his perilous stand, and nursed him till the wounds he had received were healed; after which he returned to Jerusalem, to the no small surprise of his comrades. * A question here suggests itself respecting this affair, to

* Albert. Aquensis.

which an answer is not easily found;—if the knight above mentioned was left as a hostage, to assure the city of Arsur of its safety, how could it be attacked without a breach of chivalrous faith on the part of Godfrey? for the giving of a hostage was, in fact, a promise of peace; or, if this was not the case, and it was the intention of the politic chief to resume his hostile attempts upon the town whenever it might be convenient, how could he, consistently either with honour or humanity, induce his companion in arms to remain with the enemy? for it was clearly not the opinion of the unfortunate man that he was intended as a sacrifice, to procure the advancement of Godfrey's power.

But the authority of the prince was now about to be assailed in a manner calculated to deprive him of more territory than he could gain by many successful battles. Baldwin from Edessa, Bohemond from Antioch, and Raymond from Laodicea, arrived at Jerusalem shortly after his return from the above expedition. With them came a host of pilgrims from Genoa and Pisa, under the conduct of Dagobert, archbishop of the latter city. Their arrival was greeted by Godfrey and his people with every expression of joy, and they were occupied with feasts and processions during the whole of their stay in the Holy City. The Italian pilgrims conceived at last so great a veneration for the King, that they determined on taking up their abode in Jerusalem, and set themselves with laudable diligence to repair the ruined edifices in the city and its neighbourhood. Dagobert seconded their exertions, but in the meantime carried on a plot to secure his own advancement to the princi-

authority in the state. Assisted by the zeal of his countrymen, and the bad character of Arnold, who then held the patriarchate of Jerusalem, he obtained the appointment to that important dignity; and being a careful imitator of the Pope, his master, lost no opportunity of placing his power upon the strongest basis. The argument universally insisted upon by the Roman hierarchy, that the servants of Christ were entitled to the authority of their Lord, or that those who preached the gospel had a just claim to be rewarded for their humble labours, by kings becoming their tributaries, was successfully employed on this occasion; and Godfrey consented to take an oath, by which he bound himself to be the faithful defender and assistant of the Primate. He also further agreed to give up a quarter of Jerusalem and Jaffa to the possession of the Church, and to declare the patriarch his successor, in case he died without leaving heirs. The submission of Godfrey was followed by that of Bohemond and Baldwin; and these three princes became the willing vassals of the church.

The character which Godfrey bore, as the most devout of men, rendered him a fit subject for the machinations of the ambitious Dagobert; but it was only when a superstitious veneration for his spiritual superiors blinded him, that Godfrey lost any of the firmness which became his station. By the valour which he displayed in all his encounters with the enemy, and by the wisdom of his counsels, he had won the respect not only of his subjects, but of the cities which still continued hostile to his rule. Many of them were induced to yield to him out of regard for his character of justice and moderation, and his name was pronounced with affection through every part of his increasing territory. But his reign was terminated by death, within a year from its commencement; and his subjects, as they deposited his remains on Mount Calvary, wept over him as children over a beloved and affectionate parent.

As soon as the throne of Jerusalem was left vacant, Dagobert insisted upon his right to the inheritance; and a violent struggle commenced between him and the barons, who declared Baldwin, the brother of Godfrey, to be his lawful successor. Messengers were immediately sent, on the part of the Patriarch, to Bohemond, and on that of the barons, to the Prince of Edessa. The former returned with the discouraging tidings that Bohemond, so far from being able to assist the Holy Father in this extremity, was himself a prisoner to the Turks, into whose hands he had inopportunely fallen. Nothing, therefore, remained to oppose the claims of Baldwin; and after a perilous march from Edessa with four hundred knights and a thousand foot-soldiers, that prince entered Jerusalem in triumph. A short and successful expedition, which he made almost immediately after assuming the royal authority, convinced the Patriarch of the uselessness of any farther opposition, and he consented to crown him at Bethlehem. Tancred was the only one of the nobles who refused to acknowledge Baldwin as their sovereign; but his dislike of the Prince of Edessa yielded to the pacific persuasions of his companions; and he was shortly after called to the government of Antioch, left vacant by the captivity of Bohemond.

It would occupy more of our space than we can

spare to recount all the circumstances which attended Baldwin's contests with his neighbouring enemies. He was sometimes successful, but at others exposed to such imminent personal peril, that he was reported to have been slain ; and his trembling subjects awaited in hourly terror the arrival of the Saracens at the gates of their city. One anecdote, however, of these petty wars, we must not pass over. Baldwin, in riding along the banks of the Jordan, after having subdued a party of Arabs, discovered a woman labouring with the pains of child-birth. With a humanity which has been strangely lauded by historians as next to divine, he refrained from slaughtering her, and afforded her some refreshment out of the stores which could be at the moment obtained. Water and fruits were presented to the suffering woman, and a female camel provided nourishment for the infant. Both mother and child were then restored to the disconsolate Arab, who, proving to be a man of great distinction among his countrymen, declared he would never forget the generous conduct of the Christian prince.

Soon after this occurrence, Baldwin was obliged to seek refuge in Ramla, which was every hour in danger of being taken by the enemy. At the moment when his peril and anxiety were at the highest, a message was brought him that a stranger desired to be admitted to an immediate audience ; on approaching the King, who thus addressed him :—" Thou hast acted generously towards a wife who is dear to me, and having saved her life, restored her to her family. I now brave a thousand dangers to recompense this service. The Saracens surround the city into which you have fled for safety. To-morrow it must be taken, and not a single one of its inhabitants will escape death. I come to offer you the means of safety ; I know all the ways which are not guarded ; hasten then, time presses ; you have only to follow me, and before the morning you will be safe among your friends. " The Mussulman had spoken truth, and the prince arrived at Arsur in safety.

But the subjects of the sacred territory were not blind to the hazardous situation in which they were placed. Had it not been for the casual recruits which their little army received from the pilgrims who continued to arrive from Europe, they would have been without any sufficient protection against their enemies. It was with reason, therefore, that complaints were continually made respecting the conduct of the Emperor Alexis. Originally, this prince was bound by no obligation to aid them in their schemes of conquest ; and the conduct of the first crusaders afforded him a sufficient plea for wishing them far removed from his dominions. But he had latterly entered into a solemn engagement with the European chiefs ; and by receiving from them an oath of allegiance, had promised, both by implication and reality, to assist and defend them in their progress.

A union, however, such as this, was not likely to remain unbroken. Craft and policy on the one side, and ambition, enthusiasm, and the love of gain on the other, are bad allies ; and it would be a difficult matter to determine, in a strict compass, the respective justice or dishonesty of the two parties. Alexis, when the complaints of the Europeans reached his ears, made some show of attention to their requests, and paid the ransom of se-

veral knights and noblemen who had fallen into
the hands of the Moslem. But against the states
of the fallen Bohemond he waged almost continual
war ; and when that prince escaped from captivity,
he prepared to defend himself, by assailing the
emperor from the ships of Pisa and Genoa. But
Bohemond was soon reduced to seek protection by
flight; and so narrowly was he watched by the enemy,
that he only succeeded in escaping his vigilance by
concealing himself in a coffin. In Europe, however, he
was received with the most flattering honours. The
King of France gave him one of his daughters in
marriage, and the Pope bestowed upon him the
standard of Saint Peter. Thus supported, he summoned the knights of France and Italy to fight for
him, and the cause of truth, against the faithless
Emperor ; and having collected an army sufficiently numerous, began his march to the East. But
his expectations of conquest were destroyed by
the prudence or superior power of Alexis ; and
having laid siege to Durazzo unsuccessfully, he
shortly after died of chagrin.

The affairs of the Christians were at this time
in the most unpromising condition. Confusion and
distress prevailed in Antioch after the death of
Bohemond ; and it was with difficulty the King
of Jerusalem succeeded in reconciling Tancred—
who had hitherto governed the principality during the absence of Bohemond—and Baldwin du
Bourg, who now claimed it as his possession. The
Prince of Edessa was so reduced in his finances,
that he was obliged, it is said, to promise his beard
as security for some money which he borrowed
for the payment of his soldiers. Jerusalem was
preserved from much of the distress suffered by

these secondary states, by the concourse of pilgrims which frequented it, and still more by the
assistance which it received from the reviving
spirit of commerce. It has been already mentioned how greatly it increased in wealth and importance while its Moslem governors had the prudence
to encourage the mercantile intercourse of its inhabitants with the people of the West. Several
of the sea-ports of Syria had fallen under the successful attacks of the crusaders. The maritime
cities of Italy closely pursued every advantage
which had been gained by their more chivalrous
precursors; and thus, while succours were afforded the latter, without which thousands who escaped the general carnage must have perished, Europe was also benefited by the market which was
opened for her commodities, and the encouragement thus given to her enterprising merchants.

A. D. 1112. Tripoli, Biblos, Sarepta, Sidon,
and some smaller fortresses, were added to the territory of the Christians about this time; and such
was the terror which their successes inspired, that
armies, which seemed fitted to annihilate a force
ten times as numerous, dispersed, without venturing a battle. We must also refer to the same period the death of Raymond, Count of Tholouse,
who fell in the siege of Tripoli, and that of the
noble and generous Tancred, who perished from
wounds received in battle.

The King of Jerusalem, encouraged by the success which had hitherto attended his arms, prepared for wider conquests. The Emir of Damascus afforded him an opportunity of distinguishing
himself against the Turks of Bagdad, who, having
had reason to suspect the fidelity or proper con-

duct of that governor, sent an army against him which was to deprive him both of his principality and his life. Seeing no other means of safety, the Emir applied to the Christians for succour; and with their united strength, they succeeded in driving the boasting forces back to their angry master. After this, Baldwin made an expedition into Egypt, and arrived within three days' journey of Cairo. Having pillaged the town of Pharamia, he returned with the confident expectation of being shortly able to make himself master of the great capital of the Moslems in that quarter of the world. But he was suddenly taken ill, and died; employing his last breath in comforting his weeping friends, and exhorting them to pursue the successes they had obtained, and to bury him beside his brother Godfrey.

A.D. 1118.   Baldwin du Bourg had been nominated by the late King as his successor; but this disposition of the crown was at first disputed by some of the nobles, who desired to elevate Eustache, the brother of Godfrey, to the vacant throne. The opposition, however, was not long continued, and the will of the deceased prince was followed.

Although the kingdom of Jerusalem, with its dependencies, formed a state entirely independent of those which had been founded by Baldwin and Bohemond, no part of the Christian possessions could be exposed to imminent danger, without the rest being endangered likewise; and it was probably owing to the want of a closer union between the rulers of the three principalities, that they were so frequently on the point of falling into the hands of their former masters. The evil effects of a disjointed interest were strongly felt by Baldwin the Second, in the first year of his reign. Antioch was attacked by the united armies of Persia and Syria, under the Prince Ylgazi ; and the Christians, overpowered both by the numbers of the enemy, and their vain terror at some supposed prodigy, were totally routed. The plains of Artesia were the scene of this fearful conflict, which gave to the spot on which it was fought, the appellation of the " Field of Blood." The terrified citizens of Antioch were comforted, however, in the midst of their panic, by the arrival of the King of Jerusalem ; who, having received the benediction of the Patriarch, proceeded at once in pursuit of the victorious Moslems. His arms were attended with brilliant success : the chiefs of the hostile army fled in the midst of the battle ; and he returned to his own territories, crowned with honour, and with the blessings of the people he had delivered.

The assistance which Baldwin had afforded to Antioch, he next endeavoured to extend to the State of Edessa, now suffering under equal distresses. But on this occasion he was less fortunate. The nephew of Ylgazi had taken the Prince of Edessa and his cousins prisoners, and loaded them with irons. Baldwin, soon after his arrival, shared their fate, and his subjects were thrown into the deepest affliction and consternation.

A noble instance of true chivalrous valour was given on this occasion. Fifty Armenians determined to attempt the delivery of the princes from the fortress, in the dungeons of which they were confined. Having gained an entrance under the disguise of merchants, they instantly put the guards to death, broke the chains of the captives, and

from the harbour of Ptolemais, where it had been anchored.

Closely beset both by sea and land, it might have been expected that Tyre would speedily have fallen beneath the attacks of the allies; but the vigilance or bravery of its defenders protracted the siege for several months; and the soldiers of the Christian leaders were beginning to grow weary of their toils, unrecompensed by any of those splendid prizes which they hoped would fall to their lot, whenever the city should be taken. To promote the speedier completion of their design, the Venetians agreed to join the troops in an immediate assault; and in the middle of the sixth month from the commencement of the siege, the town surrendered to the triumphant Christians. Nothing could exceed the delight with which the news of this conquest was received in Jerusalem. Banners were displayed in every quarter of the town; flowers and olive branches strewed the streets; the ringing of bells added to the calm and serious gladness which becomes a religious festival; and the *Te Deum* was chanted with gestures of devout joy.

One of the good consequences of this victory was the delivery of the King from his captivity in Charan, who persuaded the discomfited Moslem to accept a ransom for his liberty. His return to Jerusalem was hailed with the most loyal enthusiasm; and he immediately put himself at the head of his army, and defeated the Turks, who had been making attempts on Antioch. But he did not live long to enjoy his triumphs, or extend the conquests of his people; and, after a reign of twelve years, several of which had been passed in captivity, he died, leaving his throne to Foulque of Anjou, who had married his daughter Melisinda. His life is reported to have been spent in acts of the most humble piety, as well as in deeds of valour.

A.D. 1131. The new monarch of Jerusalem had been led to Palestine, to recover himself from the melancholy with which he was overwhelmed for the loss of his former wife. He came to the crown when the sacred territories were disturbed by internal causes of weakness. The late King had imitated the example of Baldwin the First, and called a council, by the aid of which he endeavoured to improve the state of manners among his people, and repress the disorders which were beginning to destroy the morality of all classes. But the absence of the prince from his dominions, and the unsettled state in which an incessant warfare kept his territories, prevented the re-establishment of order; and Foulque had scarcely ascended the throne, before he was summoned to assist the distressed inhabitants of Antioch, whom civil dissensions, as well as the approach of the Moslems, kept in a continual state of anarchy and peril. By a prudent piece of policy, he restored tranquillity for a time to the distressed state; and having married the defenceless daughter of the late prince to Raymond of Poictiers, left him as the best defender that could be found for her and her subjects. A few years after, Antioch was threatened by the Greek Emperor; but the storm was eluded, and the monarch generously retired from the city, to make a pilgrimage to Jerusalem, from which, however, he was deterred by an inti-

mation which was given him, that he must enter
it not as a monarch, but as a simple pilgrim.

A. D. 1145. Foulque was more than sixty years
old when he was crowned King of Jerusalem, and
of an infirm constitution; and, after a short reign,
in which it is supposed the Christians lost much
of their military vigour, he left his dominions to
his son, Baldwin the Third, at the time of his
father's death only twelve years of age.

As soon as the young prince escaped from the
trammels which his ambitious mother Melisinda
would have placed upon his actions, he exhibited
his want of prudence, and the impetuosity of his
character, by attempting to surprise Bosra, the
siege of which he had been induced to undertake,
by the vain promises of an Armenian stranger.
Opposed in his march by an active enemy, and
suffering under the burning heat of the sun, where
the scanty water-courses had been all poisoned before his approach, he was only able to support the
spirits of his followers by the promise of the rich
booty which it was expected they would find at
the end of their distressing march. The Armenian
who had persuaded him to the enterprise, was the
governor of Bosra, under the Prince of Damascus,
to whose territory it belonged. No difficulty,
therefore, was to be anticipated, if they could reach
the city in safety, and with this encouragement
they patiently supported all the fatigues and dangers of the route. But, to their astonishment and
grief, on their arrival before the gate of the town,
a defiance was sent them by the wife of the governor, who, despising the treachery of her husband,
had summoned the garrison to arms, headed it
herself, and was now prepared to resist the King

of Jerusalem, with his galled and disappointed
troops.

Their retreat was attended with still greater
evils than those which had pursued them in their
approach. The Saracens, not being able to destroy them by a direct attack, set fire to the brush-
wood with which the arid plains over which they
had to pass were thickly covered. The flames and
smoke, which soon enveloped them, filled them with
horror and consternation; their faces and armour
were frightfully blackened; and in expectation of
utter destruction, they besought the Bishop of
Nazareth to pray for heavenly succour. The supplications of the prelate were, it is said, heard.
The wind changed; a knight, mounted on a white
horse, and bearing a red standard, was suddenly
seen at the head of the army; and they at last
reached Jerusalem, rejoicing in their unexpected
and miraculous delivery.

But the most powerful enemy of the Christians
at this time was Zengui, the celebrated founder
of the Atabeck dynasty, and who had established
himself in Mosul, Aleppo, and other Syrian cities,
from whence he threatened the Christians, by the
boldness of his troops, and the skill with which he
led them to battle. The city of Edessa had for a
long time tempted his rapacity and ambition; and
the weakness of the young prince, Jocelin, son of
Jocelin de Courtenay, now afforded him a favourable opportunity for attempting its conquest.

At a moment when the city and its prince were
sunk in a treacherous feeling of security, Zengui
surprised them from their slumbers, and immediately prepared for the assault. What added to
the terror of the inhabitants, was the absence of

Jocelin, with his principal nobles, at his country seat, and succours were in vain looked for, either from him, or any of the distant Christians. The siege was therefore carried on by the Saracens with every certainty of success; but, though scarcely a hope remained to the inhabitants of being long able to hold out, his summons to surrender was proudly rejected. They then prepared themselves, by mutual exhortations, to suffer as martyrs, rather than fall into the hands of the infidel; and in this disposition Zengui found them, when, after a siege of twenty-eight days, he forced the barriers, and entered the city with his victorious army. A terrible massacre followed this event. From the rising of the sun, to three o'clock in the afternoon, the slaughter continued without intermission; and the Moslems celebrated their triumph, as that of Mahomet and his faith, over a race of people who adored a stone, or an empty sepulchre. But the triumph of the chief was of short duration; and he perished by the hands of his slaves, soon after he departed from Edessa.

The death of Zengui encouraged Jocelin to attempt the recovery of Edessa; and having collected some of his most faithful followers, he succeeded in making his way into the city during a dark night; and, opening the gates to the rest of his party, he regained possession of his capital. But the attempt, though thus far successful, threatened them with immediate ruin. Nourredin, one of the sons of the late conqueror, suddenly appeared before Edessa. The messengers which the prince had sent to implore the aid of the Christian brethren had not been prosperous in their mission; and he found himself enclosed in a place which, being unpro-

vided with the necessary means of defence, served
as a prison, in which he and his companions were
prevented from escaping the fury of their enemies,
rather than as a fortress, in which they had any
chance of resisting his attacks.

In this state of despair, no hope of safety appeared to present itself, but in an attempt at flight.
Means were therefore immediately taken to render the enterprise as safe as circumstances would
allow. In the middle of the night the gates were
silently opened. The impatient multitude hastened forth, followed by Jocelin and the soldiers,
and made the best of their way towards the camp
of the enemy. But before they had left the city
a sufficient time to allow of their escape through
the slumbering ranks of the besiegers, the Saracens, who had retained possession of the citadel,
were roused by the trampling of the fugitives,
and, calling to arms, instantly pursued them. Nourredin, by this time apprised of what was going
on, rushed upon the Christians with the foremost
of his troops, and rage and despair prevailed on
every side of the gloomy battle-field. The darkness of the night, however, greatly assisted the
Christians, whose little band of warriors would
otherwise have been crushed under the numerous
forces of the Moslem. Having succeeded in forcing a passage, several of the fugitives fled into the
neighbouring plains, but were pursued and slaughtered by the enemy; so that before the conflict
was ended, thirty thousand Christians had perished
in the contest for Edessa, and no less than sixteen
thousand been made prisoners. Nourredin banish-
ed all who remained in the city, and destroyed its
citadel, its ramparts, and churches.

Our attention must now be directed to the rising influence of the Hospitallers and Templars, who, by uniting in the closest manner, all the duties of monks with those of warriors, became the foremost supporters of the Holy State. The origin of these orders is traced back to the year 870, when a monk named Bernhard instituted an hospital in the valley of Jehosaphat, near the church of Saint Mary, for the reception of pilgrims from the West. This edifice was gradually enlarged through the succeeding centuries, and became an extensive monastery, to which the piety of its inhabitants added another hospital for their poor brethren, and dedicated it first to St John, the Patriarch of Alexandria, and subsequently to St John the Baptist.

About the time when Jerusalem was first recovered from the Saracens, Gerhard of Provence arrived in the Holy City and determined to devote himself to the service of his fellow-believers in the hospital of St John. But so great was his charity, that he extended it even to unbelievers, and every tongue spoke the praises of his incomparable benevolence. Several young cavaliers united themselves with this excellent man; and, separating from the monastery which confined their exertions within too narrow a circle, they took a particular vow, and assumed a black habit, with a white cross worked upon the breast, as the garment of their order. With the most faithful devotion to their office, they relieved the poor, attended the sick and wounded, and supported the infirm, wherever they were to be met with. Their self-denial and patience of fatigue aided them in their benevolent pursuits; and when Godfrey saw the good they were every where diffusing by their pious labours, he bestowed upon the order the rich lordship of Montboire in Brabant. Baldwin also bestowed upon them a part of the booty which he obtained in his victories over the Moslems; and by these gifts and those of succeeding princes, the Poor Knights of Saint John acquired possessions of great value and extent. The order, consequently, was shortly after established in Europe; and several houses dedicated to its service were erected in Sicily, Spain, and various parts of Italy. But with the possession of wealth, it lost its primitive simplicity and usefulness; and by a bull of the Pope, which freed it from subjection to the Patriarch of Jerusalem, room was made for the introduction of corruption and misrule.

Gerhard died in the reign of Baldwin the First, and Raymond Dupuy was chosen to succeed him as chief of the order. The disposition of the new master was less mild and humble than that of the founder; and having remodelled the statutes, to which he added many new obligations, he made it a part of the Hospitallers' duty to fight against the infidel as well as attend the sick. But his laws' were marked by great severity; and the discipline which he inculcated was fitted to raise the dignity, and support the pretension of the order. To those of the brethren who performed the functions of religion, he gave directions that they were to perform all their offices in white garments, and exercise their duty with becoming seriousness and regularity. The Grand Master, who possessed a general authority over all the affairs of the order, was to be obeyed in the most uniform manner; and to him it belonged to preside in the supreme council, in which he had two votes, and to appoint all the officers concerned in the affairs of the so-

ciety, whether in Palestine, or in any of the states
of Europe. With regard to the common members
of the order, they were forbidden to wear any
costly raiment, especially the skins of wild beasts;
in which prohibition, it seems probable, allusion
was made to the passion which had long existed
among persons of rank for rich and expensive furs.
In their journeys, they were directed to travel two
or three together; but to choose their companions,
not according to their private likings, but as their
undertaking might be best promoted by their associates. When they came to any place in which
there was a house belonging to the order, they
were obliged to take up their lodgings with the
brethren, be content with whatever fare was set
before them, and not wander about to seek any
better accommodation. A curious direction is
also added to the above, namely, that they should
each of them provide himself with a light, which
he should take care to keep burning during the
night near where he slept, lest his life might be
put in danger by the wicked enemy. The errors
into which any of the brethren might fall, were
punished with the severest penances; and bread
and water were, during a certain time of their mortification, the only nourishment allowed them. The
general habit of the order has been already mentioned; but soon after its assuming a military character, those who engaged in war were allowed to
wear a scarlet surcoat, with an embroidered cross
of silver.

A. D. 1119. While the Hospitallers, or Knights
of Saint John, were rising into power and distinction, another order of a similar nature was gradually preparing to rival it, both in splendour and

influence. Among the many brave knights who had followed Godfrey to Jerusalem, there were nine whose deep piety and fervent devotion to the cause of the faithful acted as a strong incitement to their uniting with each other in strict and affectionate friendship. Hugo of Payence, and Godfrey of Saint Omer, were at the head of this little band of pious warriors ; and they bound themselves by a vow to pass a life of chastity and humiliation ; to fight for the protection of the objects which claimed their veneration ; and travel through the most dangerous and least defended parts of the Holy Land in furtherance of their devout profession. In the reign of Baldwin the Second, when a great number of other knights professed their desire to associate themselves with these noblemen, the society subjected itself to the rules of Saint Augustine ; and the King, in order to encourage an institution so calculated to increase the glory of his reign, and assist in the general advancement of the Christian cause, gave the members of the new establishment a part of his palace for their residence ; and this being near the Temple of Solomon, they thence took the title of *Knights of the Temple,* or *Templars.* Many valuable benefactions soon increased the power of this order. Foulque, Count of Anjou, had so high an esteem for it, that he contributed yearly thirty pounds of silver to its support. Many other noblemen showed an equal desire to contribute to its splendour and usefulness ; and it continued to increase in importance, till it was doubtful whether the valour, or the pride and luxury of its members, were the greater.

. The manner in which these monks of chivalry were introduced to their order, recalls to our recollection what has been already said respecting the ceremonies generally performed at the admission of any chevalier to the honour of knighthood. But, in the present case, the spirit of the warrior was entirely subjected to the vows of the religionist; whereas, in others, it was allowed as much freedom as it could desire, if they were ready to assist the church in its particular extremities.

When a noviciate was to be admitted to the order of the Templars, the chapter of the society met during the night in some church or chapel; and the customary rites having been performed, the knight who presided sent two of his brethren to demand of the candidate, if he desired to be admitted into the order? This message was three times repeated; and the novice having, in return, asked for bread and water as many times, he was introduced to the assembly of the brethren, and the president then addressed him in this manner: " The perils which you will have to meet, in pursuance of the vows you are about to take, are many and imminent. The rules of our order, also, are severe and strict. You will have to suffer hunger and thirst, when you desire to eat and drink; to watch when you wish to sleep, and to pass into another country, when you desire to remain in the one where you are dwelling." Having thus warned him of the hardships to which he would expose himself, by becoming their associate, the chief continued: " Is it your desire to become a knight of this order? Are you sound of body? Are you married, or under an engagement of marriage? Do you belong to any other order? Have you any debts which you or your friends are not able to pay? If the answers to these inquiries were such as satisfied the chapter, the candidate was next called upon to take the following oath :—" I swear to devote my conversation, my strength, and my life, to defend the faith of one God, and the mysteries of the Gospel. I promise to be submissive and obedient to the Grand-master of the order. Whenever the Saracens shall attack any possessions of the Christians, I will pass the seas to deliver my brethren. I will render the aid of my arm to the church and to kings, in battle against the infidel. Whenever I am opposed by but three enemies, I will combat with them, and never flee; I will contend with them alone, if they be infidels."

The duties which the Templar imposed upon himself by this oath, rendered him, if religion could in any instance be propagated by the sword, the most faithful missionary the church ever had. The foundation of all his other obligations was, to war without ceasing against the disbelievers; and so strongly were they bound to consider this by the exhibition of the highest Christian virtue, that they were not permitted to proceed to battle without having taken part in the celebration of the most holy ordinances of religion.

The influence of these orders upon the affairs of Christendom, was as prejudicial both to private and general piety, as it was favourable to the schemes of a corrupt church. When chivalry was first instituted, it may be argued with justice, the power which the ministers of religion acquired over the turbulent spirits of the age, contributed to restrain their violence within narrower limits, and to soften many of the barbarous usages of war. But here religion, or the voice of her ministers,

was in opposition to that of the men who delighted in blood and violence. It consecrated their
swords, only that it might prevent their being
drawn, when truth and justice manifestly forbade
the conflict; and, if it sometimes roused the warrior to battle, its commands were always mingled
with some sentiment that gave at least an outward
grace of humanity to the valour and desperation
of knightly prowess. But when the church began
to regard the sword as her rightful weapon against
the infidel, and taught the bloody doctrines of war
as a part of her ritual, the most cruel dispositions
of man's nature seemed better aids to salvation than
the purest breathings of the spirit; the blood of
his Saviour was hardly more efficacious in the
work, than that which he made to flow from the
heart of the disbeliever; and the best sign which
he could give of faith, and all the graces which
should accompany it, was the joy he felt in trampling to death the miserable objects of his wrath.

    Much, of course, must still have depended on
the personal dispositions of the individuals who
composed the religious orders of knighthood. Humanity is not easily perverted by rules which con-
tradict its laws; and many instances were no
doubt continually occurring, in which these champions of Christendom, who, by the laws of their
society, were to suffer degradation if they withdrew their hand from the work of destruction,
manifested a love of mercy, and only the generous
virtues which belonged to chivalry in its purest
forms. But in theory, the principles upon which
the military orders of the church were established,
struck at the heart of all that was good and excellent in her profession, and converted the bra-

very of soldiers into the savage cruelty of fanatics. What was to be expected from such a system? In a short time, the feelings exhibited by the founders of the institutions, men of pious and enthusiastic, but humble dispositions, were no longer to be seen exercising any influence over their disciples; pride and licentious luxury rendered their vows of poverty, and every rule of their discipline, a mere mockery; continual and destructive contests were waged between the members of the one, and those of the other fraternity; and before any very long period was past, the church itself was obliged to take into consideration the scandalous vices of which its warlike children were accused of committing.

In the establishment of the monkish orders of chivalry, the principles in which chivalry itself commenced reached their full and most perfect development; they had triumphed completely over every barrier to their diffusion. In the first stage of their progress, they had created a religious soldiery; in the second, and more remarkable one, they raised up a military priesthood. The flower of European knights took upon themselves the vows of a monastic life, renounced every object of hope or ambition which was not in common with those of their order; and, retaining all their passion for war, wild adventure and desperate daring, were subject to a discipline of self-denial, penitence, and humility, which might vie in strictness with those of any of the purely religious fraternities. The eloquent preacher of the Second Crusade described them as in every way answering to what was to be expected from a society composed according to the strictest rules of ecclesiastical dis-

cipline. " They live," he said, " without having
any thing as their own, not even their will. Simply clad and covered with dust, their countenance
appears burnt with the heat of the sun, and is
haughty and severe. When they approach to battle,
they arm themselves with faith inside, and with
fire outside ; their courage is unshaken in danger,
and they fear neither the strength nor the number
of their enemies.   They place their whole trust in
the God of armies ; and in fighting for his glory,
they seek a certain victory, or a holy and honourable death.

But it may reasonably be doubted whether chivalry did not suffer greatly by this union of its
light and brilliant spirit, with the strange and unnatural institutions of which we are speaking. Its
gallantry, its gay and festive bearing, its courte-
ousness and grace, were changed for severer characteristics ; but in most cases they were bartered
for only an affected severity of manners, and thus
knighthood lost its best and brightest principle,
the devotion to truth—its fearless and constant
following of what was esteemed generous and memorable. Bound to the observance of rules which
they were continually tempted to violate, they at
last became schooled in the same arts of hypo-
crisy as their ecclesiastical predecessors ; and the
proud, noble-hearted knight, learnt to look with
little horror on a species of trickery which it ill
became a fearless and honourable knight to practise. By giving him, however, a rubric for his
guide, instead of the pure and simple precepts
which had hitherto been deemed sufficient to carry
a knight through all temptations and difficulties,
the feeling of personal responsibility, and the su-

finement and delicacy of honour, founded on personal feeling, were greatly weakened; and a cold and formal observance of chivalrous maxims supplied the place of that willing service which had been yielded by the primitive knights, and in the days of their freedom.

This is a most important epoch in the history of chivalry; and it is deserving of a much longer consideration than can be here given to it. The power which the Roman Pontiffs acquired by the institution of military orders of churchmen, was of the utmost consequence to their security and grandeur. While the Christians of Palestine rejoiced in the increase and establishment of champions in whom they had reason to place the utmost confidence, Europe had another chain forged for her by the same occurrence; and the free diffusion of truth was rendered more distant than ever by the boldness with which the great spiritual oppressor of the nations was now enabled to defy all enemies whatsoever. The influence of the powerful combination thus effected between the church and the chivalry of Europe, was not, it is true, immediately taken advantage of; but the discovery of what might be performed by such a union was early made, and no means were left unemployed by the Court of Rome to pursue the prize which seemed offered to its eager grasp. It is impossible to measure the exact extent to which any one event influences those which follow; but it is not unlikely that the tyranny of the Popes would have been destroyed centuries before it was, had it not been for the principle introduced at the time of which we are speaking; the principle, namely, of making avowed religionists of the men

who could best fight for the interests of the church.
It is also equally probable, that the doctrine, which
made it an act of the greatest devotion that a
churchman could perform, to slaughter as many
Moslems as he was able, afforded no slight nourishment to the furious spirit of persecution, which,
a few centuries after, poured itself out, like a vial
of wrath, upon the states of Europe. It had been
declared by the authority of popes and cardinals,
that the sword ought not to be sheathed while disbelievers were in the way of the church, or opposed the conquering progress of her sons. The
right, in a word, of blood-shedding had been le-
galized by the most sacred of princes, and of blood-
shedding from motives purely religious or ecclesiastical. When circumstances therefore arose, which
turned the attention of the church towards heretics instead of infidels, or rather towards those of
its own community, who hated its corruptions,
it made no hesitation in dooming the offenders to
destruction ; it had familiarized itself to the slaughter of its opponents ; and there was nothing strange
in the sight of blood, so long as it flowed from
men who disbelieved in its pretensions to universal power, and infallible righteousness.

It was about this period, also, that the great
theatre of Christian conflict had another set of actors upon its stage.   We can but barely allude to
that extraordinary people, the Ismaelians of Persia
and Syria, or, as they are more generally termed,
the Assassins ; but Oriental antiquarians have a-
greed in describing them as a race of fanatics, of
whom it is difficult to say whether they were more
remarkable for their desperate acts of valour, or
their devotion and attachment to their chief. They

had their origin in the multiplied disputes which a-
rose among the disciples of Mahomet, almost the
moment he expired, and acknowledged as their founder, Hassan, the son of Sabbah, a native of Cho-
rassan. Soon after the first Crusade, they established a colony between Tripoli and Tortosa;
and to the chief of this band, the Christians gave
the appellation of the *Old Man of the Mountains*.

The adventurous enterprises which were undertaken by the followers of this prince, surpassed
the wildest achievements of the knights of Christendom; and no instance can perhaps be found
of such a complete prostration of self-will and
reason to the command of another, as was exhibited by the subjects of the *Old Man of the Mountains*. From his ten castles near Mount Libanus,
he diffused terror, by the fame of his exploits, over
Europe as well as Asia. He had only sixty thousand subjects; but they were armed with daggers,
which, at the signal of their chief, they were ready
to plant in the hearts of monarchs on their thrones,
and to make their way through the most fearful
perils to effect their object. The means which he
had employed to gain this complete ascendancy
over the minds of his people, were appeals to the
imagination, which it only required a belief in his
divine mission to render omnipotent. Paradise
was seen opening its golden portals to the faithful
missionary of his will; and that hope might not
grow sick with too long an expectation of delight,
the passage was spread with the real luxuries of
life. When the appetite was in danger of flagging,
it was stimulated by delicious liquors; and in the
moment of intoxication, the objects most calculated to inflame desire were presented before the

deluded votary, as evidences to the truth of the prophet's doctrines.

By these artifices the Ismaelians were alike prepared to serve their chief, whether he called them to the banquet or the battle-field; whether to listen to his promises of felicity, or undertake the secret destruction of his enemies. The inventions which they employed to effect their purposes were frequently as remarkable as the courage necessary for the execution. They professed any religion, when it might serve to assist their designs; travelled under every variety of disguise, and introduced themselves into houses and palaces, as professors of all kinds of learned arts. A curious instance of this facility in personating the character required, is related by M. Jourdain. A celebrated Persian doctor, says he, was accused of secretly inclining to the doctrines of the hated Ismaelians. To clear himself of an accusation so dangerous to his reputation and his life, he mounted a pulpit, and publicly declared his innocence, by pronouncing several maledictions against the sect. Information of this occurrence having been conveyed to the chief of the Assassins, who had emissaries ready to give him intelligence of whatever was done by his most distant friends or enemies, he charged one of his faithful guards with the duty of taking revenge on the learned Persian.

The Ismaelian having gained an introduction into the house of his intended victim, continued there seven months, no opportunity occurring in that time to aid him in his purposes. One day, however, being alone with the doctor, he suddenly fastened the doors of the apartment, drew his dagger, and precipitating himself upon the asto-

nished Persian, held him down by sitting on his
breast. The doctor demanded the reason of this
violence, and the Assassin replied, " I intend to
rip thee up from the navel to the breast. "—" For
what reason ? " said the Persian ; and he was informed that intelligence had reached his master
of the curses which he had publicly pronounced
against the Ismaelians. Without hesitation, the
doctor denied having spoken willingly against
them ; and the Assassin, freeing him from his grasp,
said, " I had no order to kill thee ; if it had been
otherwise, I should not have delayed or failed
to do it. Know, now, that Mohammed salutes
thee ; he desires that you would honour him by
coming to his castle ; you will then become an
all-powerful governor, for he will obey thee blindly."
To this strange salutation he added, " We reckon
as nothing the discourse of the people. Their
insults have no effect upon us ; but for you,
you ought not to speak against us, or to censure
our conduct ; for your words imprint themselves
in our hearts, as the lines of the graver on the
stone. "—" It is impossible, " replied the doctor,
" that I should go to the castle ; but I will willingly promise to speak no more in a manner that
may be displeasing to your sovereign. " At hearing which, the Assassin drew from his girdle three
hundred and sixty pieces of gold, and said, " Behold your pension for a year ; and it has been resolved by the *sublime divan* that you should every
year receive a like sum. I have also with me two
robes of yemen, which your domestics must take, for
our master sent them for you. " Having said this,
the Ismaelian instantly disappeared, and the doctor

continued for several years to receive the promised
pension. *

The terror with which the Old Man of the Mountains inspired his enemies, rendered him a valuable
ally; and his assistance was often sought by monarchs, who found the power and wealth of a kingdom unable to effect what the chief of the Ismaelians could perform by a word. The Christian
princes did not disdain to employ his resources
against their foes; and as there was a bitter enmity existing between the tribe of the Assassins
and the Turks of Syria, the former were not unwilling to unite with the crusaders in their assault
on the Mussulman cities. To Baldwin the Second
they offered to give Damascus, which they agreed
to assist him in surprising, in exchange for Tyre;
but six thousand of them fell in the defeated
scheme. Paneas, however, was delivered up to the
Christians by an Ismaelian governor; and the
prince of Mouseul was murdered in the middle of
a mosque, to do them pleasure.

But to return to our narrative: The fall of
Edessa filled the inhabitants of Jerusalem and the
other Christian cities with dismay. It formed,
with Antioch, the strongest barrier which they
possessed against the power of the Moslem; and
when they heard of its destruction, they wept in
despair, as if the enemy might be hourly expected
at their gates. The military spirit which had
glowed so fervently in the first year of their conquest, lost much of its ardour as the nobles began
to settle themselves in their several possessions:

* Lettre à M. Michaud, sur les Assassins, par M. Amed.
Jourdain.

and the infirmities of Foulque of Anjou, by preventing him from pursuing his advantage with the
vigour of more active princes, contributed to hasten
the decline of martial prowess. The Templars
and Hospitallers had, it is true, arisen as the champions of the faith; but they were not yet sufficiently numerous to stem the torrent which seemed ready to pour down on all sides from the high
places of Mahometan power. With the successes
of the valorous Zengui, the Moslems recovered
their hopes, and began to regard the Christians as
less invincible than they had hitherto conceived
them to be. The concord, also, which several of
the Mahometan chiefs found it necessary to encourage among themselves, contributed greatly to
augment their force, and make it more formidable
to their former conquerors. None of these circumstances escaped the attention of the Christians,
who, having once lost the enthusiastic idea of their
invincibility, fell at once into the most gloomy
despondence. Miraculous signs in the heavens,
which invariably presented themselves, when either success or misfortune wrought much upon the
feelings of the faithful, added to the general notion
of some great and imminent peril; and the Church
in the East again cried for succour to the princes
of Europe.

CHAPTER II.

SAINT BERNARD—THE SECOND CRUSADE.

A.D. 1147.   FORTY-EIGHT years had now passed since the Holy City had been made the prize
of Christian courage.   During that period, it had
been threatened with many calamities, as the capital of the sacred territory, but it was still unshaken.
The excitement, in the mean time, which had first
roused the Christians of Europe to undertake its
delivery, continued unabated ; and thousands who
had before been deterred by their dread of the infidel from attempting the journey, now dared to
look forward, with devout anticipation, to the peace
they should win while worshiping at the sepulchre
of the Saviour.

It was with feelings of the deepest consternation, therefore, that the faithful heard of the success which attended the arms of the Saracens.   A
fearful apprehension pervaded the Christian world
that Jerusalem, with all its venerable edifices, so
lately reconsecrated by the prayers of the believers, was again about to fall a sacrifice to the
Moslem.   In the meantime hospitals had arisen,
and bands of holy men established themselves a-
round the sepulchre of the Saviour, to worship him
by their deeds of charity, as well as prayers.

Churches and monasteries invited Christians from all quarters of the world to enter their wide-spread portals; and the remembrance of how much had been done and suffered by the faithful soldiers of the Cross, gave the sanctity of a martyr's grave to the whole land of Palestine.

Thus glorious, both in its present as well as ancient state, every report of its danger was regarded by the most zealous of the Western Christians, as a summons to renew the contest with the infidel. There were many circumstances in the situation of the European princes favourable at this time to the project of a second crusade. Their characters were, for the most part, rendered impetuous by a love of war, and the haughty spirit of independence; but the church, either by its laws or its authority, held them in close subjection to her will; and, from the two opposing principles thus kept in constant operation, feelings were created which fitted the proudest and most powerful nobles for a warlike pilgrimage.

In commencing the history of the second great expedition to the Holy Land, a new set of actors present themselves to our notice; and we are interested by observing the strong likeness which exists between the different generations of enthusiastic devotees who wrought in the same field. Urban, the politic instigator of the former crusade, had been long dead; and Eugenius the Third was now on the Papal throne. According to the ancient historian,[*] he was filled with the most pious desire to promote the glory of God; and having a paternal solicitude for his afflicted children in the

* William of Tyre.

East, he formed the design of summoning the faithful to undertake their cause. The situation of Eugenius at this period afforded some reason for his desiring to excite a spirit of enthusiasm in Europe. His tranquillity had been disturbed, as well as Urban's, by the pretensions of an anti-Pope; and a busy spirit of sedition and heresy was abroad in several quarters of the Pontifical States. Nothing could be so well adapted to destroy this dangerous inclination to disunion in the church, as an enterprise, which, by engaging personal ambition or vanity on the side of devotion, might revive the flame, and restore them to obedience. It is not improbable, that the Roman See would have lost its power over the churches of Europe long before the great revolution which stripped it of so much of its authority, had it not been for the crusades. An opinion of this kind seems to have existed in the minds of the Pontiffs, who exerted their influence so strenuously in their favour; and the finest and most favourite stroke of policy in these spiritual rulers during the middle ages, appears to have been the subjecting of princes so to the power of the church, that they must either break with it, and so be fit objects for its anathemas, or yield to its penances, and be the foremost in supporting the views which might best serve its intentions.

But the most remarkable of the personages with whom we have now to do was Saint Bernard. This celebrated man was born of a noble family of Burgundy. His mother was conspicuous for her piety and benevolence; and the disposition of this her favourite son was in accordance with her own mild and devout temper. From his earliest age, he de-

lighted in solitude and reflection ; and his medita-
tions were attended even in youth with celestial
visions. On one Christmas evening, after he had
been long reflecting on the mystery of the incarnation, and other sacred subjects, he beheld our Saviour in a dream, as if still in his mortal infancy ;
and the sight so charmed him, that he thenceforth
could think of nothing, but how to serve God in
the best way he might.

After various doubts and temptations, he formed
the determination of entering the monastery of Ci-
teaux. This resolution he shortly after communicated to his brothers and several friends ; and so
delighted were they by his persuasive eloquence,
that they resolved, to the number of thirty, to forsake the world, and unite with their friend in de-
voting themselves to a life of holiness. Only one
of the saint's brothers remained behind with their
aged father, who had some time before lost his
wife ; and when they bade the child farewell, tell-
ing him that they left him to enjoy all the wealth
of the paternal house, for that they were going to
seek a heavenly inheritance, he told them that the
change would be an unfair one for him, and soon
after followed them, and assumed the habit of a
monk.

The pious exercises and continual austerities to
which Saint Bernard subjected himself, rendered
him in a short time the wonder of the society to
which he belonged, and his reputation spread far
and near. His food was, both at this and in the
after-periods of his life, only coarse bread softened
in warm water. The mortification which he considered it his duty to practise, extended not only
to his food and bodily comforts, but to his mental

enjoyments. Thus, one day he happened to be visited by some lay friends, and, betrayed into forgetfulness, he was guilty of the sin of being amused with their conversation. For this offence, he bound himself to a rigid penance for twenty-five days, and during that time would continually prostrate himself before the altar, and there pray long and fervently for pardon. This constant endeavour to abstract his thoughts from every thing external was at length successful; and he is reported to have been so insensible to surrounding objects, that he knew not whether his cell was roofed, or naked to the sky—whether it had one, or three windows. An instance of his blindness to whatever affects the senses was also afforded, when he one day rode to visit the brethren of a neighbouring monastery. A monk who came to meet him, was surprised at seeing the saint mounted on a horse, which, for its splendid accoutrements, it only became a knight or a baron to ride. On expressing his astonishment at the circumstance, the holy Bernard expressed his also; but explained the mystery by saying, he had borrowed the horse, and had forgotten to see whether it had a bridle or saddle of any sort.

The celebrity which he acquired by his devout character, and the humility of spirit for which he was equally famous, attracted the regard of Hugh, Earl of Troyes, and that nobleman founded a monastery for him in the midst of a wild and lonely district, about eleven leagues from Langres in Champagne. Having been appointed abbot of this retired spot, he proceeded thither with several of his companions, who sang hymns of thanksgiving as they travelled to their new residence. It was

with the greatest difficulty they provided themselves with food or shelter when they arrived at
Clairvaux, the name afterwards given to the district. But the commencement of their subjection
to Saint Bernard's rules was a fit introduction to
what followed. The only nourishment they were
allowed to receive, was coarse bread made of
the bad corn which they cultivated themselves.
Frequently they had not even this, and they were
then obliged to live on beech-nuts, vetches; and
even the leaves of trees, which they boiled into a
sort of soup. These austerities were at length
carried so far, that those of the little community,
who wanted somewhat of the strength and fervour
which distinguished the chief of the new order, began to complain of their decaying frames; and the
abbot wisely discovered his error, and lightened the
heavy load he had placed upon his feeble brethren.
But he would not allow himself the same indulgence which he granted others. He would continually say to those with whom he conversed on
the subject, " Did you know what is required of
a monk, you would not eat a morsel of bread that
was not first moistened with your tears." And
when any one desired admittance to his order,
he was accustomed to observe, " If you desire to
enter this house, you must leave your body without—only spirits can enter here."

The health of the saint was speedily destroyed
by his abstinence, and he was frequently at the
point of death. On one of these occasions, the
good Bishop of Challons, who admired him for his
great piety, contrived to save him from the grave,
by an ingenious artifice. Having obtained from
the Pope a right to order and control the customs

of Bernard, he proceeded to the Abbey of Clairvaux, and, showing his authority, compelled the saint to leave his cell, and take up his abode in a neat and healthy cottage in the neighbourhood, where he interdicted his attending to any of the rules of the order, and obliged him to follow the directions of a skilful physician, who prescribed for him a wholesome and nourishing diet.

By means such as these the life of Bernard was preserved; but his pale countenance and emaciated form gave him the appearance of one long since ready to sink into the grave; and it was only by the constant beaming forth of his devout and rapturous spirit, that he could be regarded as a living being. Notwithstanding his constant bodily infirmities, he laboured unceasingly in the duties of the priesthood. His preaching turned the hearts of the proudest and most dissolute hearers to his holy purpose; and such was his fame, that princes and even bishops would call upon him to settle any disputes which might arise between them. As a controversialist, his talents were employed on the most trying occasions; and he was long engaged in combating the errors of the celebrated Abelard, who at this time disturbed the church by his novel and heretical opinions. But the learning of Bernard derived its chief force from the solitary meditation to which he devoted so many of his hours; and he was accustomed to say, that the trees of the lonely forest were his only masters in the scriptures.

The monastery at Clairvaux, having such a distinguished saint for its abbot, greatly increased in the number of its austere inhabitants; and the fame of the order reached England, Spain, Italy, and

Germany, in all of which countries establishments
were shortly after founded, and governed according to its severe rules.

But the power of Bernard's eloquence and reputation was now about to be tried in a still more
conspicuous manner than it had hitherto been
done. Letters and ambassadors had arrived from
the distressed Christians of Jerusalem and Antioch,
supplicating for immediate aid in preserving the
Holy Land from the arms of the infidel. The earnest and afflicting style of these addresses moved
the hearts of all men; and it was the general persuasion that immediate measures should be taken
for sending a powerful armament of Christian warriors to Syria.

The King of France appeared as a fit and willing leader for the expedition. Godfrey of Bouillon
had been instigated to assume the cross, from
his remorseful penitence at having insulted the
sacred authority of the Pope. The same feeling
was at this time operating on the mind of the
young King Louis VII. In a war with one of his
rebellious barons, the Count of Champagne, he
had pursued his vengeance in spite of the commands of the Pontiff, and the exhortations of his
bishops. In the siege of the city of Vitry, he had
put many hundreds of the innocent inhabitants to
death; and ended a contest, undertaken to support
the just pretensions of the crown, by acts of the
most flagitious violence.

A universal consternation reigned through the
states of his kingdom as Louis returned from this calamitous war. He was met on all sides by the lamentations of his subjects, and the reprobation of the
clergy. The holy Bernard himself wrote to him or

the assailant, and no means were spared to convince
him of the crime of which he had been guilty.
For some time these appeals were ineffectual, but at
last they reached his heart. His repentance was
then as violent and uncontrollable as his cruelty had
been. He wept continually at the thought of his
offences; refused to partake of any pleasure or
even nourishment, and no longer regarded with
satisfaction any of his former pursuits. Every
measure was employed to restore his mind to some
degree of tranquillity; but nothing availed, till the
letters of the Eastern Christians, and the exhortations of Eugenius, published the call to a second crusade.

During the festival of Christmas, Louis summoned an assembly of prelates and barons at Bourges,
and declared to the august meeting his intention
of setting off forthwith to the Holy Land. The
announcement was heard with surprise; and some
of the bishops and noblemen present hesitated
whether or not to approve of the design. Suger,
the Abbot of Saint Denis, saw much to dread in
the kingdom's being left without a ruler, and zealously advised the impetuous monarch to consider
well the consequences of the step, before he ventured upon such a difficult, and, in all respects,
perilous undertaking. Not having sufficient authority, however, to sway the king by his own
advice, he persuaded him to seek the counsel of
Bernard, which was done; and the holy abbot
returned an answer, exhorting the King to pursue a course so useful to Christendom and creditable to his piety. The Pope having been also
applied to respecting the King's intention, returned a similar answer; and another assembly was

summoned to meet at Vezelay, a small town in Burgundy.

The Pontiff, owing to the circumstances of the papal dominions, was obliged, like his predecessor Urban, to excuse himself from partaking actively in the enterprise, and even from personally attending the present meeting. But he deputed his authority and the support of the cause to Bernard. He also sent letters to all the princes of Europe, beseeching their aid, and promised the same rewards to those who should now assume the cross, as had been offered at the preaching of the first crusade. The advice which accompanied these exhortations and promises, was creditable to the good sense and policy of Eugenius. Many of the miseries suffered in the former expedition, were the result of the thoughtlessness of the knights and others who led the forces. He cautioned the chevaliers, therefore, on this occasion, not to burden themselves with hounds and falcons, nor other useless accompaniments, but to be provided with good clothing, armour, horses, and weapons.

Bernard, by his reputation for wisdom and sanctity, had been often engaged in public affairs of considerable importance, and had had sufficient power to heal one of the greatest schisms which had ever existed in the church of Rome. But at the time when he was called upon to rouse the princes of Europe to attempt the second restoration of Palestine, he had passed three years in his cell, without having ever left it, except once in each year, when he attended the general meeting of his order. His character, however, and the fervent devotion of his soul, were better assistants in his work, than either bodily strength or acquaintance with the world ;

and with only his piety to support his emaciated and sinking frame, he commenced his arduous undertaking. The spiritual eloquence of this faithful apostle of the crusades, produced the most astonishing effects; and hundreds who would have remained unaffected by proud and studied orations, were melted into love and obedience by the humility, the meek and gentle tone, which distinguished all the addresses of Saint Bernard.

A. D. 1146. The Council of Vezelay took place at Easter; and the number of knights and others who attended the meeting was so great, that the city could not afford sufficient room for the purposes of the assembly. It accordingly adjourned to an open field on the descent of a mountain, a short distance from the town, and there, from a lofty platform, the venerable abbot, surrounded by bishops and princes, addressed the immense audience. His exhortations were received with repeated exclamations of the well-known war-cry, " *'Tis the will of God! 'Tis the will of God!* " and when he had finished, the King of France, with whom was his consort Eleanor of Guienne, fell at his knees, and devoutly received the consecrated cross from his hands. The uncle and brother of Louis followed his example, as did also a crowd of other noblemen. These were imitated by persons of an inferior degree; and such was the multitude of those who demanded the sacred badge of crusaders, that the crosses which Bernard had brought for the occasion, were not sufficiently numerous to supply the demand; and he, and many other persons present, tore their vestments to make more of these holy ensigns.

The success which had thus attended the first

efforts of the Saint, established the high reputation he had acquired in his monastery. Every
tongue spoke his praises; and the moment it was
known any where that he was employed in pub-
lishing the crusade, the greatest confidence prevailed as to its prosperous issue. So strongly was
the opinion fixed in the minds of the people that
his sanctity was the best guerdon of success, that
in a council held at Chartres, he was appointed to
be the head and leader of the design. For some
time he resolutely refused to accept of a station
for which he felt himself totally unfit; but the
commands of the Pope prevailed over his repug-
nance; and he at length consented to proceed with
the enterprise to which he had already so greatly
contributed.

In prosecution of the design which had been
formed of obtaining the assistance of the most
powerful European princes, Bernard set out for
Germany, immediately after having received the
important charge above mentioned. He arrived
at Spires just as the Emperor Conrade the Third
had summoned a diet of the States, to deliberate on the affairs of the empire. The renown
of the missionary secured him respect; but Conrade had lately suffered greatly from the disturbed
state of his dominions, and was unwilling to hazard
an enterprise which would require his absence,
and probably plunge his government again into
disorder. Bernard, however, replied to all these
considerations of the Emperor, by assuring him
that the church, which had given him the imperial crown, would also take care to preserve him
in its enjoyment; and one day, while performing
service before the princes who composed the diet,

be burst out into such a passionate display of eloquence on the subject so near his heart, that his
astonished auditors yielded to his persuasions, and
most of them, Conrade being the first to set the
example, threw themselves on their knees, and
with tears and exclamations of the most devout
emotion, swore to follow the will of their Saviour,
whithersoever it might carry them.

The flame thus kindled, almost instantaneously
enveloped, in one general blaze of wild enthusiasm,
nearly the whole of Germany. Bernard was every
where seen, and his presence produced the effect
of a celestial vision. Miracles were said to attend
his steps; and the crowds who followed him tore
his garments, in order to possess some relic, however trifling, of so glorious a saint. Wherever he
preached, the inhabitants of the district left their
homes, and assumed the cross, whatever might be
their age or rank in society. The world thus
seemed again to undergo the great moral convul-
sion which had attended the preaching of the first
crusade; and the progress of all ordinary affairs
was stopped, as being no longer worthy of regard.

On the Abbot's returning to France, he found
that, during his absence, the arrangements for the
expedition had made little progress. His presence, however, quickly restored a spirit of activity and zeal; and in a meeting held at Etampes,
measures were finally taken for the departure of
the armament. Deputies also from the King of
Sicily, whose dominions had been threatened by
the Saracens, offered to provide the crusaders with
ships and provisions; but the chiefs, blind to the
advantages of a route by sea, rejected the valuable
proposal.

The several divisions of the two armies of Louis and the Emperor, assembled under their respective chiefs at Mentz and Ratisbonne. But difficulties were experienced at the very outset of the expedition, from the want of money; and it was only by laying large impositions on the Jews, and by levying enormous taxes from all classes of people, that the enterprise was enabled to proceed. The misery to which Louis reduced his people by these proceedings, did not hinder his belief in the merit of his undertaking; and his devotion continued to burn with equal ardour as at the first. But the wise and cautious Abbot of Saint Denis, whom he left in charge of the government, apprehended the direst effects from the procedure of the King, and wept over him, as if he already saw the misery which would ensue from the ill-timed expedition.

Louis, shortly after this, arrived at Constantinople, at the head of a hundred thousand pilgrims, and he was speedily followed by the Emperor Conrade. But the march of the German crusaders was attended with many difficulties; and a frightful storm overthrew their tents with destructive violence, when they had nearly reached the imperial city. The troubles, however, which assailed them on their advance to Constantinople, were not to be compared with those which pursued them from that stage of their journey. The throne of Alexis was occupied by Manuel his grandson, who now exercised the same arts as that monarch employed against the leaders of the first crusade. The most bitter hatred existed between the rival Emperors of the East and West; and the dislike which had long been harboured by the

rulers of the two great divisions of the Roman
world, was at present further increased by the rumour which had gained ground respecting the hostile
intentions of the Germans against the successor of
Constantine. In every part of their march, therefore, the crusaders found themselves assailed by
the troops of Manuel, who, not daring to proceed
to open warfare, fell upon and destroyed whatever
stragglers were found from the main body, and, by
prohibiting the inhabitants of the cities near which
they passed from furnishing them with provisions,
reduced them to the greatest distress. Wearied
by this harassing march, they reached the mountains of Cappadocia, when they were nearly sinking unto the earth by the united effects of sickness,
fatigue, and want of food; and in this condition
they were obliged to meet the sudden onset of the
Saracens, who had watched their approach, and
now put thousands of them to the sword.

The French, who had been equally convinced
of the perfidy of Manuel as the Germans, pursued the route of the latter, full of indignation a-
gainst the subtle and deceitful Greek. As they
approached Nice, rumours reached them of the
fatal defeat of their companions; and Louis, impatient to know the extent of the misfortune, hastened to meet the Emperor Conrade in his retreat.
The two monarchs fell into each other's arms, and
wept bitterly over the misfortunes which they had
experienced, and at the apprehension of the worse
woes which still threatened them. Conrade had
himself been twice wounded in the late battle, and
nearly the whole of his army had perished. Of the
knights who attended him, all had lost their horses
and stores; and only a miserable wreck was left of

this proud and boasting armament which set out from Ratisbonne. Reduced to this miserable plight, the Emperor in vain endeavoured to persuade his barons to continue the enterprise. They had already experienced enough of the generalship of their master, and of the resistance which they had to expect from the enemy. He was, therefore, obliged to take a mournful farewell of Louis, and return to Constantinople, receiving, when he arrived there, the most flattering attentions from Manuel, who was willing to hide the satisfaction he felt at his defeat, under the smiles of a pretended friendship.

A. D. 1148. It was now the depth of winter, and the French crusaders were pursuing their toilsome march through the desolate country of Phrygia. Every obstacle which the rigour of the season, or the bleak and depopulated nature of the land, could oppose to their progress, assailed them on the way; but their courage remained undaunted; and they at length reached the banks of the Mæander, where the enemy appeared to dispute their passage. The battle which ensued was fought with desperate courage on both sides; but the French were victorious, and they resumed their route with the most fervent hopes of final success. These, however, were speedily damped by the untoward event of a defeat, which followed close upon the late triumph. Having to traverse a lofty mountain, the first division of the forces, under the command of the Seigneur de Taillebourg, received orders to halt on the heights till the rest of the army should come up, when the whole was to descend into the plain in order of battle.

Meeting with nothing to impede their march,

the troops of the Lord de Taillebourg quickly reached the spot where they were ordered to wait for their companions. But the wild and dreary aspect of the mountains offered little temptation to repose; and the Queen and several other ladies, who were under the protection of the Seigneur, persuaded him to continue his route till they should find a place for encampment more suited to their taste. But no sooner had the French squadrons forsaken their strong position on the hills, than it was occupied by the Turks. In the mean time, the remainder of the Christains came up; and as they had no idea but that the figures they saw moving about in the distance were their comrades, they hesitated not to break their ranks, and prepare for pitching the tents. Suddenly every rock and defile were teeming with Mussulmans. The crusaders, unable to recover from their panic, perished before they could offer any resistance; and Louis owed his life to the loyalty of a few of his nobles, who rallied round him at the moment of danger. Thirty of these brave men perished in the defence of their master; and after their defeat, Louis placed his back against a rock, and continued the fight alone, till the Saracens who attacked him growing weary, and not knowing his rank, left him, to pursue an easier and more profitable victory.

The news of this battle, with a report of the King's death, quickly reached Europe, and the most lively distress prevailed throughout the dominions of the unfortunate monarch. But even the desperate defeat which he had suffered, was not sufficient to persuade him to return to Europe, without sacrificing more blood and treasure to the

undertaking. He resigned the command of the
forces to Gilbert, an old and celebrated warrior,
and to Everard des Barres, Grand-master of the
Templars. Their march through Pamphylia was
attended with the usual evils of famine and disease, and their only hope lay in the expectation of
finding in the Greek city of Attalie some relief to
their sufferings. But what was their consternation, on arriving at this place, to find its gates
fast closed against them, and their application for
shelter from the tempestuous and bitter atmosphere treated with indifference!

The misery of the crusaders was now complete.
They had neither clothing nor provisions, and were
exposed, without a chance of shelter, to the destructive effects of the season. Every day saw their
numbers thinned by the most cruel of deaths. But
nothing could afford a stronger proof of the King's
devotion and firmness of character, than his conduct on this occasion. He implored his followers
to remain with him, and pursue their design,
whatever might be the difficulties of the way,
promising to share with them all he had, and to
shrink from no peril or suffering which it might
be necessary to endure. But his barons, however
moved by these supplications, saw the utter im-
possibility of remaining where they were, or endeavouring any further progress, without bringing
upon themselves inevitable destruction. They,
therefore, refused to listen to his entreaties, and
only blamed him for not turning his arms against
the false and barbarous Greek.

As the Christians saw no other means of deliverance from their misery, it was with some
degree of satisfaction they received an intimation

from the governor of Attalie, that he would furnish them with a certain number of vessels, in which they might return to Europe, or proceed wherever they chose. The offer was accepted; but several weeks passed before the ships appeared; and then it was found, that only a part of the army could be transported in the small and ill-prepared fleet. To those who were to remain at Attalie, and pursue their journey over land, Louis gave liberal supplies of money, and appointed two noblemen of rank and character as their leaders. But the fate of these poor wretches was of the most calamitous kind. The Turks, finding them reduced to so small a number, attacked them without intermission. The Greeks continued to refuse them admission into the city. Their two leaders forsook them, and they all perished either by the sword of the Saracens, or in a vain attempt to march into Cilicia. Louis had directed his course towards Antioch, and arrived there in safety with his queen, and the small portion of his army, which he had been able to save from the disasters that had attended his route. Raymond of Poictiers, who was then prince of Antioch, was zealously employed in defending himself against the approaches of the Saracens. The arrival of Louis gave him hopes of being able to form a powerful army to meet the enemy; and he used every means likely to persuade the King to remain in his principality; but nothing availed to induce Louis to defer his visit to Jerusalem. Raymond, however, continued his entreaties; and, finding himself so unsuccessful with the King, he next turned the whole force of his persuasions towards the Queen, who was his niece. The character of Eleanor was no ornament to the cause in which she had pretended to engage herself. She is reported to have been devoted to gaiety and voluptuousness; and, when her persuasions excited the suspicions of the King, and convinced him still more of his duty to leave the court of Antioch for the sepulchre of the Saviour, she united with her uncle in a project to dissolve the marriage between herself and Louis. The King, on finding this to be the case, had her secured one night; and, having brought her into the camp, immediately took his departure.

Louis lost no time in pressing his march towards Jerusalem; and when he arrived in the neighbourhood of the Holy City, he was met by multitudes of the inhabitants, who came out to escort him into the town, and who, in almost impious imitation of the scene which took place on Christ's entry into Jerusalem, carried olive branches in their hands, and made the air resound with their exclamations of—" Blessed is he who cometh in the name of the Lord!" The arrival of the French King was rendered still more joyful by that of the Emperor Conrade, who reached Jerusalem about the same time; and the most flattering hopes were conceived by the inhabitants of the Holy City, that they might now again defy the power of the Moslem.

In an assembly, which was shortly after held at Ptolemais, it was determined that an attempt should be immediately made to obtain possession of the strong and important town of Damascus. Various other projects had been formed by Raymond of Antioch, and others of the Christian princes; but the quarrel which had taken place re-

specting the imprudent Eleanor, prevented the
presence of the former; and among the high-born
women, who formed part of the noble assembly at
Ptolemais, the Queen of France had no place.
Disputes of other kinds prevailed over the minds
of several of the chiefs whose union was necessary to the success of any great undertaking; and,
encouraged as the faithful were by the presence of
so many distinguished princes and warriors, they
had yet reason to tremble for the effects which
discord might hourly produce among them.

The command of the army was shared between
Baldwin the Third, King of Jerusalem, the Emperor Conrade, and the King of France. Early in
the spring it began its march, and, after some short
delays, encamped about June, within sight of Damascus; and on the spot where Saint Paul is supposed to have seen the awful vision to which he
owed his conversion. Situated in the valley formed by the two mountainous ridges known by the
names of Libanus and Anti-Libanus, this ancient city
was celebrated, as well for the loveliness of the
surrounding country, as for its splendour and opu-
lence. The rivers of Abana and Pharphar poured
their delicious waters along its plains; and its groves
of fig-trees and of the most fragrant shrubs resounded continually with the melody of birds and
the murmur of cooling fountains. " The head of
Syria is Damascus," * was the language of the
Prophet; and the Emperor Julian, or the writer of
the letters attributed to him, breaking out into rap-
ture at the thought of its lovely valleys, and ferti-
lising rivers and streamlets, claims for it the appellation of the Eye of the East.

* Isaiah vii. 8.

The power of Noureddin at the time when the Christians appeared in the plains of Damascus, had been increased by the continual successes of his victorious arms. The wisdom of this distinguished Musulman was equal to his valour; and he secured his conquests by a prudence and policy as admirable in the eyes of his subjects as his heroism. Of all the inferior states of Syria, the city of Damascus was the only one which retained its independence, and that had already been threatened repeatedly by Noureddin. The character of the governor, who was slothful and unwarlike, tempted the assailants to renew their preparations for the conquest of so important a place; but the Christians suddenly appeared in the field, and the Saracens were compelled to pause in their career.

The rich groves and vineyards by which the northern and western sides of Damascus were surrounded, served as places of concealment to numerous bodies of archers, who were stationed there immediately on the approach of the crusaders. Lofty walls defended the city on the other sides; and the Christians preferred attempting to pass the ambushes and intrenchments of the north and west, to attacking these formidable ramparts. After a long and fierce encounter, which, from the nature of the defence, was frequently slackened and again commenced, the enemy began to retreat from his several holds, and fled to the river which bathed the walls of the city. Here the conflict was recommenced with fresh fury. The three kings performed prodigies of valour; and the Emperor Conrade waged single combat with a gigantic Saracen, hurled him from his horse, and with a single blow severed him in two.

Nothing now appeared to oppose the speedy reduction of Damascus; and the chiefs, before following up their success, employed several days in considering who was to enjoy the government of the splendid city. The Count of Flanders succeeded in obtaining a decision in his favour; but the other chiefs, no longer caring about a conquest from which they were to derive no personal advantage, speedily lost their zeal for the prosecution of the enterprise; and, after many disputes, the siege was recommenced, under every disadvantage which could result from indifference and dissension. By an unfortunate error in generalship the army was removed from the post it had gained with so much difficulty, and from which the assault of the town was comparatively easy, to one in which its attacks were opposed by the strong towers and ramparts, in which the besieged placed their principal reliance. A large body of new forces was in the meantime added to the reassured garrison; and after a few feeble attempts, the Christians raised the siege, and fled before the princes of Aleppo and Mosul, who were said to be on their march to Damascus. We cannot stop to inquire to whom the disgrace of this defeat, in the moment of victory, chiefly belongs. It is most likely to have resulted from the general spirit of discord which almost invariably prevailed among the leaders of the army, when any prize lay in the way which could not be easily divided. The evil consequences, however, of the event were immediately felt. In an assembly of chiefs held shortly after their retreat, the siege of Ascalon was proposed as an en-

terprise likely to prove successful. But neither
amity nor enthusiasm any longer existed among
the several divisions of the army, or the princes
who led them. The Emperor Conrade, therefore,
bade adieu to the Holy Land, without farther
tempting the calamitous fate which had hitherto attended him, and Louis followed him to Europe a
few months after.

Thus ended the second crusade, the events of
which are far less worthy of attention, than the
characters which they bring into notice. Immense
masses of the populace of France, Germany and
Italy, were roused by a sudden and tumultuous excitement of passion and devotion ; but after the first
fervour of enthusiasm passed away, the misery
which had been caused by the taxes and extortions
of the princes engaged in this expedition, was felt in
its full extent. The operations of the army were
marked, from beginning to end, by the weakness
and incapacity of its chiefs. The narrative of its
progress is one continued detail of disgrace and
suffering ; and not a single instance occurs of any
event which might relieve the gloomy uniformity
of the recital. Not even the influence of enthusiasm can be discovered as affording alleviation to
the distresses of the perishing crusaders. The
flame seems to have burnt itself out, almost as
soon as they left their native land ; and they yielded unresistingly to the alternate attacks of the Mussulmans and disease and famine.

But it was not from the want of personal bravery in the chiefs, or of ability and undaunted devotion in the principal instigators of the expedition, that it failed of success. Bernard was far
superior to Peter the Hermit, both in learning

strength of intellect, and general reputation. He
placed a reliance on the external signs of penitence,
and sacrificed his health to austerities, which a
more rational view of religious duty teaches us to
regard as contrary to the simplicity of our faith.
But it was only in the excess of his mortifications
that he differed from the greatest and most universally venerated ornaments of the church, and in
an age when rigid fastings and corporeal penances, were an essential part of practical piety, the
strictness of his life is only an additional proof of
his faith and sincerity.

Saint Bernard had many qualities, both of
mind and disposition, which claimed the respect
of his cotemporaries, and ought to render his
memory venerable to posterity. He was thoroughly versed in all the learning of his profession:
and his mind, deeply imbued with the sanctity of
spiritual meditation, was richly stored with thoughts
and images that gave a powerful charm to his discourse. Amid all his attentions to the burden-
some ordinances of that superstitious age, he retained a clear apprehension of the pure doctrines
of our faith; and used to say, when speaking of
God, that he took hold of him by his two feet,
his justice, and his mercy; by the one, that he
might never sink into slothfulness or forgetfulness
of his condition; and by the other, that he might
be safe from despair. Of his humanity, and superiority to some of the most frightful errors of
the times, we have a memorable instance in his
conduct respecting the Jews of Germany. When
the first crusaders were traversing that country,
thousands of the miserable Israelites perished, it
will be remembered, by the Christian sword. The

same savage barbarities were again about to be committed by the followers of Louis and Conrade. But Bernard came forth as the protector of the trembling Jews. "They are not to be destroyed or persecuted," said he, "but to be converted;" and this enlightened address saved them from the massacre which impended over them.

On the return of the crusaders from Syria, the whole blame of the disasters which had accrued from the expedition was ascribed to the venerable abbot. But he bore the abuse so plentifully heaped upon his name with the most perfect resignation, and rejoiced that he was calumniated, rather than Providence blasphemed.

Louis the Seventh, though greatly wanting in the prudence which it became him as a monarch to cultivate, possessed many qualities which entitled him to respect; and had it been his lot to have engaged in the first, instead of the second crusade, there is reason to believe he would have been a powerful assistant to the cause. His valour was of the most chivalrous kind; and in the disastrous battle in which he lost the flower of his army, he equalled, by his prowess, the actions of the ancient heroes. We must also regard with respect a man who, notwithstanding all the misfortunes which he suffered, and the many temptations he had to swerve from the course, continued to follow what he deemed his duty, when deserted by nearly all his friends, and in the face of danger and even ruin. The bravery of Godfrey, though perhaps cooler and steadier, shone not more conspicuously in the fierce onset of battle, or in the endurance of suffering. Nor was the piety of that chief superior to the devotion of the

King of France, if we are to judge of them by
their resolute performance of the task to which
they had pledged their faith. In the midst of all
his troubles, Louis never dreamed of freeing himself, by returning to Europe, without finishing his
pilgrimage; and when most harassed by his own
sufferings, and those of his army, he as scrupulous-
ly attended to all the exercises of devotion, as
when at home in his palace.

The Emperor Conrade appears to have been
a prince whose greatest error was his indecision
of character. He had wisdom enough to perceive the danger to which he would be exposing
himself, by leaving his dominions; but his resolution and judgment both forsook him at the first
impulse of enthusiasm. He was brave and devout, but unskilful, it would seem, in the conduct
of an army; and the rude multitude, who had only
Peter the Hermit for their guide, were not exposed to a more terrible destruction than that
which overwhelmed the imperial forces.

There are many other interesting portraits presented to us in the narrative of this crusade; but
we must not dwell longer on them. Suger, Abbot
of Saint Denis, would otherwise merit our regard. His prudent advice to the King was calculated to save France from some of the worst
calamities to which that nation had been yet exposed; and his shortly after determining to head
a crusade himself, represents him in the character
of a devotee, who had sincerity, patriotism, and
good sense to save a kingdom from ruin; but
enough of fervour to brave, at the age of seventy,
and when his personal good only was concerned,
the perils of a desperate warfare. This excellent

man, however, died before he could carry his design into execution; but he had proceeded into Germany, and collected a large body of persons ready to follow him as their leader.

The second crusade, though monarchs headed the enterprise, and men of the greatest piety furthered it by their prayers, wanted many of the aids to success which had attended that of the Hermit. The excitement, if as general, was not so essentially popular. The funds by which it was supported, were derived from taxes and impositions, instead of the free devotion of the people; and the host of high-spirited and generous nobles, who sold their estates to arm their bold retainers for the war, had their place ill supplied by the princes of two impoverished kingdoms.

CHAPTER III.

ACCUMULATING DISASTERS OF THE EASTERN CHRISTIANS.— JERUSALEM SURRENDERS TO SALADIN.—THE THIRD CRUSADE.

A D. 1152. THE same difference may be perceived between the first crusade, and the after expeditions known by that name, as between the first wild burst of a mountain torrent from its bed, and the current of its waters when they have reached the plain, and run on in a languid course, which only reminds us of its origin, when some accident of the elements widens or quickens it. It is the observation of Gibbon, that, " however splendid it may seem, a regular story of the crusades would exhibit the perpetual return of the same causes and effects ; and the frequent attempts for the defence or recovery of the Holy Land, would appear so many faint and unsuccessful copies of the original. " Were the story of the crusades, indeed, only valuable for the splendour with which common opinion may invest it, the remark of the historian would be as correct, in regard to the importance of the narrative, as it is in respect to its interest. But history is not written to affect the mind with brilliant exhibitions or romantic incidents. If it often chance to have the charm of fiction, it is only because

truth is sometimes as strange, or " stranger
than fiction." Its proper object is to build a
bridge over the dark chasm of the past; to be in
all respects the reflex of prophesy, and aid us to
look back, by the skilful employment of human
learning, as the latter, by a divine power, enables
us to look forward. But the record which is given
us of past events is, therefore, equally valuable,
whether they have flown on in a regular or interrupted course, whether one age has been the pat-
tern of another, or totally its opposite. In the
one instance, we shall be able to discover how
long certain motives of action can exist without
being worn out; and, in the other, how suddenly
they can be destroyed or neutralized by a change
of circumstances.

If there were nothing else worthy of notice
in the accounts which have been handed down
respecting the various crusades, there would be
sufficient to interest us in the picture which they
present of so many thousands of men, not merely of different countries, but of different periods,
uniting in one grand and uniform pursuit—it being the second great phenomenon in the Holy
Wars, that they were so many times revived, and
continued to excite popular passion in their favour
for nearly two hundred years. But to return to
our narrative.

The discouraging termination of the second
crusade, added greatly to the distresses of the Syrian Christians; and the fame of Nouraddin seemed
to threaten them with immediate ruin. Raymond
had fallen in battle with the Saracen shortly after
the siege of Damascus, and his death was followed by the dismemberment of his principality, many

of the towns of which, left without a master, resigned their liberties to the Moslem chief without
a struggle. Baldwin of Jerusalem had, with difficulty, in the beginning of his reign, freed himself from the controul of his mother Melisinda;
but since that time, she had continued to recover
or retain a considerable part of the royal authority.
She was a conspicuous personage in the council
assembled at Ptolemaïs, on the arrival of Louis
and Conrade, and she made her voice to be heard
in every debate of any importance. At the period of which we are now speaking, she had
carried her ambition so far as to dispute openly with
her son for the enjoyment of sovereign authority;
and the schism offered the enemy a strong temptation to attack the kingdom thus badly governed.
An assault was actually made on the Holy City
by a band of adventurous Saracens; and had Melisinda and her son been the only defenders or
counsellors of the state, it must have speedily fallen
into the hands of the enemy; but this misfortune
was averted by the bravery of several members of
the orders of religious knights.

The principality of Edessa, whose late unfortunate master Jocelin died in a Turkish prison,
was soon after depopulated of its Christian inhabitants, and returned to the possession of the Saracens. The desolating conquests of the enemy,
which were thus daily threatening the dominions
of the faithful in the East, if they could be witnessed in Europe with only so much of enthusiasm
that it ceased with the influx of distress and famine, operated differently on the minds of the
Syrian Christians themselves. They had come
out as pilgrims, but they were now the settled in-

habitants of the land ; and many of them had been
in the country, and felt attached to it, not only for
its holiness, but for its being the land of their nativity. Where none of these feelings operated, and
the subject was considered as a mere matter of
ordinary concern, there were many reasons to make
the approach of the Saracens an event dreadful to
the Christians. They might worship the Saviour
in any part of the earth, and in their native country, or that of their forefathers ; they might quickly form new feelings of patriotism and affection ; but it would not be so easy for them to find
a home in the parent-land, or the means of existence ; and this apprehension extended from the
meanest burgher to the proudest knights and nobles, and to the King of Jerusalem himself.

. It was not, therefore, out of a mere principle of
chivalry or devotion that Baldwin proceeded to
the siege of Ascalon, but from motives of interest,
which greatly added to the vigour with which the
spirit of knighthood inspired him. Ascalon was
an important post of defence to Egypt; and its
possession would be, in the present situation of
affairs, a most valuable advantage to the Christians. But it was protected by fortifications that
seemed to defy attack ; and its bold and well pro-
visioned garrison was sufficiently strong to meet the
threats of the besieging forces. The Christian name,
however, still continued to be dreaded in Ascalon ; and it was only by the greatest exertions the
Saracen chiefs could preserve the people from despair. The siege had continued for two months,
when a fleet arrived from Europe with several
bands of pilgrims on board. Gerard of Sidon was
already at the head of fifteen vessels ; and this re-

inforcement, both of the sea and land forces, produced the most joyful excitement throughout the Christian camp.   Had it not been for the cautious and unceasing activity of the Mussulman chiefs, Ascalon must have at once fallen into the hands of the besiegers; but every precaution was used to preserve the defences of the city; and at night huge glass lanterns were suspended from lofty buildings, to prevent a surprise during the darkness.   By these means they continued a successful resistance to all the efforts of the Christians; and five months had passed without the latter having gained any important advantage.   A fleet from Egypt brought reinforcements about this time to the city; and this seems to have urged the Christians to a more vigorous attack.   From a moveable tower of prodigious size, they assailed the enemy with such force, that it seemed impossible the ramparts should be any longer defended, till at length the Saracens determined upon attempting the destruction of the formidable machine.   In order to effect this important project, they cast a quantity of wood under the part of the walls by which the tower was placed.   On this wood they poured oil and other combustibles, to which they immediately set fire, expecting that the sudden combustion would speedily destroy the machine.   But, as when a similar experiment was tried at the siege of Jerusalem, the wind drove the flames with great force against the ramparts, and the fortifications speedily took fire.   Through the whole of the day and night the wind continued to fan the flames; and just as the morn was dawning, the terrified inhabitants heard the walls tumble with a horrid crash to the earth.   The Chris-

tian warriors roused themselves at the noise, and
ran towards the breach. A party of Templars
rushed into the city, and others of the army prepared to follow them; but, to their astonishment,
the holy knights had placed guards against the
place of entrance, either to forbid their fellow-
warriors to follow, or to give them false intelligence.
While, however, they were engaged in pillage,
which they hoped to enjoy entirely by themselves,
the Saracens recovered from their consternation,
rallied a few of their best soldiers, and, turning
upon the Templars, speedily put them to flight.
In vain the dishonourable chevaliers looked for
help. None of their comrades were near, and they
perished nearly to a man.

The success with which this first band of their
enemies was repulsed, encouraged the Moslems to
make a still further resistance to the approach of
the besiegers; and in a little time the latter were
obliged to retreat to their camp, and give up all
idea of the immediate possession of the city. So
disgusted were the King of Jerusalem and several
of the noblemen in the army with this event, that
they proposed raising the siege, and returning
home; but the prayers of the ecclesiastics, and the
advantageous position which they now held, induced them to determine on renewing the assault
the following day. At the hour proposed, the
besiegers commenced their attack; the Saracens
gave way; and it was evident to the inhabitants
that the city could hold out but a short time
longer. Uttering the most melancholy laments,
therefore, they implored the chiefs not to continue
a defence which would only expose them to still
greater evils, or uselessly prolong their present

sufferings. A deputation was accordingly sent to the Christian camp, and a proposal made to surrender the city, on the condition that the inhabitants should be permitted to leave it in safety in three days. The chiefs assembled in council received the surrender of the place with the greatest astonishment, and, as they had entertained little hope of such speedy success, attributed it solely to the providential interference of God.

A. D. 1163. We must pass rapidly over the events which intervened between this period and the preparations for the Third Crusade. Baldwin continued to resist the arms of Noureddin with various success; but shortly after, having succeeded in repressing the attempts of the Turks in the principality of Antioch, he died by poison, administered to him by a Syrian physician. His character rendered him, in general, the favourite of his subjects; but instances are on record of his disregard of truth and justice, when his personal advantage required their sacrifice. Thus, for example, he had given permission to some Arab tribes to settle themselves on the pasture-lands of Paneas, where they had remained for some years in perfect confidence of his good faith. But it so happened that he found himself in want of money, and, without regard either to his knighthood or his religion, he seized the flocks and herds of the Arabs, and, with the price they brought, paid his debts. But he was amply punished for his dishonesty, by the defeats which he shortly after suffered; and many of his bravest knights and barons, among whom was the Grand-master of the Templars, were taken prisoners by Noureddin.

Baldwin was succeeded by his brother Amaury,

who was abhorred by every class of the people, and was threatened, at the commencement of his reign, by a faction which proposed to change the order of succession, in order to exclude him from the throne. But having overcome his domestic enemies, he turned his thoughts towards Egypt, the condition of which was favourable to his hostile intentions. The rivalship which existed between the pretenders to the favour of the Caliph, destroyed the peace of the country; and when the King of Jerusalem reached the borders of the Nile, he met an army, which speedily yielded to his better disciplined forces. At length the Vizier Dargam, whose authority was threatened by the approach of his rival, under the protection of one of the Emirs of Noureddin, solicited the assistance of the Christians, and offered to requite their services with the most liberal rewards. But he was slain in battle before his allies could render him the aid required, and his enemy Chaver was put in possession of the government. The latter, however, now began to discover the error into which he had fallen, by calling in an ally so powerful and ambitious as Noureddin. The captain of that victorious Moslem refused to leave the country, which he had reduced to the will of Chaver; and the latter, seeing no method of freeing himself from his treacherous friends, determined to seek the alliance of the Christians, who were on their march towards Cairo. By their assistance, he succeeded in forcing the enemy into Bilbeis, from whence, after three months, he was obliged to retreat by capitulation. Soon after this, Noureddin suffered another defeat near Tripoli; and the Moslems began to tremble for the safety of their possessions, till the enthusiasm of their renowned leader restored their courage, and again led them to victory. A new and formidable expedition was then determined on by Noureddin and the Caliph of Bagdad, and Egypt was threatened with an invasion by their united forces.

Amaury, on receiving intelligence of these proceedings, assembled a council at Naplousa, and an army was quickly raised to assist the Vizier of Egypt in the defence of the country. The treaty of alliance having been ratified, the Christians offered the enemy battle near Cairo, and succeeded in driving him from his intrenchments; but the advantage thus gained was not pursued; and the Saracens retreated without much loss to Alexandria. The consequence, however, of the defeat which they had suffered, was the present tranquillity of Egypt; and the King of Jerusalem returned to his dominions, loaded with the munificent presents of the Vizier Chaver.

But the riches and magnificence of Cairo had awakened the ambition and avarice of Amaury. On his return to Palestine, he is said to have looked with contempt on the narrow boundaries of his kingdom, and to have regretted that he had left Egypt unconquered. His marriage with the niece of the Greek Emperor Manuel did not contribute to lessen his ambitious desires; and he at length invited his uncle to join with him in an attack on the country which had so strongly excited his avarice.

When the enterprise was proposed in council, opinion was greatly divided on the subject. The Hospitallers, whose luxury had begun already to make large revenues necessary to

their support, were greatly in favour of the besiegers; most of the barons also, to whom the
same necessities rendered so rich a prize an object
of desire, expressed similar sentiments; but to
the honour of the Templars be it spoken, they resisted with energy and eloquence the prosecution
of a design, which they declared would be a violation of Christian faith.   The treaty which had
been made it was not for them to break, without any reason but their desire of spoil; and, even
considered in a political point of view, the state
of the kingdom was not such as to render an undertaking of great hazard and difficulty advisable
at that time.   But these reasons were overruled
by the King and his less honourable counsellors,
and the invasion of Egypt was finally determined
upon.

A.D. 1168. The Christian army directed its first
movements towards Bilbeis, which it took by assault, and put the whole of the population to the
sword. . From this place, it proceeded by rapid
marches on the route to Cairo, where the terrified
Egyptians expected to see its banners displayed
in triumph over their ruined country.   But all the
efforts which despair could make, had been employed to avert the coming blow.   Noureddin had
been summoned to their assistance, and the troops
assembled on which confidence could be best
placed in this extremity.   In addition, however,
to these measures, they employed one which promised a still better chance of success, and sent
ambassadors to Amaury, offering him a vast sum
of money to withdraw his forces. . The King of
Jerusalem had been already rendered doubtful as
to the final issue of the contest. The preparations

made by the Egyptians, convinced him that the
conquest would not be so easily achieved as he
had at first imagined, and the approach of Noureddin's troops, filled him with apprehensions for his
safety. Without any great unwillingness, therefore, he assented to the proposals made him by
the ambassadors, and suspended his march. But
his base violation of the treaty was now met by a
cunning, which, if not equally base, was well fitted to punish his treachery. The Egyptians, having gained time by the negociation, hastened before its conclusion to bring fresh forces into the
field, and improve the defences of the provinces.
In vain did Amaury, day after day, expect the
payment of the stipulated sum; and at length he
found himself duped by the sagacious enemy, and
was obliged to precipitate his retreat to Jerusalem,
in order to avoid the increasing number of his
foes. Chirkou, the captain of Noureddin's forces,
entered Cairo as a conqueror, and in that character retained possession of the country. The Vi-
sier Chaver was shortly after put to death by
his infuriated subjects; and the conqueror himself lived only a few weeks to enjoy his triumph
and his new dominions. The Christians, in the
meantime, though greatly depressed by the unfortunate termination of the late expedition, ceased not to pursue measures for renewing the attempt. Assisted by a Greek fleet, they laid siege
to Damietta, but were defeated with great loss;
and Amaury, in despair, proceeded to Constantinople, to implore, in person, the assistance of the
Emperor. His success, however, does not appear
to have been very decided; and he returned to
Jerusalem only to see his states ravaged by earth-

quarter as well as war, and to terminate his existence when nothing but trouble and desolation menaced his subjects. He was succeeded by his son Baldwin, then only thirteen years of age ; and the government was given, during his minority, to Raymond, Count of Tripoli.

But while the kingdom of Jerusalem was threatened by disasters both from within and without, a new enemy had been raised up by the events of the times, whose genius and courage were likely to prove still more formidable to the tottering throne of its princes. Saladin only wanted to be a Christian, to be ranked among the first and the most glorious of chivalrous heroes. This celebrated captain was descended from a tribe of Curds, and was the nephew of the famous Chirkou. When the latter besieged Alexandria, Saladin distinguished himself by the noblest deeds of valour, and is said to have solicited and obtained knighthood from the Christian chief, who admired and rewarded his virtues. On the death of his uncle, the Caliph of Egypt chose him from the rest of the Emirs in the army, as the successor of his deceased relative. His courage and policy soon made him master of Egypt ; and on the death of the Caliph, he retained the supreme authority in his hands, and put an end to the Fatimite dynasty. Whether the conqueror achieved this object of his ambition by the murder of his master, or whether he was solely aided by the situation of the Caliphate government, is matter of doubt ; and the brilliant successes with which his usurpation was followed, soon rendered it difficult to discover what was the real character of his succession. But whatever doubts may exist as to the guilt which he incurred on ascending the throne of Egypt, it is a matter of little difficulty to determine with what degree of fidelity he served his original master Noureddin. That prince, on learning the measures which his lieutenant was pursuing in the conquered provinces, began to be doubtful as to his loyalty, and put it at once to the proof, by claiming his assistance in Syria. But the death of Noureddin relieved the ambitious Saladin from his perilous situation; and he prepared himself either to resist or attack the less formidable power of the chieftain's son and successor. The young prince had shut himself up in Aleppo; and having solicited the aid of the Christians, hoped successfully to resist the arms of his rival. Saladin, too prudent to risk his new authority, when it was not necessary to hazard it, bribed the Christians to enter into a truce with him, and return to Jerusalem. Another instance of bad faith on the part of the Franks followed this event; and as soon as Saladin had collected an army sufficient for the purpose, he hastened to punish them for their breach of the truce. Baldwin, the young king, prepared to meet him, but was terrified at the reports he heard respecting the greatness of his army, and sought protection within the walls of Ascalon. Having, however, recovered from his panic, he made a bold attack upon the camp of the enemy, and routed him with great loss. But the success was only a passing one; and he was obliged to renew the truce which had been so dishonourably broken.

But tranquillity was restored for only a very short period. Renaud de Chatillon was a cheva-

lier,· who,· having captivated the affections ·of Con-·
stance, widow of the Prince of Antioch, had ascended the throne of that territory. But he was
soon after taken prisoner by the Saracens; and, on
returning from a long captivity, found his wife
dead, and his son seated on the throne, which he
had forfeited as much by his cruelty to·the people, as by his imprudence in·war. He next married the widow of the Lord of Carac, and became
master of some castles on the confines of Arabia.
But·his restless spirit would not suffer him to re-
main·unoccupied in his little domain; and having
associated with himself several Templars, he· ra-
vaged· the country, and laid the caravans which
came in his way under heavy tribute. Saladin declared· to the King· of Jerusalem, that he
should consider ·these freebooting excursions of the
Lord· of Carac as violations of the treaty, unless
speedily restrained by his authority. Baldwin,· in
vain, urged the· necessity of peace upon his refrac-
tory vassal; and Saladin again prepared to invade
Palestine. For the present, however, he content-
ed· himself with having merely intimated his intention of ravaging Galilee, and then drew off his
forces to meet other enemies. Renaud de Chatillon, on the retreat of Saladin, immediately renew-
ed· his predatory excursions; but, in a desperate attempt to reach Medina, his party was totally vanquished; and the enraged monarch,· after taking
vengeance on the prisoners, swore on the Koran
to resent still further the insult he had suffered.

The unsettled condition of Jerusalem offered
every advantage to the enemy. The King was at
last reduced, by the infirmity of his constitution,
to· appoint a regent; and Guy of Lusignan was

chosen to fill that august office. This nobleman had obtained the affections of Baldwin's sister, but possessed no better qualities than those of a graceful person. Their marriage raised him to the first situation in the state; and every opportunity was afforded him of doing good service to his subjects and brethren. But he shortly proved himself totally unqualified for the duties of a prince. Saladin was allowed to ravage the lordship of Carac unresisted; and the King saw his sceptre wielded by a man whose hand seemed too impotent to hold a sword. Again, therefore, assuming the supreme authority, he appointed the Count of Tripoli as regent, and declared Baldwin, son of Lusignan's wife by a former marriage, his successor. The young King, who was only five years of age, was crowned with great solemnity; and the anxious Christians looked forward with hopes to his future reign.

A. D. 1185. But these were not destined to be completed. Shortly after the death of Baldwin the Fourth, and while the disputes relative to the regency were at their height, the youthful monarch suddenly expired, and left the kingdom in a fearful condition of helplessness and anarchy. Sybilla immediately preferred her claims to the inheritance, which were strongly opposed by the Count of Tripoli. But by the advice of the Patriarch, and of the Grand-master of the Templars, she employed cunning to overcome the influence of her rival. Having proclaimed her determination to renounce Guy of Lusignan as her husband, and give her hand to a warrior who might be able to defend the kingdom to which she laid claim, she proceeded to the Sepulchre, and there heard the sentence of divorce pronounced by the Patriarch Heraclius. At the conclusion of this ceremony, the holy father desired her to give herself and her crown to him whom she deemed most worthy of them. To the astonishment of the spectators, Sybilla immediately approached her husband, and placing the crown upon his head, observed, that those whom God had united, man could not separate.

The accession of Guy to the throne of Jerusalem, was opposed by several of the most powerful of the barons. His incapacity was universally known, and the loss of the Holy State was prophesied as the almost necessary consequence of his elevation. The situation of the Christians had never been worse than it was at this time; and signs in the heavens were again seen and interpreted as prognostics of the most terrible disasters. " Impetuous winds, " it is said, " tempests and storms, arose from all quarters of the sky. The sun was darkened for several days, and hailstones fell of the size of an egg. The earth itself, shaken by frequent and terrible convulsions, foretold the ruin and destruction which were approaching, the wars and miseries which would shortly ravage the land. The sea even could not be contained within its proper bounds, but, raging and bursting its limits by the fury of its waves, represented the anger of God. Fires were seen in the air, as if a house was burning; and all the elements, and the whole architecture of God, seemed to declare their abhorrence of man's impiety, and the ruin which was to come. " *

* Continuation of William of Tyre.

The terror which these supposed, or, perhaps, real, signs of the Divine anger inspired, was fully justified by the actual condition of the people. The men who could alone defend them, were either retiring in disgust from the scene of strife, or were wholly engaged in forwarding their own designs. The Seigneur de Carac continued, in the mean time, to provoke the wrath of Saladin by his devastations ; and when the Moslem approached his states, five hundred of the bravest knights, of the orders of the Temple and of St John, perished in their attempt to defend him. The news of this bloody battle filled the King of Jerusalem with despair; and having no hope of safety from his own exertions, he sufficiently subdued his pride to solicit a reconciliation with the Count of Tripoli, the late regent. Their friendship was only established in time to enable them to concert what measures were required to resist the threatened invasion of Saladin. At the head of fifty thousand warriors, and accompanied by the bravest of his barons, the King, together with the Count of Tripoli, proceeded towards Sephouri. But scarcely had they assembled on the plains to which they had directed their march, when intelligence was brought that Saladin had taken Tiberias; and was likely to be soon master of the citadel, in which the wife and children of Raymond were lodged during his absence.

It was the instant advice of most of the chiefs, that the army should be immediately led against the Saracen. But the Count, with a noble disregard of his own interest, declared himself of a contrary opinion, and pointed out to them the danger of exposing the forces, on which their last hope of safety depended, to the danger of such an expedient. "Willingly would I," said he, "abandon the county of Tripoli, and all the possessions which I hold, to save the city of Jesus Christ." But so little, unfortunately, had the warriors of this period been accustomed to that devotedness of zeal which distinguished their ancestors, that the advice of Raymond was treated with suspicion and coldness; and the Master of the Templars succeeded in persuading the King, that he was in secret correspondence with the enemy. Lusignan, ever open to such suggestions, immediately gave orders that the forces should be put on their march against Saladin; and with unwilling minds the barons found themselves obliged to submit to this indiscreet command. When they came in sight of the hostile army, they beheld it strongly posted on the hills which overhang the Lake of Tiberias. Their safety, it was now evident, depended on their being able to force their way to the Jordan; and exhorted by the priests, inspired by the sight of the true Cross, and urged forward by dread of the destruction with which they were menaced, they fought with a desperation that astonished Saladin, and drew from him expressions of admiration. The battle continued till night, and on the following morning it was renewed with equal fury. "It is Wednesday," said Saladin, exhorting his soldiers, on the previous evening, to fight valiantly, "a festival for the true believers, and the day on which Mahomet hears the vows which are addressed to him. Let us pray that he may give us victory to-morrow." These inspiriting words were not lost on the ears of the faithful Moslems, who rushed upon the Christians as if they formed the only barrier between them and the blessed valleys of Paradise. Their onset was irresistible. The Christians gave way; and after one or two ineffectual attempts to rally, the whole army was thrown into confusion. A fearful slaughter now commenced; and to increase the despair of the vanquished, the Cross, which had alone continued to comfort them in their misery, was seen in the hands of the enemy; and soon after, Lusignan, the Seigneur de Carac, the Grandmaster of the Templars, and several other distinguished noblemen, were made prisoners by the triumphant infidels. Of the few who escaped the sword, or were not made captives by the Moslems, the Count of Tripoli was one; but he shortly after died of despair, some say from having been traitorous to the cause of his brethren; but others, with more probability, from the sorrow which he suffered at the gloomy prospect which their affairs presented.

It is almost difficult to decide, from the exaggerated descriptions given of this terrible battle, whether the number of the prisoners or of the slain was the greater. Saladin, however, on returning to his camp, had a tent prepared for the King of Jerusalem, and received him with kindness and respect. Having given him some wine, the luxury of which was increased by its having been cooled in snow, the unfortunate Lusignan presented the beverage to the Lord of Carac; but the Moslem held back his hand, exclaiming, that a traitor like him should not drink in his presence. The menaces with which this was followed, enraged Renaud; and he manifested his contempt for them, as if he had still been at liberty, and in his own good castle. But Saladin, forgetting what his prisoner was unarmed, and totally defenceless, or else wanting in that nobleness of disposition which has been ascribed to him, struck him with his sword, and suffered his guards to murder him before his face. The following day, a scene of far greater horror took place. The conqueror, seated on a throne, and surrounded by Emirs and the most learned men of his court, summoned before him the Hospitallers and Templars, and, as a particular honour, gave his counsellors the privilege of each killing a captive with his own hands.

Ptolemais, Naplossa, Jericho, and several other cities, opened their gates to the conqueror; but Ascalon only surrendered, on condition that the King should be restored to liberty, and that the women and children should be sent in safety to Jerusalem. To the Holy City, Saladin himself hastened with all possible speed; and the inhabitants, terrified at the certain approach of ruin, came out to hear the proposals of the conqueror. He offered to permit them to depart without bloodshed, and to provide them with a settlement in some other province, if they would at once resign themselves and the city to his clemency. But this they declared their duty forbade them to do; and in spite of the threats of Saladin, the terrors of a supernatural darkness, and the mournful lamentations which resounded through the desolate streets, they hastened to prepare themselves for battle, and make the best resistance which their situation would allow. To obtain money for the purchase of the necessary stores, they despoiled the churches of their treasures; while the citizens armed themselves, repaired the fortifications, and chose Ibelin de Balean for their chief, who imme-

diately created fifty chevaliers from the towns-
people, in order to supply the place of the noble
knights who had fallen in the late battle.

Saladin fixed his camp on the spot which had
been formerly occupied by the tents of Godfrey;
but a few days after he removed his forces to the
north side of the city, and began by undermining
the ramparts, from the gate of Jehosaphat to that
of Saint Stephen.   In vain did the Christians
sally forth from the town, and attack the enemy
with the desperation of men that feared not death
half so much as defeat.   In vain did they rush
against the strong towers and destructive engines
which menaced them with instant ruin; the steady
and confident courage of the Saracens defied all
their bravery and despair; and sinking, under the
conviction that instruments of human warfare
could no longer avail them, the disheartened citizens fled back into the town, and were met by the
shrieks of their wives and children, the disregard-
ed exhortations and prayers of the clergy, and vain
promises of the most liberal rewards, if they would
return to the charge.   But nothing could prevail
on them to renew the conflict; and the streets of
Jerusalem were filled with bands of armed men,
who, forsaking the ramparts, joined in the processions which the priests led in terror to the sepulchre.

At length it was determined that a deputation
should propose to Saladin the surrender of the
city; on the terms which he had originally proposed.   But the conqueror rejected the offer with
disdain, and declared his determination to take Jerusalem by storm, and put the inhabitants to the sword.
On hearing this, the captain of the Christians,
Ibelin de Balean, used all his arts of persuasion to

restore some degree of spirit to his troops; and having gained a trifling success over the enemy, he declared to Saladin, that, before they suffered him to enter the Holy City, they would destroy the objects most venerable in their eyes, and that they would each of them purchase an entrance into Paradise, by sending ten Mussulmans to Hell. The resolution and despair evinced by this declaration, induced Saladin to pause before driving the vanquished to the extremity with which he had menaced them; and he desired some hours to consider their proposition. On the next day, he gave his assent to the proposals which had been originally made, and the treaty was signed in his tent. According to this agreement, the Christians were to be safe from the swords of the Moslems, but were not to have their liberty except at a given price, according to their sex and age. Thus, the ransom of a man was fixed at ten pieces of gold, that of a woman at five, and of a child at two. All who were unable to raise this sum, were to remain in slavery with their vanquishers.

October 1187. Where could a painter find a subject more fitted for the best efforts of his art, than the departure of the Christians from the Holy City? On the day appointed for that gloomy purpose, Saladin mounted his throne in the full pride and glory of a conqueror. The weeping inhabitants were summoned forth, and passed in solemn procession before their master. First came the Patriarch and the clergy, bearing the vessels and ornaments of the church of the sepulchre. The Queen Sybilla followed, lamenting both the miseries of her people, and the calamities of her captive husband. With her came a number of disarmed knights and barons, and a crowd of women and children, whose unrestrained lamentations added to the melancholy of the scene. In this manner they proceeded to the gate of David, the only one which had not been closed by the commands of the monarch, and bid a long adieu to objects on which their hearts were now fixed with a tenfold strength and affection.

: Saladin was of a generous and noble nature; and though it is a gross absurdity of language, to call a warrior merciful, he was frequently open to feelings of pity and compassion. On the occasion of the Christians' banishment from Jerusalem, his conduct was marked by as much humanity as could be expected to remain in the breast of a man so accustomed to scenes of blood and violence. To several orphans and indigent people he gave freedom, without insisting upon any ransom. Women, who were weeping bitterly at parting from their husbands and children, were comforted by having them restored to them before they departed; and the Queen received the kindest and most respectful attention from the conqueror. When the exiles had all left the city, only thirteen or fourteen thousand Christians remained in captivity, and of these the greater part were children.

The devotion of Saladin was equal to his courage; and he valued, it is said, his conquest the more, because it was achieved on the day of the week when Mahomet ascended in his famous vision from Jerusalem to heaven. His first care, after the departure of the Christians, was to purify the streets, mosques, and every part of the city from the pollutions it had undergone during its possession by the Franks. The mosque of Omar, that sacred monument of the Moslem's ancient triumph, obtained his especial regard ; and its walls and pavement were purified with copious showers of water distilled from the fragrant roses of Damascus. On the Wednesday which succeeded his triumphant entry into the city, his army and followers were summoned to attend him in the principal mosque ; and, from the hallowed pulpit which had been erected by the command of the founder, the most learned doctor of the law pronounced the thanksgivings of the faithful, for the victory which had been granted to the arms of their devout and valorous chief.

Having thus given a brief view of the circumstances which led to the third great expedition of the Western Christians to Palestine, we must turn our attention from the desolated Jerusalem, to inquire into the effect which the intelligence of its fall produced in Europe. The calamitous loss of the Holy City was ascribed, both in the East and West, to the crimes of the inhabitants. Their pride and licentiousness ; the quarrels which had been allowed to disturb the peace of the devout worshippers at the Sepulchre ; and the avarice which had made every other object yield to the selfishness of the powerful ;—these were all now declaimed against with becoming warmth ; and it seemed as if the eyes of the Christian world had suddenly regained the faculty of discerning between good and evil. It would have been well, if these feelings had led to the moral renovation which they appeared to prognosticate ; but they were mixed up too closely with the dread of miracles and omens to work steadily either upon the

reason or the heart. The painted images of our
Saviour and the saints were reported to have shed
tears of blood at the fall of the Holy City ; and
the awful prodigies; which the Jewish historian
relates respecting the destruction of Jerusalem by
Titus, were said to have been repeated on this
occasion. But these, and similar relations, of
which we have such an abundance in the chronicles of this age, bear upon their front the signs of
mere copies. In the instance of their real occurrence, the voice of Heaven was alone heard in the
terror-stricken land—the arm of Omnipotence
could be alone seen in the fiery darkness ;—but
in all those referred to, and, we may add, in all
instances of imagined prodigies, we hear the preach-
ings, the threats, or exhortations of men ; and human hands may be seen busily astir, beckoning the
multitude to follow their directions. The earthquake which makes a desart of peopled cities, is
alone thought of when the scene of ruin is visited,
and the relation of its violence is listened to with
awe ; but the feeling is inspired by no effort of
him who tells the story, to persuade us to build
another city in the place of the one destroyed. If
he should mix up exhortations of this kind with
his narrative, and let us evidently see that he is
less moved with the terrible remembrance of the
spectacle he has witnessed, than by the desire to
make it profitable to his purpose, we should, if
we had only his words to judge from, at once
doubt the veracity of his account.

But from whatever sources the marvellous relations were drawn which were dispersed at this
time through all parts of Europe, they had the
effect of drawing the attention of both high and

low to the history of the real calamities which
had been suffered by the Christians of Syria.
Many whom we may believe to have been out of
the reach of the fables which engaged the regard
of the less enlightened, were so strongly affected
by the miserable events which had occurred, that
they sunk beneath the weight of their sorrow.
Urbane the Third, who was then Pope, and resid-
ing at the time at Ferrara, was one of those who
felt the deepest affliction at the loss of Jerusalem;
and he shortly after died of grief. His successor,
Gregory VIII., soon after his accession to the pontifical throne, issued a bull, in which he exhorted
the faithful immediately to take arms for the recovery of the Holy City from the infidel. " Having learnt," said he, in this apostolic epistle, " the
awful severity of the judgments which the Divine
hand has exercised against Jerusalem and the Holy
Land, we and our brethren have been penetrated
with so great a horror, afflicted with sorrows so
lively, that in the painful uncertainty which we
have felt on this occasion, we have only been able
to exclaim with the Psalmist, ' Lord! the Gentiles
have seized thine heritage; they have polluted
thy holy temple; Jerusalem is now but a desart;
and the bodies of thy saints have served for food
to the beasts of the earth and the birds of the air!
For after the suggestions of the devil had produced dissensions in the Holy Land, behold Saladin
came with a powerful army to desolate it. The
King and the Bishops, the Templars and the Hospitallers, the barons and the people, rush to the
encounter, bearing with them the cross of the
Lord,—that cross which, in memory of Jesus Christ,
who suffered on it, and purchased man's redemp

tion on it, was regarded as the surest defence a-
gainst the attacks of the infidel." Then, after
alluding to the frightful slaughter which had followed the successes of the Saracens, and showing
how great cause all Christians had to weep at the
calamities which had befallen their brethren, he
continues, " Language is not able to express, the
senses cannot comprehend, what has been our affliction—what ought to be that of a Christian people, in learning that the Holy Land now suffers as
it did under its old inhabitants ; that land, rendered illustrious by so many prophets ; from which
the lights of the world have gone forth, and, which
is yet greater and more ineffable ; that land, in
which God, the creator of all things, became in-
carnate ; in which, by infinite wisdom and incom-
prehensible mercy, he submitted to the infirmities
of the flesh ; to the sufferings of hunger, thirst, and
the punishment of the cross, and, by his death and
glorious resurrection, wrought out our salvation.
We ought not, then, to attribute our misfortunes
to the Judge which punishes, but to the iniquities
of the people who have sinned, since we see in the
scriptures, that when the Jews returned to the
Lord, they put their enemies to flight, and that
one of his angels was sufficient to annihilate the
formidable army of Senacherib. But this land
has swallowed up its inhabitants : it has not been
able to enjoy a long tranquillity ; and the trans-
gressors of our divine law have preserved it but
for a short time, to give this example and instruction to those who sigh for the heavenly Jerusalem,
which can only be attained by good works, and
through manifold temptations. Already had the
people of these countries to fear that which has

now occurred, when the frontier cities fell into the hands of the infidels. Would to heaven that they had then had recourse to penitence, and that they had sought to appease, by a sincere repentance, the God whom they had offended; for the vengeance of God is always tardy; it surprises not the sinner; it gives time for repentance, till at last wearied mercy yields to justice. But we who, in the midst of the desolation which overspreads this country, ought to pay attention not only to the sins of its inhabitants, but also to our own, and to those of all Christian people, and who ought yet more to fear the destruction of the small portion of the faithful who still remain in Judea, and the ravages with which the neighbouring countries are menaced, in the midst of the dissensions which exist between Christian kings and princes, between towns and villages; we who see nothing on all sides but scandals and disorders, we ought to weep, and say with the prophet, ' Truth and the knowledge of God are not on the earth. I see lying, murder, adultery, and blood-thirstiness, rule in their place.' Repentance must every where prevail; our sins must be effaced by a voluntary penitence, by a returning to the Lord in sincerity and piety, in order that, being corrected of our vices, and observing the malice and ferocity of the enemy, we may do for the cause of the Lord, that which the infidel fears not every day to do against him. Think, my brethren, for what object you are come into this world, and how you ought to go out of it. Think that you will pass away as all things else. Employ your time, then, in good actions and in repentance; give that which you possess, because you have not made yourselves and you have nothing of your own; for to create even a worm is beyond all the powers of the earth. We will not say, ' Restore us, O Lord; but permit us to enter into the heavenly granary which thou possessest. Place us amidst those divine fruits which fear neither the injuries of time nor the attempts of robbers. We will strive to reconquer this land, on which Truth descended from heaven, and where she disdained not to endure the reproach of the cross for our salvation. We shall have seen neither the love of riches, nor a perishable glory, but your holy will, O God! Thou who hast taught us to love our brethren as ourselves, and to consecrate to you those riches, of which the disposition is, after this life, so little dependant on our will. It is not more wonderful to see this land struck by the hand of God, than it is to see it afterwards delivered by his mercy. The will of the Lord could alone save it; but it is not permitted to us to ask why he has done this; perhaps he has desired to prove us, and to make us know that he who, when the day of penitence is arrived, embraces it with joy, and sacrifices himself for his brethren, although he die in his youth, embraces a great number of years. Remember with what zeal the Maccabees were inflamed for their holy law, and for the deliverance of their brethren, when they precipitated themselves into the most fearful dangers, sacrificing their possessions and their lives, and mutually exhorting each other rather to perish than see the profanations of the holy things of their religion. Yet they lived under the law of Moses, whilst we have been enlightened by the incarnation of our Lord Jesus Christ, and by the example of so many martyrs. Show then your courage ; fear not to sacrifice those earthly possessions, which can endure for so short a time, and, in exchange for which, you have the promise of those which are eternal, of which the senses cannot comprehend the glory, and which, according to the Apostle, are worth all the sacrifices which we can make to obtain them.

" We promise, then, to all those who, with a contrite heart and a humble spirit, will not fear to undertake this painful journey, and who shall determine thereon from the motives of a true faith, and with the desire of obtaining a remission of their sins, a plenary indulgence from their offences, and eternal life as the consequence.

" Whether they perish or return, let them know, that, by the mercy of Almighty God, and by the authority of the holy Apostles Saint Peter and Saint Paul, and by ours, they are freed from all other kind of penitence which may have been imposed upon them; always providing, that they have made confession of their sins.

" The possessions of the crusaders, and their families, shall be under the special protection of the bishops and archbishops, and other prelates of the church.

" No inquiry shall be made in regard to the right of possession whereby a crusader holds any property whatsoever, till his return or death be certainly ascertained ; till either of which events, his property shall be respected and protected.

" If he be indebted to any one, he shall not be obliged to pay interest for the debt.

" The crusaders shall not travel clad in costly raiment, with dogs, birds, or other such objects, which are signs of luxury and ostentation; but they shall provide themselves with what is necessary, shall be simply clad, and have the appearrance of penitents rather than of men bent on the pursuit of vain glory."

This remarkable document will enable the reader to judge of the methods employed on this occasion to rouse the sinking spirits of the Christians of the West. It contains a singular mixture of good sense and piety, with false notions as to the objects of religious duty, and the wretched fallacies of genuine Romish dogmas. But Gregory followed up his exhortations with well-directed exertions, and had just succeeded in uniting the commercial cities of Italy in amity, when an end was put to his labours by death. His unfinished task was resumed by his successor Clement III.; and William, the eloquent Archbishop of Tyre, who arrived in Europe about this time, both encouraged and aided him in his pious design. Shortly before the fatal disasters which had deprived the faithful of the Holy City, Heraclius, the Patriarch of Jerusalem, had visited the West, to endeavour, by his representations, to awaken the sympathy of the European monarchs. After having in vain sought succour in France and Germany, he turned his attention to Henry II. of England, who, it will be remembered, was at this time suffering under the opprobrium of having been privy to the murder of Becket. But though he had taken a vow to perform a pilgrimage to the Holy Land, and was now urged by all the arguments which the zeal of the Patriarch could invent, he remained unmoved, and only professed his willingness to give his pecuniary assistance in the war with the infidel.

The Archbishop of Tyre arrived in France at the moment when the King, Philip Augustus, and Henry II., were on the eve of waging battle. But the mournful tidings which every day made a deeper impression on men's minds, and the entreaties of the Church, induced them to suspend hostilities; and William had the satisfaction of addressing both the monarchs in an assembly which they had mutually convened near Gisors, and which met for the purpose of determining what measures ought to be pursued for the relief of Palestine. The topics which he urged upon the attention of the assembled princes, were similar to those which were employed in the letter of Gregory; and he inflamed the devotion of his auditors by a particular detail of the barbarities which had been perpetrated by the Moslems. His words penetrated the innermost hearts of his auditors; and Henry, who must have deeply repented his indifference to the holy cause, when his aid might have averted many of the disasters which had occurred, at once declared himself a soldier of the Cross. His example was followed by the King of France, who was equally moved by the representations of the prelate; and several of the bravest knights in Christendom then pressed forward to receive the sacred badge of warriors for the Sepulchre of Christ. Among these were Richard, the celebrated son of Henry, and many of the principal noblemen of France.

The hopes of those who looked forward to the recovery of Jerusalem, as an event of the utmost importance to Christianity in all parts of the world, heard with delight of the accession of so many brave and distinguished warriors to the cause. The Church also failed not to use her efforts to support the excitement she had succeeded in awakening, and appointed proper psalms to be used every day of the week, in reference to the subject of her anxiety. But the measure which seemed most fitted to insure the success of the undertaking, was resolved on in a council of the chief promoters of the design, both lay and ecclesiastical. By one of their decrees, all those who did not personally engage in the war were to pay a tenth part of their revenues and moveable property towards its expenses. Peter de Blois alleged, in opposition to this ordinance, which extended even to the possessions of the Church, that the clergy contributed an ample share of assistance to the enterprise by their continual prayers for its success. But his objections were overruled; and all priests, as well as laymen, were threatened with excommunication if they resisted the decree of the council. One or two religious orders were, therefore, alone exempted from this heavy tax, which, on account of its origin, has been called Saladin's Tithe.

But after the various sums collected by these means were put together, the expenses of the war seemed still insufficiently provided for. The manner in which the tax had been levied was arbitrary in the extreme, and the mode employed in collecting it was not less so. A Templar, an Hospitaller, an Archbishop, and a Priest, with other functionaries, attended in every district, and when any one was considered to have paid less than a tenth of his income, a committee of four persons in the parish was elected to decide the question.

The most inquisitorial survey, therefore, was made of the private affairs of every individual, and the enthusiasm of the faithful here received its most formidable check. But thus far the proceedings of the crusaders were colourable, by the supposition that all was done for the good of the church, in whose prosperity and tranquillity every Christian was alike interested. The disgraceful violence which was exercised against the unfortunate Jews, was neither to be justified by any reasons of this nature, nor was it palliated by the caution with which common humanity might have taught their persecutors to proceed in their work. At the word of a fanatic, the Kings of France and England violated every principle of law and justice; and the property of the terrified Jews was seized without scruple to support the holy designs of these pious princes.

But the whole design was, shortly after its commencement, endangered by the disputes which took place between Henry and Philip. The ungenerous policy of the latter having drawn Prince Richard into an unnatural quarrel with his father, the tranquillity of Christendom was destroyed by the contest of the two great supporters of the crusade. In vain did the Cardinal Albano, the Pope's legate, fulminate his excommunication against Richard, and threaten Philip with the same punishment, for his disobedience to the commands of the church. They persisted in their designs against the dominions of Henry; and at length that monarch was obliged to agree to a peace, on terms which it became not a prince of his power and capacity to accept, and much less a son to impose upon his father. The unfortunate King, however, did not long survive the mortification he had felt in being reduced to purchase such an ignoble peace with Richard and his confederate ; and his death put the former in possession of the crown, which he had employed so many artifices to obtain during the lifetime of his father.

The first appearance of Richard on the scene is not calculated to excite any interest in his favour, for he was not only guilty of the basest conduct as a son, but consented to employ a species of falsehood and cunning in his proceedings, which, according to the right principles of chivalry, ought to have covered him with shame and reproach. He is represented, however, as feeling the deepest sorrow at the remembrance of his past conduct; and as some atonement for his guilt, he immediately exerted himself in aid of the expedition to Palestine. He had taken the vow of a crusader at Gisors ; and the time now appeared come - in which he might at once cover his sins, and reap immortal glory by his bravery. The want of money was the only difficulty with which he had to cope on the occasion ; and this was soon removed, by his determination to rifle the rich coffers of his Jewish subjects. But his offence against justice, in respect to this persecuted people, was not limited to robbing them of their wealth. The rude multitude, whose passions were always awake when any opportunity was afforded them of treating a Jew with barbarity, perceived the disposition of their monarch with a terrible sagaciousness, and every part of the kingdom was defiled with the blood of some miserable family of Israelites. In York, such was the horror with which these poor people expected the approach of their persecutors,

that five hundred of them murdered their wives
and children in the building to which they had fled
for refuge, and, having thrown their bleeding bodies
over the walls to the infuriated rabble, they set
fire to the house and perished in its ruins.* When
Richard had largely increased his funds by this
iniquitous oppression of the Jews, he proceeded
still further to augment them by the sale of the
crown lands and revenues, and even of the principal affairs of state. He then endeavoured to provide for the safety of the kingdom, thus pillaged
by its sovereign, during his absence, by compel-
ling his brother John, and also Geoffrey his natural brother, to bind themselves by oath not to
enter the country while he was abroad; but he saw
reason to remove or modify the prohibition, and
having appointed the Bishop of Durham and Ely
as regents, he departed in full confidence of having done every thing necessary to the security of
his dominions.

A. D. 1189. In the plains of Vezelay the two
Kings met, and embraced as friends that were
bound to each other by the most solemn ties of
faith and duty. The calamities which had destroyed the former armaments, had warned them
from attempting to lead the present expedition to
Syria by land, and taking an affectionate leave of
each other, they separated, Richard directing his route
for Marseilles, and Philip proceeding to Genoa, where
their fleets were respectively ordered to await their
arrival. But while the Kings of France and England were thus preparing for their expedition, the
Emperor Frederic Barbarossa, nephew of Conrade,

* Hume.

was far on his way to Palestine. Moved by the persuasions of William of Tyre to take a part in the expedition, he had quickly collected an army composed of the best disciplined and bravest of his troops. Having sent Saladin a formal declaration of war, and desired the Emperor of Constantinople and Sultan of Iconium to grant him a free passage through their territories, he set out from Ratisbonne. He had scarcely arrived within the boundaries of the Greek empire, when he found himself on all sides surrounded by the troops of the perfidious Emperor. But he fought his way through them, and reduced their master to supplicate a peace on any terms. He then passed the Hellespont, and had just reached Laodicea, when he was assailed by an army of Turks, which he routed, and proceeded to Iconium, where his soldiers, after a short siege, were suffered to repose themselves from their arduous march. Refreshed by this interval of rest, the Emperor led his forces towards Syria; but having reached the banks of the Cydnus, or the Selef, * he was tempted, by the beauty of the stream, to bathe, and almost instant death followed the imprudent indulgence of the desire. His army, after the loss of its brave leader, was speedily diminished by desertions and the difficulties of the way; and a very small portion of it, under the conduct of his son, reached the city of Ptolemais.

The Kings of England and France had in the mean time put to sea; but, as if they were to meet with as many difficulties by water, as their predecessors had on land, a violent storm attended

* Michaud.

their course, and they were driven to seek shelter
in the port of Messina. Their detention here during the whole of the winter, again threatened the
success of the undertaking. The most bitter enmity took place of the friendship which had been
professed by the two monarchs. The late King
of Sicily had been married to Richard's sister, who
was still living, but suffered many indignities from
Tancred, the reigning prince. The anger of the
English monarch was, therefore, justly dreaded by
the new sovereign; but he had still greater reasons to fear the power of Philip. The Emperor
of Germany, with whom the French King was in
close alliance, had married Constantia, the rightful heiress to the crown of Sicily; but Tancred,
her natural brother, had contrived to possess himself of her inheritance; and thus the approach of
the crusaders filled him with the greatest apprehensions for the safety of his throne. For some
time he succeeded in warding off the anticipated
evil, but the jealous temper of Richard was excited by some supposed affronts upon his authority; and while he was consulting with Philip, in
an open field, upon the subject, his guards attacked the Messinians, and entered the city sword
in hand. By his command the English ensign
was hoisted on the walls; and Philip, who was
encamped within the town, regarded this circumstance as a gross insult upon his dignity. The
obnoxious standard was removed at his request;
but animosity is supposed to have long existed
from this event. The next cause of quarrel was
Richard's refusal to marry Alice, the sister of
Philip; but this dispute was also terminated without any farther consequences, than the dislike

which generally remains in the minds of such men as Philip and Richard, after a difference of long continuance.

Shortly after the reconciliation of the monarchs took place, Berengaria, the daughter of the King of Navarre, arrived in Sicily, accompanied by Richard's mother; and Philip having already resigned his claims upon him in regard to Alice, and set sail for Palestine, the English monarch determined on espousing the Princess Berengaria. Having divided his fleet into two squadrons, in one of which his intended bride and the Queen-dowager of Sicily embarked, he set sail, but had scarcely cleared the port, when a violent storm arose; and the vessel on which the princesses were aboard, was wrecked on the coast of Cyprus. Isaac, the Emperor, as he styled himself, of the island, rejoiced at the rich spoil which this and the other ships stranded on his coast afforded him, immediately made prisoners of the crews, and left Berengaria and the Queen to the fury of the storm, and the bad shelter of their stranded vessel. But Richard soon appeared off the island; and hearing of the barbarous conduct of the monarch, he disembarked, entered his capital by storm, and having obliged him to surrender, threw him into a dungeon, but, out of compassion for his misfortunes as a sovereign, bound him with fetters made of silver instead of iron. He then appointed governors to protect the island; and having celebrated his nuptials with Berengaria, again set sail for Syria, taking his bride with him, and the daughter of Isaac.

A. D. 1191. When Philip arrived at Ptolemais, the siege of that city had already lasted more than two years; and the blood of both Christians and Saracens had flowed in ample streams beneath its walls. The sight of the King of France, with his brave army, filled the Christians with a joy which they had rarely felt since the loss of Jerusalem. But Philip declared his determination not to attempt any conquest till the arrival of his associate, the King of England. It was not long, however, before the fleet of that monarch hove in sight. By the way, he had attacked and sunk a vessel of the enemy, laden with stores; and his name was already a terror to the Moslems, and a promise of success to the faithful, who awaited his arrival. But before detailing the operations of the two princes, each ardently bent on the acquisition of glory, and equally desirous of outshining his companion, we must revert to the events which had taken place in Syria before their appearance on the scene.

CHAPTER IV.

CONTINUED SUCCESSES OF SALADIN.——RICHARD OF ENGLAND
AND PHILIP OF FRANCE ARRIVE IN PALESTINE.——SIEGE OF
PTOLEMAIS.——CONRADE CHOSEN KING OF JERUSALEM——HIS AS-
SASSINATION.——VALOROUS EXPLOITS PERFORMED BY RICHARD.

THOUGH Jerusalem was lost, the spirit which had
animated the faithful to achieve its conquest was
not subdued; and Saladin, so long as the vanquished people valued a grave in the holy soil of
Palestine, more than a lordly dwelling in any
other part of the world, was still but half master
of his new dominions. The little remnant of
brave warriors which existed after the sweeping
destruction of the late conflict, was closely shut
up within the strong fortifications of Tyre. To
this place, therefore, important both for its situation and its strength, the conqueror directed
his arms, soon after his conquest of the Holy
City. But, just as it was on the eve of surrendering to the numerous forces of the Saracen,
Conrade, son of the Marquis of Montferrat, who
had lately distinguished himself in his defence
of the Greek Emperor against his seditious subjects, and had been rewarded with his daughter
in marriage, appeared in the city, and offered
to take part in its defence. The chivalrous devotion of the noble warrior to the falling cause re-

newed the courage of its other defenders. The
fortifications were repaired; and Saladin saw himself obliged to prepare again for the assault of a
town, which he had every moment expected would
open its gates to receive him. The father of Conrade was now his prisoner, and he threatened to
expose him in the front of his ranks, if the city
were not speedily surrendered. The answer of
the son was, that he would not cease to defend
the city for such a threat; that if it were necessary to the cause, his own arrow should pierce the
heart of his father; and that he should then glory
at being the son of a Christian martyr. The boldness with which the citizens proceeded to the defence of their walls nobly seconded this brave defiance. Even children and women busied themselves in the preparations; and the desperate courage of the besieged at length compelled Saladin to retire from the place, and direct his forces
against Tripoli, which, like Tyre, still resisted his
arms.

A Spanish chevalier is mentioned as having distinguished himself by the most valorous exploits
in the defence of Tyre; and he is again celebrated
in the accounts of the siege of Tripoli, where his
deeds were crowned with such brilliant success,
that the Moslem was again obliged to retreat without having effected his purpose. Saladin was, however, more successful in his attacks on the castle
of Carac and on Tortosa; and he had sufficient
confidence in the security of his situation, to restore the captive Lusignan about this time to his
liberty. But, previously to dismissing him, he exact-
ed an oath, by which Lusignan bound himself to renounce all pretensions to the kingdom of Jerusalem,

and to return to Europe. The liberated captive, however, had scarcely left the tent of his conqueror, when an assembly of bishops freed him, by their decrees, from the obligation of his vow. He then proceeded to Tyre; but Conrade refused to admit him, or allow his claim to the city; and the unfortunate King, as a last resource, collected a band of about nine thousand men, and determined on laying siege to Ptolemais. The attack was commenced immediately on their arriving before the walls; but they were terrified from continuing their bold attempt, by a report that Saladin was on his march to the relief of the town at the head of his powerful army. To their great delight, however, a fleet of fifty vessels approached the shores, bearing twelve thousand Christian warriors from Denmark and other states of the North, well-armed and provided with large quantities of valuable stores. These were followed by a troop of English, headed by the Archbishop of Canterbury, and another from Flanders; and thus reinforced, the little army of Lusignan took up a strong position on Mount Turon.

Saladin paused not an instant in his march to Ptolemais, now threatened by so formidable a band of besiegers. By a valiant attack upon the Christian lines, he made his way to the city; and reassuring the garrison by his words, and leaving two of his most experienced generals to take charge of the defence, he fixed his camp on Mount Kaisan, from whence he determined to make an assault upon the forces of the besiegers. These were every day increased by fresh troops of pilgrims from the West, who, having been incited to undertake the voyage, by the exhortations of the

Pope and the venerable preachers of the crusade,
preferred setting out in small detached parties, to
joining the royal armaments of Richard and Philip. The siege had now continued forty days;
and the Christian army, impatient of further delay, received the signal for battle. The numerous
forces immediately descended into the plain, which
separated them from the enemy; and the gallant
appearance of the knights and barons, armed with
lances and swords, and covered with glittering
mail, inspired the Moslems with apprehension.
Several bishops are mentioned as having appeared
in full armour at the head of the troops; and the
King of Jerusalem was preceded by four chevaliers who bore the holy Gospels.

Saladin regarded the preparations and far-stretching lines of the Christian force with apprehension,
and had the mortification to see the left wing of
his army give way almost immediately after the
commencement of the engagement. The Christians followed up the advantage thus gained with
desperate resolution. The enemy was driven from
his encampment, and the victorious believers
were masters of the hill on which he had posted
himself. But suddenly the Moslems rallied;
the Christians, surprised in their eager search after booty, were assailed at a disadvantage; an A-
rab horse, which had broken loose from its rider,
was pursued by a party of soldiers; the idea seized
the rest of the army, that their speed was occasioned by the pursuit of the Saracens; and, in
an instant, the field was covered with the scat-
tered forces of the faithful, all seeking to escape,
by the rapidity of their flight, the swords of the
enemy. Saladin hesitated not to take immediate

advantage of the panic which had seized his adversary; and, in his pursuit, he killed or took prisoner, the best and noblest of the Christian warriors. But such was the impression which the
previous success of the enemy had made on the
mind of Saladin, that he did not attempt to pursue his victory by any farther attack on the hostile
army. The feeling which he had himself on the
subject was partaken by his principal officers; and
it was debated in council, whether it would not be
the most prudent measure to retire from a city, the
defence of which had already cost them so dearly.
The Moslem forces were finally led to the mountain Karouba, where they were encamped for the
winter; and the Christians were left to pursue the
siege, without any present interruption from the
assaults of Saladin. But messages were sent continually to warn him of the danger of the city;
and, as no other carriers could be so well trusted,
or had so fair a chance of escaping the pursuit of
the enemy, pigeons were employed to convey these
messages to his camp.

As soon as the spring had rendered the country
more passable, Saladin again descended into the
plain, and advanced towards the Christian tents.
The besieged, encouraged by his presence, employed all the most formidable arts of defence; and
the engines which the Franks had placed against
the walls were burnt to the ground, either by
flaming arrows, or naptha, which was hurled upon
them in pots filled with that inflammable material.
The troops, in the mean time, were attacked
without ceasing by the forces of Saladin, and almost every day was witness to a pitched battle
between the two mighty armaments. The fleets

also, which came laden from the east and west
with supplies for the respective camps, were seen
joining in furious conflict as they pressed towards
the port; and the whole circumference of plain,
mountain and ocean, appeared covered with hosts
of warriors all engaged in desperate conflict. On
the festival of Saint James, however, the Christians, impatient of the partial success which had
attended their occasional encounters, pressed their
chiefs to risk a more general engagement. The
desire was granted; but their conduct scarcely answered to the anxiety with which they had solicited to be led onward. After a sudden and impetuous onset, they were totally routed by the
Saracens; and the garrison, making a sally at the
same time from the city, their camp was pillaged,
and several of their women and children were carried away by the conquerors. The news which arrived about this time of the death of the Emperor
Barbarossa, and of the dispersion of his forces
which took place shortly after, increased their discomfiture, and several of the chiefs began to me-
ditate a retreat. A victory, however, which their
fleet gained over the vessels of the enemy, re-
inspired them with hope; but this was once more
dissipated by a similar circumstance in favour of
the Saracens; and thus the combatants shared success and defeat almost equally between them. But
as the winter season again approached, the Christians began to be less frequently supplied with
stores by the arrival of vessels from Europe, and
famine and disease made fearful ravages in their
camp. To describe the miseries which were suffered on this occasion, would be only to repeat
what has already been said in the account of the

sieges of Antioch and other places during the former crusades; but such was the extremity of misery to which they were soon reduced, that many of the bravest and most faithful warriors sunk beneath their misery, and were driven, by their sufferings, to offer to renounce their religion for the sake of receiving succours from the Moslems. Frederic, who had taken the command of the German crusaders, after the unfortunate death of the Emperor, perished of want and sickness in this calamitous period. The Queen of Jerusalem, also, died about the same time; and the ambitious Conrade increased the distress and confusion of the Christians, by marrying her sister Isabella, whom he caused to be divorced from her lawful husband Honfroy de Thoron, and then laid claim to the crown of the sacred territory.

"Conrade, it will be remembered, had already a wife living, the daughter of the Greek Emperor, whom he had left at Constantinople, when he set forth on his chivalrous expedition to Palestine. This circumstance, together with the divorce which he was obliged to procure for Isabel, occasioned great displeasure to the more conscientious of the faithful; and the weak and unfortunate Guy of Lusignan lost no opportunity of exclaiming against the usurper of his throne. But Conrade had many claims to the respect of the army. He had performed prodigies of valour in the defence of Tyre; he was master of that important city; and was on the whole, perhaps, the prince in whose bravery and experience the discomfited Christians might the most safely place reliance. Opinion was thus divided on the important question of who should be King of Jerusalem, and the most ruinous consequences would probably have followed from the dissensions between the two parties in the army; but the Bishops prudently proposed that the decision should be referred to the Kings of England and France, who were every day expected; and they thus obtained the advantage of putting off the danger of the contest, till they should have more authority to ward off its evil consequences.

The arrival of the two monarchs was celebrated by the Christians with the greatest expressions of delight; and as Saladin cast his eye over the vast plain covered with their tents, he trembled for his newly acquired dominions. But the power of the crusaders was threatened with a fearful diminution, by the pride and dangerous rivalry of Richard and Philip. The latter, it is said, promised three gold pieces a month to the knights in his army who were without money. Richard, on hearing this, immediately promised four to those of his chevaliers who were in a similar situation; and from this and other circumstances of a like nature, the former animosity which existed between them regained possession of their minds. When the subject, therefore, of Conrade's pretensions to the crown of Jerusalem was proposed for discussion, Philip, who seconded his claims, was immediately opposed by Richard, who contended for the rights of Lusignan. In the midst, however, of these disputes, the contest with the Saracens was carried on with equal vigour as at the first; and it was not till the two monarchs fell sick that any pause took place in the conflict. The generous conduct which was evinced by Saladin on this occasion has been deservedly celebrated. T

refresh the Christian princes in their illness, he
sent them supplies of Damascus pears and other
delicious fruits, and an intercourse was kept up
between the three kings, which manifests a high
refinement of sentiment in the warriors of that
period.

Neither Richard nor Philip had suffered their
sickness to keep them entirely from the battle-field;
but instantly on their recovery, the proceedings of
the army again commenced with wonted vigour.
Success, however, still hung doubtfully between
the two armaments, and equal valour was displayed by the Christian and the Moslem. But
the deeds of one chevalier are particularly commemorated in the narrations of the continually renewed contests which took place between the hostile forces. On one of these occasions, the camp
of the believers was attacked by the enemy, who
were on the point of pushing their way beyond
its defences. Without any companion, this renowned hero opposed himself to the charge of the
Moslems, and armed with his heavy cuirass, which
entirely covered him, he received, unflinching, the
vollies of darts and javelins which were incessantly hurled against him. At length, finding that no
weapon could reach the heart of this redoubtable
knight, the Saracens had recourse to the Greek
fire, which, enveloping his head in flames, speedily
destroyed him.

Never did a more general display of valour
take place, than during this long and celebrated
siege. At length, the Saracens began to tremble
within their fortifications. They saw the moats
filled with the dead bodies of their comrades, and
the Christians every day gaining some more advan-

tageous position for carrying on the assault. While a mine was dug on one side, huge mounds of earth were raised on another; and from these hillocks, or their moveable towers, the besiegers poured their destructive missiles into the city. Their perseverance soon began to show some promise of success. The ramparts were in several places broken down, and the garrison became every day less spirited in its resistance. The governor of the city, convinced that he could hold out but for a short time longer, at last consented to follow the wishes of the inhabitants, and endeavour to make terms with the enemy before their power of defence was quite exhausted. He accordingly proceeded to the Christian camp, and there offered to surrender, on condition that the inhabitants should be permitted to retire in safety, which, said he, was granted to the Christians, when, four years before, the Mussulmans had taken possession of the city. But the chiefs of the crusaders refused to accept the offer, and declared they would only spare the inhabitants on condition that Jerusalem, and the other towns taken since the battle of Tiberias, were also surrendered. The Moslem, rendered desperate by this answer, returned to the garrison, and made another bold attempt to save the city. But his efforts were vain, and he was obliged to avert the fury of the conquering Franks, by agreeing to pay two hundred thousand gold pieces to the chiefs, to restore the wood of the true cross, with sixteen hundred prisoners, and to give hostages till these stipulations should be fulfilled.

The siege of Ptolemais had lasted two years, and formed one of the most remarkable periods in the history of the crusades. The chivalry of Europe was put to many a signal proof during its continuance; and the heroic deeds of Richard of England, and other less exalted, but equally brave knights, rendered the plains of Ptolemais famous in the records of chivalric daring. Several encounters, it is related, took place between the chiefs of the hostile armies, which appear to have had their origin in the sole wish of the warriors to try their strength.; and the battle-field was not unfrequently converted into the scene of a splendid tournament. By this means, a close intercourse was kept up between the Christian and the Moslem, and the ferocity of each was softened by the obligations of knightly honour. The courtesy of Saladin, when his royal enemies were confined by sickness to their tents, has been already noticed; and if the rude spirit of the Frank felt at any time the humanizing effects of an intercourse with the more polished Saracen, the siege of Ptolemais was one of the events to which the advantage is to be ascribed. But whatever were the consequences of this occasional interchange of attention between the two enemies, the annals of war have no picture more fearful than that which is presented in the history of this siege. No less than sixty thousand Christians fell before they achieved the victory; and such was the madness that pervaded both the besieged and the besiegers, that multitudes of children were suffered to rush from the respective camps, and destroy each other in the presence of their parents and countrymen.

But in the midst of all this martial fury, and chivalrous glory, we have still before us an odious spectacle of licentiousness and debauchery. The soldiers of the cross openly gave themselves over to every species of vice. Three hundred women are said to have arrived at one time in the camp, who immediately resigned themselves to prostitution; and the moral condition of the army was in all respects in harmony with this affair. The frightful disorders which took place during the first crusade fill the mind with horror; but our astonishment at the atrocities which were then committed by men professedly engaged in the service of God, is greatly diminished by the consideration, that most of those who composed the earlier armaments were drawn from the most untaught and the rudest of the people;—that they were left free both of law and discipline, and were led by men who had little authority over them, and who, for the most part, were as ignorant and devoid of principle, as themselves. No such palliation, however, is to be alleged, in apology for the licentiousness of the army under the Kings of France and England. They were at the head of troops who owned their sovereign authority;—they possessed a general and important influence over the whole vast multitude, and were accompanied by several of the most accomplished cavaliers of the time. The disorders, therefore, which occurred are a plain indication of a general dissolution of manners, not merely in the inferior ranks of the crusaders, but among the boasted ornaments of chivalry; and the gay and sparkling picture of knighthood and its times, is, in this portion of history, changed into a revolting representation of dark and terrifying vice.

But there are circumstances which, in

gloomiest annals of our race, cast a ray of light
over the melancholy spectacle of human degradation.   Frequently has it been the case, that, when
war has reigned in its worst forms, charity and
mercy have found some plea to appear on earth,
and exercise their divine ministry on the very scene
of destruction and misery.   The plains of Ptolemais furnished an example of this kind.   While
thousands of Christians were every day perishing
in battle, and the most powerful of the ecclesiastics were engaged either in the actual conflict, or
in urging the warriors to the fight, a poor English
priest employed himself in consecrating a spot of
ground for the burial of the dead ; and having built
a small chapel there at his own expense, he suffered
no Christian to return to the earth, without paying his remains the last offices of brotherly charity.   The Teutonick Order of Knights had also its
origin about this time, and arose from the benevolence of some German chevaliers, who united
themselves into a body for the protection and support of their wounded countrymen.   Their asso-
ciation was subsequently approved of by the Pope,
and a code of laws was drawn up for the future
government of the society.   The initiation of the
members was nearly the same as that of the Templars ; and, like them, they were to have a cross
embroidered on their vestments, which were
white, and on their banners.   The grand-master
had also the privilege of having the *fleurs-de-lys*
added to the cross, which honour was granted
him by the King of France ; and by these, and
other similar means, the order shortly acquired
considerable distinction.   When, in a subsequent
age, it established itself in Europe, it obtained

by conquest, and the gift of the Pope, a sovereign authority over the principal part of Prussia; but the original spirit of the institution seems to have been worn out before this period; and, under the pretence of bringing the unfortunate inhabitants of the devoted provinces within the pale of the true church, they, perpetrated many and diabolical enormities. But to proceed with our narrative:—

The Christians had scarcely time to enjoy their triumph, before discontent reigned throughout the camp. The pride and impetuosity of Richard appear to have been the first cause of this occurrence. Leopold of Austria was publicly insulted by him, and had the mortification of seeing his standard, which he had fixed on one of the city towers, pulled down and thrown into a ditch by the haughty Englishman. Conrade retired in almost equal disgust; and Philip, moved, it is probable, by a feeling of a similar kind, declared his intention of immediately returning to Europe. Besides these dissensions among the chiefs, a feeling of dissatisfaction very generally prevailed through the army. Nearly the whole of the spoil had been divided by Richard and Philip between themselves; and both the clergy and the troops were loud in their complaints against such a disposition of the booty. But the courage of Richard was not to be daunted by difficulties; and his first wish was to be left sole master of the field. It was with no little pleasure, therefore, that he saw the several rivals of his authority prepare for their departure; and when the last of them took farewell of the ambitious chief, he turned to the work of forcing the enemy to complete the performance of

the capitulation. This, it appears, Saladin was
backward in doing; and the principal articles of
the treaty remained unfulfilled. Richard, therefore, determined on giving the Saracen a proof of
what he would do in prosecution of his right, if it
were any longer withholden; and, on the Wednesday after the Feast of Assumption, he sent seven
hundred of his Moslem prisoners without the
walls of the city, and there had them butchered
by his followers, who are represented as rejoicing
in this work of blood. * The conduct of the monarch has been sometimes excused by the asser-
tion, that Saladin had committed a similar cruelty
towards the Christians in his power; but there is
not evidence sufficiently strong to convict him of
this crime; and the lion-hearted conqueror must
bear the whole weight of the iniquitous proceeding.

Saladin, however, though he determined on resisting the claim of the Christians as to the execution of the treaty, had not sufficient confidence
in his strength to venture on meeting his conquerors in the field, and they were left to enjoy, for
a short time, the pleasures and security of the
noble city they had subdued. But again the cla-
rion sounded through the camp, and at the summons of the English King, the army began to
march towards Joppa. A fleet accompanied
it on its way; and the sacred standard was
borne in a sort of car, mounted on four wheels,
for the purpose. The usual miseries attended its progress, and the troops were infested
continually by numerous insects, harassed by

* Vinisauf.

the close pursuit of the enemy, and oppressed by
the great weight of their armour and accoutrements. They were, therefore, obliged to proceed so slowly, that three leagues was the utmost
distance they could march in a day, and at night
they halted for repose. Before their retiring to
rest, a herald cried with a loud voice, " Lord, succour the Holy Sepulchre!" which he repeated three
times, and the response was made by the whole
army. A similar form was used in the morning
when the march was recommenced; and after six
days the Christians arrived at Cæsarea. The confidence of the chiefs had by this time somewhat
abated, and they would willingly have entered into a negociation with the enemy; but his proud
rejection of all proposals in which the surrender
of Jerusalem was mentioned, made them determine to pursue their fortune, till a battle should
decide the fate of the Holy Land. At length
they reached the plains of Arsur, and there the
troops of the enemy were assembled to meet them.
No less than two hundred thousand Moslems
formed the army of Saladin on this occasion. But
Richard, without hesitation, prepared to engage
him, and about three in the afternoon the battle
was begun by a mixed troop of Bedouin Arabs,
Ethiopians and Scythians, all armed according to
the costume of their respective countries. Their
wild and furious attack, however, made little impression on the faithful, who went forward on
their march, the commander having ordered them
to remain on the defensive till he should give
the signal for attack. But his precaution was rendered useless by the impatience of the army to
commence the assault; and some of the most ar-

dent of the knights rushing forward against the
enemy, they were followed first by the Hospital-
ers, and then by others, and the battle in a
few moments became general. At first, the confusion of the conflict hardly permitted either party
to discover its precise position, and many Christians are said to have fallen under the misdirect-
ed weapons of their brethren. At length the Saracens began to give way, and the faithful saw
themselves masters of the field. They are described as remaining for some minutes so astonished at their sudden success, that they forgot to
examine the real condition of the hostile forces,
and in this situation they were surprised by twenty thousand of the enemy's troops, who, unexpected-
ly rallying, rushed upon them with a courage rendered furious by the desire of retrieving the favour of their master. But Richard flew to the head
of his army, his presence restored its confidence, and
the Moslems were again beaten; so that altogether
Saladin lost in this battle above eight thousand
soldiers, and thirty-two of his principal officers or
Emirs.

The Christians, after this important victory, pursued their route to Joppa; but Saladin had preceded
them, and demolished the fortifications of the town,
as he proposed to do those of the other cities which
he had reason to dread might fall into the hands
of his enemies. It thus became a matter of doubt
to the chiefs of the crusaders, what measure it would
be most prudent for them in this case to pursue.
But Richard succeeded in persuading his companions to remain for a time at Joppa, and commence
rebuilding its fortifications. After enjoying a short
but luxuriant repose, the army resumed its march

in September, and then again fixed its camp, the situation chosen for that purpose being between the castle of Desplants and Mahei. It was while it remained here that Richard gave one of the most shining instances of his bravery and generosity. A small body of Templars having ventured from the camp to ravage the country in search of forage, they were suddenly assailed by a numerous party of Saracens. Overpowered by numbers, they were on the point of sinking beneath the swords of the enemy, when Richard discovered their hazardous position. Mounting his favourite Cyprus barb, he darted towards the scene of action, when his attendants, perceiving the overpowering numbers of the Moslems, begged him to retreat; and it was then he returned that answer to their entreaties, so honourable to him as a brave and faithful knight. "While these warriors," exclaimed he angrily, "have followed me as their chief, I also have promised never to abandon them. If they should perish without help, should I be worthy of commanding them? or should I again be able to bear the name of King?" Without saying more, he rushed upon the Moslems; death followed every stroke of his sword; the dispirited knights recovered their courage; in a little time the infidels were nearly all killed or taken prisoners; and the Christians returned, with Richard at their head, in triumph to the camp.

But notwithstanding all the bravery of Richard, and the readiness with which he always exposed himself to the greatest dangers of the war, he was unable to silence the voice of envy, which was the more clamorous against him, the more he merited the respect of his companions in the holy enterprise. Convinced of the obstacle which was thus opposed to his designs, he repeated the proposal to Saladin, or rather to his brother, Malek-al-Adel, of ceasing from any further prosecution of the war, if he would consent to resign Jerusalem to the Christians, and the wood of the true cross. But again the Saracen rejected the proposition with disdain; asserting, that he could not, without committing the greatest crime, resign a city to infidels, which had been rendered holy in the eyes of Mussulmans, by its having been the chosen scene of their prophet's miraculous vision, and by its still being the spot where the angels loved to assemble. As for the wood of the true cross, the Saracen declared that he considered it as an object of scandal, as an outrage upon the Divinity; and that no consideration or advantages whatsoever should induce him to give up to the Christians that shameful object of their idolatry.

The negociation failing on this ground, it was renewed in a manner less consistent with the principles which seemed to have originally guided the English monarch in his treaties with the Moslem. The widow of William, the late King of Sicily, had a short time since arrived in Syria; and, strange to say, Richard now proposed that a marriage should be effected between Malek-al-Adel, the brother of Saladin, and this Christian princess. Should this take place, he proposed that they should each reign over Jerusalem, and thus provide both Christians and Mussulmans with a ruler of their own faith. This strange proposal was accordingly sent in due form to Saladin, who, it is reported, expressed no disinclination to the arrangement; but, as it was rea-

sonable to expect, both the Christian and Mussulman army manifested the strongest indignation at
this temporizing conduct of their chiefs; and they
were obliged to break off the unpopular conference.
No slight evil appears to have resulted from the
difficulty which the crusaders lay under to settle
the government of the Holy City, even when they
had still to fight for its possession. The most
violent disputes had arisen on account of the doubtful right of succession to the throne; and Philip
and Richard had made this one of the many
sources of their personal dislike. Before the former, however, left Syria, a sort of compromise
had been agreed on by Conrade, who claimed the
crown in virtue of his marriage with the princess
Elizabeth, and the feeble Lusignan. According
to this treaty, it was settled that the latter should
enjoy the kingdom for life, but that, at his death,
it should descend to Conrade, or the heirs of
that prince. That while they both lived, the revenues of the state should be divided between
them; that Conrade should enjoy, as a reward for
his services, Tyre, Berytus and Sidon, which
should belong to him as hereditary possessions;
and that Lusignan should, in the same manner,
be endowed with the lordship of Joppa, with the
provision, however, in both cases, that these states
should be held as tributary to the kingdom of
Jerusalem.

But events were about to occur which speedily
put a termination to this settlement; and how little it was regarded by the principal leader of the
crusades, may be sufficiently learnt from the mention we have made of his negotiations with Malek-
al-Adel. Immediately after the termination of that

affair in the manner described, Richard continued
his march, and the enthusiasm of the army persuaded him to direct his course towards Jerusalem; but the difficulties of the route, the weakness of most of the soldiers from sickness and privation, and the formidable defences which Saladin
was preparing against his approach, rendered the
greater part of the leaders fearful of the consequences of such a bold proceeding, and they
finally determined on marching to Ascalon. But
on their arrival before that city, the Christians
were oppressed with a profound melancholy. That
strong and extensive fortress had been just before
stripped of its noble ramparts by the policy of
Saladin, and now presented a miserable spectacle
of ruin and desolation. Even the Moslem, when
he gave the command for its destruction, is said
to have evinced the deepest regret at the fatal necessity which compelled him to this step.   Having consulted with his Emirs to find, if possible,
some expedient by which the city might be safely
spared, and seeing no alternative, he called one or
two of his friends to him on the morning of the
day intended for the destruction of the place ; and
having, in company with them, taken a last survey of the lofty and magnificent citadel, he exclaimed, " By the holy name of God, I would
rather lose my son than destroy one stone of this
city; but what the will of God, and the welfare
of the faithful require, let that be done." The
command was then given for the demolishing of
the gates and ramparts ; and when the Christians
arrived, Ascalon, the bride of Syria as it was called, retained no resemblance of its late strength
and magnificence.

Richard, with all his impetuosity and pride, and little inclined, as he generally was, to perform any duty but such as called for a display of his knightly acquirements, was not wanting in the penetration and foresight which, had they been oftener exercised, would have gone far in making him a skilful leader, and perhaps a wise and prudent monarch. The same principle by which the Saracens had acted in destroying the fortifications of Ascalon, ought to have induced the crusaders to pursue steadily the plan on which they at first acted, of repairing them. Could they have effected their restoration to any thing near their former strength, they would have made themselves masters of one of the most important stations in the land. Richard was well aware of the benefit which would accrue to the cause by such a procedure, and did every thing in his power to excite the enthusiasm of the army in favour of his design. At first his ardour, and the example which he gave by his personal exertion, was imitated by almost every man in the army; and barons and knights were seen labouring like common workmen in the undertaking. But their determination soon waxed faint; and some of the least willing began to excuse themselves from continuing their exertions, by throwing out expressions of contempt upon the occupation. Leopold of Austria, who had never forgotten the insult which he had received from Richard at Ptolemais, replied to the persuasions of the latter to continue his exertions, that he was neither a carpenter nor a mason. The word was taken up by other chevaliers equally disinclined to such a labo-

L 2

rious employment; and discord speedily reigned through every division of the Christian forces.

The work, however, was continued, though with less activity every day, till Lent, when the desire which had early existed in the army to proceed at once to Jerusalem, returned with all its original violence; and this, added to the discontent and faction which had of late gained ground, rendered the situation of Richard exceedingly doubtful. But he was shortly obliged, from unforeseen circumstances, to determine on measures which threatened the crusaders with direful consequences, and with a fit punishment for their bad faith towards a leader so devoted to their cause as the King of England. Conrade cherished the most violent dislike of his royal rival in arms, as well as authority, and employed every means to destroy his influence with the army. He at last carried his enmity so far, as to form an alliance with the Saracens, preferring to unite with the enemy of the faith, to seeing a man whom he hated prosper in his designs. It is not easy, therefore, to say what would have been the fate of Richard, had circumstances allowed of his longer continuing in Syria; but messengers arrived about this time from England, to acquaint him that his brother John was busily engaged in supplanting him in his dominions, and that he could only save his crown by speedily returning to the West.

Few of the crusaders were blind to the merits of Richard, however they hated him for his success, or dreaded the effects of his powerful resentment. When, therefore, he announced to a council of chiefs his intention to set out on his return to Europe, they received the intelligence with sorrow and consternation; and trembled at the prospect of the evils which they dreaded would follow his departure. Nothing is recorded of Richard more honourable to his character, than his conduct on this occasion. As some reparation of the loss they would sustain by his absence, he promised to leave with the Christians three hundred of his bravest knights, and two thousand foot soldiers. But the noblest instance of his generous sacrifice of private feelings to the general good, was still to come. Deprived of him, the chiefs of the army had reason to dread that confusion and anarchy would prevent their success in any future prosecution of the war. Richard's fame and authority had kept together the discordant elements of the army longer than might have been reasonably expected; and there was scarcely a room for doubt, that, on his influence being withdrawn, the forces would no longer be preserved in a state of organization. The first measure, therefore, which their present circumstances made it necessary to pursue, was the choice of a leader who might in some degree supply the place of the retreating monarch. Conrade presented himself as the only one of the Christian chiefs whose name or character could render him fit to be the successor of Richard in authority. When the latter, therefore, inquired whom they intended to elect as their head, they replied, that they had decided in favour of the Prince of Tyre. At first, Richard was deeply affected by this election of his bitterest enemy, but subduing the feeling almost as soon as it was awakened, he expressed his willingness to assent to the arrangement; and Conrade was chosen King of Jerusalem.

But the joy which the newly elected monarch expressed at the announcement of the messenger who acquainted him with his good fortune, was of brief continuance. Some months before his elevation, two young and devoted disciples of the Old Man of the Mountains arrived at Tyre. Following their usual mode of action, they used the wisest precautions to conceal their real character, and the design they had in view. To render themselves the more secure from suspicion, they assumed the religious habit, and were only remarkable for their austerities, and the fervour of their devotion. At length the time appeared fitted for the execution of their purpose; and while Conrade was sharing in the festivities of the city, in consequence of his election, they finally doomed him to destruction. He was returning from a feast when they met him; and both drawing their daggers, they buried them in the body of the unfortunate prince. The tumult which this sudden catastrophe occasioned, enabled one of the Ismaelians to escape into a neighbouring church; and he lay there concealed, till Conrade was brought in by his attendants. With the most desperate determination to complete his work, he sprung forth from his hiding-place, and, in the sight of the astonished multitude, again plunged his weapon into the body of the prince, who immediately expired under his blows.

The murder of Conrade was ascribed to various causes, and the guilt laid, by turns, at the door of Saladin, Richard, and the injured Honfroy de Thoron, whose wife, it will be remembered, the

Prince of Tyre had caused to be divorced, in order that he might himself marry her. But the Ismaelians preserved the most profound silence respecting their employers, or the motives which led them to commit the deed; and, though put to the most excruciating tortures, they died without revealing the secret. The attention of the people was shortly after engaged by the necessity of choosing a new governor; and Henry, the Count of Champagne, was preferred to the vacant dignity, and married the widow of the late Count.

While these events were taking place, Richard had proceeded to Ramla, and there distinguished himself by many a bold deed of arms. Ten, twenty, and sometimes thirty infidels fell every day beneath his arm; and, when the terror which his name inspired prevented his meeting with a sufficient number of enemies, to secure him his complement of trophies, he turned his spear against the wild animals of the forest, and contented himself with slaying bears instead of Moslems. While engaged in these pursuits, which delayed his proposed journey to Europe, the new King of Jerusalem arrived at his camp, leading with him sixty thousand well-armed troops, and accompanied by his bride and the Duke of Burgundy. The Castle of Daroum had just fallen into the hands of Richard, when this splendid addition was made to his forces, and triumph and festivity pervaded every quarter of the far-spreading encampment. In the general excitement which prevailed, the most distinguished chevaliers in the army made a solemn agreement that they would attempt the recovery of Jerusalem, notwithstanding any determination which the King of England might make to abandon the enterprise. But the jollity of his companions, and the enthusiasm with which they devoted themselves to their design, threw Richard into a deep melancholy; and he remained gloomily shut up in his tent, while every one else was occupied with the music and dancing, or other marks of rejoicing, which filled the plains. Nor were the rebukes of the ministers of religion, or of his conscience, wanted to depress the spirits of the monarch; and the idea of leaving Syria became at length so distressing to him, that he declared to Henry and the Duke of Burgundy, that he would defer his departure till the following Lent. A herald immediately proclaimed the joyful tidings of this change in Richard's measures to the army; and a command was shortly after given the troops, to commence their march towards Jerusalem. The confidence and delight with which the first crusaders traversed the route to the Holy City were scarcely greater than those which inspired the followers of the young King and his noble allies. The soldiers of Henry still retained the gaiety and glitter of the marriage-festival; and those of Richard were filled with the lofty feelings of men rendered proud by late triumphs, and still prouder by being the companions of a leader distinguished throughout Christendom for the splendour of his actions. All hearts were beating high with the hopes of conquest; and no army of crusaders perhaps had ever set forth on their route with more circumstances to support their courage, by brilliant associations and sparkling accompaniments to their martial array. The helmets of the warriors, adorned with a more than usual profusion of plumes; the splendid banners that floated in the air to the songs of minstrels, or the animating notes of the clarions; and the forest of spears, each of which, catching the dazzling light, might have been taken for a sun-beam,—altogether presented a spectacle which filled the beholders with joy, and led the soldiers themselves to believe for a time that they were proceeding to a glorious victory.

But every time we have now occasion to remark any breaking forth of the flame of enthusiasm among the crusaders, we see it burning less steadily, and more easily extinguished by any untoward circumstance. The army had pursued its march to within about seven leagues of Jerusalem, when Richard commanded it to halt, and took up his quarters in the city of Bethenopolis. Here, it appears, the remembrance of his country, of the evils to which he was exposing it by his absence, and of the great probability which existed that he would lose his crown if he any longer delayed to return, came again with full force upon his memory. Still, therefore, undecided as to what measures he should take, he remained at Bethenopolis, neither willing to go forward, and meet Saladin, who was using every means to resist his enemies to the utmost, nor able to overcome his dislike to leave others to reap the harvest of a field which he had himself prepared for the sickle. A month passed away, and still he continued undecided, while the murmurs of the army only served to irritate him, and convert his gloom into rage. Once, while he was in this state of mind, he approached near enough to the Holy City to catch a view of its towers, and the sight melted him to tears; but he could not be persuaded to act in conformity with the impulse which he felt; and when he began to confer again with the other chiefs, he only expressed his doubtfulness as to their chance of succeeding against Saladin, who was now so well prepared to resist their approaches.

The situation, however, of the Christian army was plainly such, that ruin must speedily follow, if some decision was not promptly taken to determine its further movements. A council, therefore, was called, consisting of five members from each of the two great religious orders of knights, five of the barons of Palestine, and five French barons. But the same difficulties opposed the decisions of the council, as had existed in the minds of the chiefs before they had recourse to this means of resolving their doubts. On one side it was alleged, that Saladin was involved in domestic dissensions with his subjects, and with the Caliph of Bagdad, which would prevent his offering any vigorous resistance to the Christian arms. On the other, it was said, that these reports had been circulated by the emissaries of the Moslem, and were only intended to lead the faithful to undertake an enterprise which would perhaps prove the total ruin of their cause, and be a lasting disgrace to themselves.

A.D. 1192. But it is singular enough that Richard, whose greatest wish now appeared to be to retreat from the Saracens, was, at every interval of rest to the general forces, employing himself, and a few of his bravest knights, in the most desperate undertakings. At Ramla and elsewhere, this was the case with our lion-hearted monarch; and whilst his partisans in the council were using every argument in their power to persuade to pacific measures, he was occupied in watching the approach of a richly-laden caravan, which he had received a report was daily expected at Jerusalem, with the most valuable merchandise of Egypt. Choosing a small party from his followers, he immediately set out in quest of the prize, and came up with it in the district of Hebron, after having marched all night. The caravan was guarded by a large band of war-riors; but the irresistible arm of Richard put them to instant flight, and he became master of the rich booty. This consisted of four thousand seven hundred camels, and a proportionate number of horses, mules, and asses, all of which were bur-dened with the most valuable productions of the East. The return of Richard, thus accompanied, to the camp, was hailed with loud acclamations of joy; and the people of Jerusalem were thrown into equal consternation by the loss of so much wealth. Had the Christians marched directly to the Holy City, they would have had every cir-cumstance in their favour, a disheartened garrison, and a tumultuous populace, confounding all the schemes which Saladin was employing to secure the defence of the place. But the council which had been chosen to consider the expediency of proceeding to Jerusalem, decided against it; and the army had the mortification to learn, in the midst of its rejoicings, that a retreat was to be immediately commenced.

Saladin, as soon as he saw the crusaders turn their backs on the Holy City, collected an army, composed of the forces of Mesopotamia, Aleppo, and Egypt, with which he proceeded to Joppa, and took that city by assault. But Richard ar-rived at the moment of the Moslem's triumph from Ptolemais ; and, jumping out of the vessel which was carrying him to shore, before it could reach land, he rushed upon the enemy, and quickly compelled him to retreat. On the third day after this valorous exploit, the Saracens renewed their attempts, and early in the morning he was roused by the cry of " To arms ! " When he rose, he found his camp surrounded by Musulmans ; and he had scarcely time half to dress himself, before he was obliged to mingle in the fray. Ten horses only, it is said, remained to the Christian chevaliers, and these were immediately mounted by Richard, the Count Robert of Leicester, the King of Jerusalem, and other equally brave knights, who followed Richard, some of them without shoes or stockings, and others without any covering but their shirts. After having made a hasty disposition of his small force, the valorous King exhorted them to fight like men whose only safety was in their courage, as they were surrounded by the enemy, and retreat was impossible. To this argument he added another equally powerful, and solemnly swore that he would cut off the head of any man whom he saw slack in his duty. The Turks now approached, with their trumpets sounding and banners flying, against this little but desperate band of opponents ; and after a short trial of strength, they were obliged to give way before the firm line of the Christians. Richard then led his men forward, and the cross-bowmen discharging their arrows, completed the discomfiture of the enemy. The chevaliers, in the mean time, rode furiously into the disordered ranks of the Moslems ; and as often as the valour of any one of them brought him into imminent peril, King Richard was im-

mediately at hand to cut his way through the
crowd. At one time he plunged alone into the
very centre of the Saracens, and for some time
was lost entirely from the view of his anxious followers. But while they were expecting to hear
the shout of triumph at the fall of their noble
leader, they beheld him riding out of the disordered ranks of the enemy, covered with dust, and
the blood of the numbers who had fallen by
his hand. It was at this period of the battle that
Malek-al-Adel displayed in a singular manner his
respect for the bravery of his enemy. Richard, as
it is commonly reported, was in the midst of the
fray, when he saw a Turk leading towards him
two beautiful Arabian war-horses, and they were
presented to him with a message from the chivalrous
Moslem, purporting that they were sent to aid
him in the perilous situation in which he stood.

The boldness of Richard carried him through
every danger; and as he flew from one part of the
battle-field to another, he strewed his path with
dead and wounded, and cast as much terror into
the minds of his enemies as if he had been St
George himself. Even the bravest of the Saracens felt a dread at encountering his arm; and one
who was most reputed for strength and skill in
the use of his weapons, having ventured to meet
Richard in single combat, fell in the sight of his
companions, the King, at one blow, severing his
head, right shoulder and arm, from the rest of his
body. Such was the terror which this and other
such deeds inspired, that the routed Moslems asserted that even the horses bristled their manes at the
name of Richard; and it was, after this, a common
expression with the riders of unruly steeds, to

say, that King Richard was in the way. But the
King had scarcely insured his success against the
enemy in the field, when his attention was called
to a large body of Saracens, who, during the battle, had secured themselves in the city. With
a few of his followers, Richard immediately made
his way into the town, and as speedily routed the
terrified Moslems from their defences. Towards
the evening, therefore, the Christians remained in
full possession of the field; and, desperate as had
been the conflict, they had the satisfaction to find,
that only one of their brave knights had fallen in
the battle, and he owed his death either to his
cowardly or thoughtlessly disobeying the orders
which Richard had given at the beginning of the
day. The Turks lost seven hundred men, and
above fifteen hundred horses. The crusaders were
so astonished at the issue of the battle, that they
ascribed their victory to the immediate interposi-
tion of Providence, and declared that his strength
only could have made them masters of the field
against such a host of enemies.

CHAPTER V.

THE defeat which Saladin had suffered in this memorable engagement, greatly afflicted both him and his Emirs ; and, though the courage and devotion of the brave Moslem remained unabated, it was apparent to him that his prosperity was on the wane, and that his life of glory and conquest might probably be terminated in an ignominious peace. In a council, however, which he assembled soon after the above events, he continued to express his hopes for better things ; and on his return to Jerusalem, received the proposals which Richard again made for peace with unwilling attention. He dreaded, he said, lest death should surprise him before he had completed the triumph of Islamism, and lest, by discontinuing a war in which God had so often crowned his arms with victory, he should be acting contrary to his will. But his ardour found no support in the disposition of the Emirs. They represented to him the defenceless state of the provinces, the ill condition of the troops, and the advantages which the Christians now enjoyed for pursuing their designs. In addition to this, they argued, that their enemies were notorious for the bad faith with which they kept their engagements, and that they would, without doubt, speedily afford them an opportunity of recommencing the war when they might be better prepared for carrying it on with success. Saladin, though not convinced, was persuaded by these arguments to enter into a negociation with the English King; and after the preliminaries had been debated, it was at length decided, that a truce should be established for three years and eight months, during which time the Christians were to have uninterrupted access to the Holy City, and to retain possession of the coast from Joppa to Tyre. Ascalon, as both had pretensions to that city which neither was willing to cede to those of the other, was again condemned to ruin; and with regard to the wood of the true cross, as this had been a fruitful cause of dispute in former attempts at a negociation, the Christian leader appears to have dropped all mention of that sacred relic. In ratification of this agreement, all the principal warriors in the two armies swore to its faithful observance,—the Musulmans taking their oath on the Koran, and the Christians on the Gospels. But Saladin and Richard, it is well worthy of record, only gave each other a mutual promise of fidelity, the interchange of their parole being deemed a sufficient gage for the truth of heroes so brave and chivalrous as the Prince of the Saracens and the King of England. It must not be forgotten either, that the Old Man of the Mountains was among those who signed the treaty, his influence having been felt both by Moslems and Christians during the war, and being still equally dreaded by each of these powerful parties. But the most singu-

lar circumstance, perhaps, of the whole affair, was
the omission of any mention of the unfortunate
Lusignan. That prince was, by the present treaty, deprived of his crown, with which Henry was
again formally endowed, and the dethroned monarch contented himself with obtaining the principality of Cyprus. The history of Lusignan is thus
a chequered one. He was exposed, from the commencement of his reign, to the dislike of his subjects, the more powerful of them hating him for
the honour to which his mere personal attractions
had advanced him, and those of inferior rank despising him for his alleged incapacity. His principal fault, however, seems to have sprung from his
being elevated above the rank which Nature intended him to occupy, and not from any want of
courage, or other knightly virtues. His conduct at
Ptolemais obtained him the temporary applause
of his associates, and Richard all along regarded
him with sufficient respect to adhere to his cause,
while there appeared any chance of protecting him
from his numerous rivals. But situated as the affairs of the Christians then were, talents even of
the first order might have been found insufficient
to preserve the possessor of the sacred diadem
from the hatred, if not contempt, of his subjects;
and Richard or Conrade, though they might have
longer wrestled with their enemies, would, it is
probable, have been as little able to retain the reins
of government in their hands as Lusignan. The royal authority was still considered by the Christians
to exist among them; and they expected to see
their nominal sovereign effecting as much in combating with the enemy, and in ordering their affairs, as if he had been seated on his throne in the

Holy City, which neither Lusignan, nor any other monarch, however splendid his accomplishments, could do. The deposed King had, in the beginning of his reign, to support the weight of a pillar lifted from its base, and prepared to fall the moment his strength should be insufficient for the burden. In a nation differently situated, he might have been able to depend on the aid of his associates; but the rivalships which had so long existed among the barons of Palestine, left him without any hope of assistance, either from their counsel or influence; and, when the time of trial came, he had to meet it with very inadequate forces, and to sustain the whole ignominy of the consequences.

As soon as the treaty was fully settled, the greater part of the crusaders began to prepare for their departure to Europe. But few of them felt that satisfaction at the conclusion of this third great enterprise, which they had expected to reap when they set out from the West. They had gone forth in the spirit of devotion and chivalry, animated with the most romantic sentiments, and desiring either to return crowned with the glory of having again delivered the Holy Sepulchre from the pollutions of the infidel, or to find a grave among their renowned predecessors. But they had hardly touched the shores of Syria, when enthusiasm, devotion, and knightly virtue, gave way to personal rivalry and the desire of gain, which every day became baser, and more destructive of the objects of the expedition. We can discern in the picture of the third crusade no characters which bear any resemblance to the gentle, brave, and noble-hearted Tancred, or to the bold, but sedate and pious Godfrey. All were intent on carrying some point of private advantage; and several of the most distinguished of the chiefs mutually accused each other, and with great appearance of reason, of having basely leagued with the enemy, in order to destroy the authority of his brethren in arms and religion. The retreat, therefore, of the forces which remained after the disasters to which the Christian army had been subject, was unmarked with any of those demonstrations of pious satisfaction which ought to have attended the return of Christian warriors from the scene of a holy warfare to the land of their nativity. Among those who were most deeply affected with these feelings of dissatisfaction and despondency, was the King of England. Message after message had arrived from England, warning him of the danger of his dominions, and soliciting his return. When he left his kingdom to set out for Syria, he had felt so entire a devotion to the enterprise, as scarcely to value either the happiness or the security of his territories. But these sentiments were put to a severe proof in the after events of the crusade; and, as he lost his hopes of succeeding in the entire conquest of Palestine, he became more and more solicitous respecting the fate of his kingdom. The intelligence which was brought from Europe increased his anxiety, and rendered him desirous of returning the moment he could do so, consistently with his reputation for courage and piety.

But the means which Richard appears to have employed to effect his object, cast a shade of doubt over his renown. Of all the chiefs in the Christian army, he was the foremost in endeavouring to bring about a peace with the Moslem; and though, in looking coolly on the narrative of these

transactions, we may feel inclined to applaud such
a counsel as consistent with prudence and good
sense, it is difficult to believe that a man of Richard's character was guided solely by these principles.   His close and frequent conferences, also,
with Malek-al-Adel gave a very plausible reason for
his associates to doubt the perfect honesty of his
views ; and it is, therefore, a questionable point
in the history of our lion-hearted monarch, whether he was not more eager after personal renown, than the successful prosecution of the general designs of Christendom.

But, however this may be, he was deeply affected as he prepared to bid adieu to the scene of his
chivalrous exploits ; and this is the strongest argument which can be brought in support of his sincerity.   But it failed to convince the different
chieftains, who had been instant in urging the probability that Jerusalem would fall into their hands,
if vigorously assaulted ; and the French, in particular, reprobated his conduct.   Others, on the contrary, regarded him with the highest respect and
veneration ; and when the time of his departure
actually arrived, numbers of the people shed tears,
and lamented him as if they were losing their last
hope of safety from the enemy.   Richard himself, whose heart was ever open to sudden impulses of passion, was also affected to weeping at
this demonstration of popular regard ; and as he
looked back upon the land of his adventurous pilgrimage, and on his affectionate followers, he exclaimed, in the grief and devotion of his soul,
" O Holy Land ! I commend thy people to God.
May Heaven grant that I may again come to visit
and succour thee ! "   Thus taking farewell of the

shores on which he had landed with such a noble resolution to annihilate the power of the Moslem, he set sail for Europe; but was fated, in his journey, to meet more and greater dangers than those with which he had to contend in his warfare with the infidel. Directing his course along the Adriatic, he was shipwrecked near Aquileia; and, fearing lest he might be discovered in that unprotected state by any of the European princes whose enmity he had reason to dread, he put on the habit of a simple pilgrim, and commenced his journey towards Germany, through which country he hoped to find his way safe to England. But his imprudent exposure of the wealth which he bore, quickly destroyed what little protection he was capable of deriving from his disguise. Desiring to obtain a safe conduct through the domain of the Count Meinhard, a friend of the murdered Conrade, he was aware that it would be necessary for him to use the utmost precaution in concealing the knowledge of his real character from Meinhard, who was strongly attached to the Prince of Tyre. He therefore demanded a passport as the merchant Hugo, and sent the Count a splendid ruby ring, by way of purchasing the favour required. Meinhard, on seeing the costly jewel, immediately exclaimed, " Not the merchant Hugo, but King Richard, sends me this ring. I have sworn not to allow any pilgrim to pass through my territory; but, from regard for the good will which the King has shown, and out of respect for his worth, I will grant him a safe conduct, but beg to return him his jewel." The fair words of the Count, however, were only intended to deceive

the King; and the latter very narrowly escaped
being made prisoner by the emissaries of the treacherous Meinhard.   Scarcely was he delivered from
this peril, when he fell into another, being pursued by the brother of his former enemy, who sent
after him a knight, to whom he gave directions to
force the house where Richard had taken up his
lodging.   But, fortunately for the King, the knight
knew him, and being friendly to him, gave him
a strong and swift horse, allowed him to escape
unharmed.   For three days and three nights he
rode without venturing to seek shelter or nourishment; but, at length, stopped at an obscure inn,
in a small village near Vienna, where for some days
he remained closely immured.   Still, however, he
had not been warned sufficiently by his late escapes
to act with prudence to secure his safety.   A large
and splendid ring, which it little became a simple pilgrim to wear, he stlll retained on his finger;
and took so little care in warning his attendant of
the necessity of secrecy, that that worthy follower
exposed the gold coins of Syria, which they had
brought with them; and when he found he had
awakened the suspicions of the people, he vainly
endeavoured to allay them, by reporting that his
employer was a rich merchant,   Not trusting, however, to the success of his attempt to undo the
mischief of this imprudent conduct, he warned his
master immediately to leave the place ; but Richard
preferred meeting the danger to resuming his journey;
and the suspicion of some people at Vienna being further increased, he was sought for, and arrested by one
of the officers of Duke Leopold, whose enmity to
Richard had been so violently excited at the siege
of Ptolemais.   The unfortunate King declared he

would surrender only to the Duke himself; and
when the latter appeared, he resigned his sword,
but though, at first, treated with some regard
to his rank and character, he was shortly after
thrown into strict confinement. Leopold was
not permitted long to retain his illustrious captive;
and Richard was delivered up to the Emperor
Henry VI., who confined him in a strong castle,
and neglected no means to prevent his escape.
But the lofty spirit of the royal chevalier retained its pride and gaiety through every adversi-
ty. He amused himself with sometimes wrest-
ling with his guards, and at others with making
them intoxicated, and then sporting with their ab-
surdities. Richard, however, was not wanting in
powers of mind which furnished him occasionally
with a more refined recreation. It was the fashion
in that age of war and minstrelsy, for the bravest
and highest-born knights to cultivate the gentle
arts of song; and while the page and the squire
were expected to be able to soothe the idle hu-
mour of their masters or mistresses with a lay of
love or battle, the chevalier himself was thought
to be more perfect if he remembered well those
accomplishments of his youth. Several of the most
renowned knights, therefore, are described as having been poets of no mean degree, and the lives of
the Troubadours are mingled with the stories of
many a gallant warrior. Thus, about the time of
Richard, Rambaud de Vaqueiras, the son of a poor
knight, gained so much reputation by his uniting
the characters of soldier and poet in his own person, that the celebrated Marquis of Montferrat,
who took so important a part in the fourth cru-

sade, encouraged him in making love to his noble
sister; and Vaqueiras divided his time between
singing the praises of his lovely mistress, or the
brave actions of his lord, and performing all the
valorous exploits which were to be looked for
from a redoubtable chevalier.   Bertrand de Born,
Viscount of Hautefort, is still more celebrated in
the annals of the time of which we are speaking,
for his excellent talents as a poet, and his bravery
as a knight.   He was the boldest of the chevaliers
of France, breathing it is said nothing but war,
and rousing the martial passions of all around him
to the highest pitch of excitement by the glowing
eloquence of his songs.   He was early engaged in
the quarrels of Richard with the French States,
and espoused the side of Henry of Gaienne against
that prince.   He was exposed continually to the
greatest dangers and disasters, owing to his impetuous disposition; and after a life of constant action
and adventure, he retired to a Cistercian monastery, in which he died. * One of the poems which
this renowned knight addressed to his mistress, to
whom he had been accused of infidelity, still exists.
"It places before us," says M. de Sismondi, "the
real knight of former times, all busied in war and
the chase, the labour and delight of our fathers,
successively appealing to every thing that is dear to
him in life, to every thing which has been the
study of his youth and of his riper age, and yet es-
teeming them all light, in comparison with love;"
which will be a sufficient apology for inserting it in
this place.

* Sismondi's Literature of the South of Europe.

I CANNOT hide from thee how much I fear
The whispers breathed by flatterers in thine ear
   Against my faith.   But turn not, Oh! I pray,
That heart so true, so faithful, so sincere,
So humble and so frank, to me so dear,
   Oh lady! turn it not from me away.

So may I lose my hawk, ere he can spring,
Borne from my hand by some bold falcon's wing,
   Mangled and torn before my very eye.
If every word thou utterest does not bring
More joy to me than fortune's favouring,
   Or all the bliss another's love might buy.

So, with my shield on neck, mid storm and rain,
With vizor blinding me, and shorten'd rein,
   And stirrups far too long, so may I ride,—
So may my trotting charger give me pain,
So may the ostler treat me with disdain,
   As they who tell those tales have grossly lied.

When I approach the gaming board to play,
May I not turn a penny all the day;
   Or may the board be shut, the dice untrue,
If the truth dwell not in me, when I say
No other fair e'er wiled my heart away,
   From her I've long desired and loved—from you.

Or, prisoner to some noble, may I fill,
Together with three more, some dungeon chill,
   Unto each other odious company;
Let master, servants, porters, try their skill,
And use me for a target if they will,
   If ever 1 have loved aught else but thee.

So may another knight make love to you,
And so may 1 be puzzled what to do ;
   So may I be becalmed 'mid oceans wide :
May the King's porter beat me black and blue,
And may I fly ere I the battle view,
   As they that slander me have grossly lied. *

But none of these warrior-poets is more celebrated than Richard ; and he is said to have sooth-
ed many hours of his long and dreary captivity in
the composition of lays, in which he recalled to
memory the events of his pilgrimage, or lamented
the hard fortune to which he was now doomed.
The following has been handed down to us as
having been composed by the illustrious prisoner,
after he had been confined fifteen months in the
Tour Tenebreuse, or Black Tower.

No wretched captive of his prison speaks,
   Unless with pain and bitterness of soul ;
Yet consolation from the Muse he seeks,
   Whose voice alone misfortune can control.
Where now is each ally, each baron, friend,
   Whose face I ne'er beheld without a smile ?
Will none, his sovereign to redeem, expend
   The smallest portion of his treasures vile ?

Though none may blush that, near two tedious years,
   Without relief, my bondage has endured,
Yet know, my English, Norman, Gascon peers,
   Not one of you should thus remain immured :
The meanest subject of my wide domains,
   Had I been free, a ransom should have found ;

* Roscoe's Translation.

I mean not to reproach you with my chains,
  Yet still I wear them on a foreign ground!

For true it is—so selfish human race!
  " Nor dead nor captive, friend or kindred find ;"
Since here I pine in bondage and disgrace,
  For lack of gold my fetters to unbind ;
Much for myself I feel, yet, ah ! still more
  That no compassion from my subjects flows :
What can from infamy their names restore,
  If, while a prisoner, death my eyes should close?

But small is my surprise, though great my grief,
  To find, in spite of all his solemn vows,
My lands are ravaged by the Gallic chief,
  While none my cause has courage to espouse.
Though lofty towers obscure the cheerful day,
  Yet, through the dungeon's melancholy gloom,
Kind Hope, in gentle whispers, seems to say,
  " Perpetual thraldom is not yet thy doom. "

Ye dear companions of my happy days,
  Of Chail and Pensavin, aloud declare
Throughout the earth, in everlasting lays,
  My foes against me wage inglorious war.
Oh, tell them, too, that ne'er, among my crimes,
  Did breach of faith, deceit, or fraud appear ;
That infamy will brand to latest times
  The insults I receive, while captive here.

Know, all ye men of Anjou and Touraine,
  And every bach'lor knight, robust and brave,
That duty, now, and love, alike are vain,
  From bonds your sovereign and your friend to save

Remote from consolation, here I lie,
  The wretched captive of a powerful foe,
Who all your zeal and ardour can defy,
  Nor leaves you aught but pity to bestow. *

The fate of Richard had been kept concealed from his subjects, by every stratagem which the policy of the Emperor could invent; and Philip Augustus offered that monarch an immense reward, if he would deliver up to him the person of his captive. The greatest consternation, in the mean time, reigned in England, on account of the absence of the King, whose renown had made him dear to his people, and whose mysterious delay filled them with apprehension. At length, the minstrel Blondel, who was more strongly attached to Richard than any of his followers, set out with the determination of travelling through every town and village, till he discovered the place of his beloved master's imprisonment. On arriving near the castle in which the King was confined, the faithful Blondel inquired, as seems to have been his custom, whether there was not some prisoner in the tower which he saw. The answer which he received to his inquiry convinced him, that the King was confined there; but, as he had no means of gaining a sight of his master, he had recourse to an expedient which became both his profession and the romance of the adventure. Richard and he, in some hour of friendship and idleness, had amused themselves in composing a Tenson, in which they responsed to each other; and Blondel now conceived the idea

* Burney's History of Music.

of singing a part of this song, so well known to his master, under the windows of the tower where he supposed him to be confined. Scarcely had he finished the first verse, when the delighted minstrel heard the strain resumed by the manly voice of Richard; and, having satisfied himself as to the correctness of his suspicions, he immediately bent his way to England, where the information which he gave was received by all classes of people with mixed sentiments of rage against the dishonourable enemies of their monarch, and sympathy with the noble sufferer. Their patriotism, it is well known, speedily delivered him from his captivity; but he returned to his dominions only to be involved in fresh troubles, and prove that, however admirable were his chivalrous qualities, he was destitute of the steady virtues and more useful adornments which render a monarch venerable and powerful among his people. The character of Richard appears great and worthy of admiration, or low and contemptible, as we behold on different sides. To the eye of the moralist, and when examined by the pure and unchanging laws of truth, men are virtuous and vicious, as they approach to, or recede from, the standard of good, which exists perfectly only in the Divine mind; but which, though less bright, is as an angel of life and knowledge enshrined in every man's conscience. But the inquiry of the historian is not respecting the primary or absolute virtue or vice of men's actions, but what were the circumstances which increased the splendour of their good deeds, or served to palliate the ignominy of their bad ones; or how far they agreed with, or contradicted the particular impulses to good, which existed in the ruling

spirit of the age in which they lived. In this respect
we must observe Richard as he spoke, thought, and
acted, amid scenes, and under influences, which affected all who lived at the same time, as well as
himself, and which were sufficiently strong to modify every feeling and sentiment which were not
indelibly stamped on the heart by nature. To act
in conformity with the plain and simple laws of
morality, was not, in that age, sufficient to satisfy
either the world or the conscience of the individual. Society, if we may use such a figure, wore
a scarlet mantle; and to shine in the splendour of
heroic deeds, alone gave the right to be clothed in
the livery of the times. Richard was a King.
He had, by nature, a warm heart and a quick
imagination. In whatever age he had lived, he
would have sought glory more than peace, and rejoiced rather in being a hero than a statesman. But
he lived at a period when the romance of his disposition was in perfect harmony with the opinions
of the world, and when, to be led unresistingly by
the imagination, was to act in concert with the
most admired of his cotemporaries. By his rank,
and the talents with which nature had endowed
him, he was fitted to take the first station in the
numerous ranks of chivalry; and with his own
feelings acting from within, and impressed by so
many outward impulses of popular passion, it is
not wonderful that Richard of England shone in
the brightest panoply of a Christian warrior. So
far as a human being may take his rule of action
from the character of his age, and deserve glory
for conforming to it, Richard merits a nobler fame
than any of his compeers. His knightly valour
was exercised on the most desperate occasions, and

when the only reason for his exposing himself to
danger was that he might perform the duties of a
chevalier without fear or reproach. In embarking
for the crusade, he freely spent the greater part of
his riches, and put his throne in peril. During his
sojourn in the Holy Land, the feelings with which
he calculated the chances of succeeding in its perfect recovery from the infidel, were excited by the
deepest anxiety to partake in the triumph, or not
leave the scene of conflict till the moment, when
to fight would be no longer of any use. When
circumstances drove him to the necessity of precipitating his departure, the gloomiest melancholy,
it is on all sides allowed, took possession of his
mind, and the tears which were plentifully shed
by the Syrian Christians when he bade them farewell, and his own sorrowful exclamations, prove
that he had been a true and faithful champion.

But the fame of Richard, and the pleasure with
which we regard his romantic heroism, are greatly
diminished at the recollection of the deeds of fearful
cruelty of which he was occasionally guilty. He
might slay his twenty or thirty in battle, and be
entitled, as men usually estimate these things, to
glory for so doing; but when we find him ordering the butchery of his prisoners in their chains,
we are forced to rank him among the bloodiest of
tyrants. His conduct to the Jews, and the tyranny
with which he oppressed his subjects in general,
are only to be in a very slight manner excused by
our knowledge of the imperfect light which then
prevailed respecting social liberty. In short, as
soon as we see Richard out of the battle-field, and
divested of his armour and his conquering sword,
we lose our respect for him, and lament that times

should have been, in which mankind knew of no greater glory, and no higher virtues, than those which this brave but ruthless and tyrannical monarch sought and exercised. The actual misfortunes of Richard's life were fortunate for his fame. Much of the interest attached to his memory results from the perils and distresses with which he had to struggle; and Richard, in the Tour Tenebreuse, is loved and pitied by the young and romantic, in spite of the dark deeds which history has registered under his name. His love of minstrelsy, is also another preservative of his glory; and when looking through the dim veil of the past, the imaginative may be excused, if they point in delight and triumph to the splendid vision of a king rejoicing alike in his lyre and sword, and not more glorious as a hero in battle, than tender as a lover and a poet. But while we allow him all the advantages which he may derive from these sources, we must be careful not to permit him to rank in our estimation with those of our monarchs in whose wisdom or virtue we have still to rejoice. Richard did nothing beneficial, either for his own age, or for posterity. He carried to an extreme the principles which had effect in society while he lived; but he neither controlled nor modified them, nor in any instance anticipated future times either in virtue or wisdom.

CHAPTER VI.

DEATH OF SALADIN.—THE EMPEROR HENRY VI. UNDERTAKES
ANOTHER CRUSADE.

A. D. 1193. In returning to our narrative, Syria now presents a scene very different from those we have of late contemplated. After the departure of Richard for Europe, the Christian chiefs who remained behind devoted themselves, apparently with great sincerity, to the establishment of the peace which had been commenced with the Saracens. The young King of Jerusalem had the good sense to perceive, that his royalty was merely nominal, and, therefore, would only allow himself, after a short time, to be called Count Henry. By this conduct, and a similar one in the other principal men of the Christians, the greatest concord prevailed between them and the Moslems. This was even carried so far, that Saladin sent Henry a magnificent turban and vest, which the latter publicly wore as a mark of affection for the Sultan. Little doubt, therefore, was entertained for the time, that Syria would enjoy a long tranquillity; but scarcely had his subjects been allowed to taste the blessings of peace, when Saladin was taken from them by death, and they were left exposed to the evils of a disputed succession.

Among the European warriors or monarchs of the age we are describing, no one appears to have so great a claim to our respect as Saladin. His first acquisition of power was marked, it is true, with a very doubtful character, and it is probable that he raised himself to a kingly station by those means which ambition is ever ready to provide and consecrate to her purposes. But according to history, the early life of Saladin was passed in luxury and dissipation, and it is a case, we believe, of frequent occurrence, that when a great and bold mind first awakens from its lethargy, and becomes conscious of its natural right to power, it will obey the sudden impulse to whatever ends it may conduct. But the character of Saladin, in the following events of his life, was rendered venerable by the moderation with which he used his successes, the enlightened generosity which influenced his conduct towards those of a different faith, and the prudence with which he managed the interior affairs of his dominions. He was a warrior from his youth, but he was ever ready to exercise the courtesies of benevolence towards his enemies ; and strove, by affording many instances of mildness and forbearance, to soften the wild and barbarous temper of his people. His devotion was deep and fervent ; and the natural gravity of his disposition inclined him to the most solemn and rigid attention to all the articles of his creed. But the greatness of his mind seems to have triumphed over all feelings of bigotry ; and he was faithfully devoted to his belief, and passed his life in defending it, without being a persecutor. Allowing for the different circumstances in which they were placed, a strong resemblance exists between the characters of Saladin and Mahomet. They both afforded splendid examples of a strong intellect, full of grand conceptions, and thus reared for themselves a kingdom, instinct only with the life which they gave it, and which ceased to exist in the same manner the moment they perished. Mahomet was the mightier, it is true; but Saladin approaches nearer to him than all his other followers, in the possession of those qualities of mind and disposition to which the Prophet owed his elevation.

Saladin was deplored by all classes of his subjects; and he is said to have given, shortly before his decease, which occurred at Damascus, many proofs of his wisdom, such as having sent his shroud to be seen by the multitude, as all which then remained to their victorious monarch. But these stories are generally rejected as fables; and his panegyrists are satisfied with resting his fame on the surer details of his history. He left behind him seventeen sons and a daughter. The three eldest of the former were Malek-al-Afdal, who had been employed by his father in many important stations; Malek-al-Asis, and Malek Addaher. But, unfortunately for the fate of his kingdom, he had neglected to make choice of a successor to his far-stretching authority; and, immediately after his decease, the three brothers, together with their uncle, Malek-al-Adel, took possession of those portions of the country which they could most conveniently seize. The weakness of one, and the ambition of another, speedily gave rise to dissentions among the young princes; and Malek-al-Adel employed his policy and experience sufficiently

well to make himself, in a short time, master of
the best portion of their dominions.

While the affairs of the Moslems were in this
disturbed state, the Christians were every day becoming weaker and more corrupt. There was no
one who sufficiently respected their cause to assume the title of King of Jerusalem, or offer himself as their ruler and champion. Although in a
state of peace, they were exposed, after the death
of Saladin, to the continual insults of the infidels;
and the pride and avarice of the Hospitallers and
Templars had long rendered the holy orders of
chivalry of little use in the defence of the faith.
About the time of which we are speaking, the
most violent jealousies existed between the two
establishments; and they had not refrained from
employing their arms against each other, whenever either jealousy, or the desire of aggression,
excited their passions.

From all these circumstances, the Christendom
of the East was daily losing its power and vene-
rableness. The lamp which had been set up, and
threw its strong and fiery light for a while amid
the sacred relics of Palestine, was burning to its
socket. The gloom of a false faith was again sinking,
without resistance, over the land; and, amid the
loud and continual prayers of the disciples of the
Prophet, few and feeble were those which the people of the Lord addressed to their Almighty King.
The vigour and devotion which had animated the
Christians of Jerusalem, when the first crusade
was projected, was now no longer visible in any
part of Syria; and it is more than probable, that
if the faithful had been suffered to remain without
interruption from the Moslem, or communication

with the West, they would, in a few years, have
so lost all their religion in the indifference and licentiousness which now prevailed, as to give the
Saracens no longer any trouble about the sanctity
of the Sepulchre.

A. D. 1196. But the feelings to which the late
important expedition owed its origin, were not
yet entirely extinct in Europe. Celestine the
Third, though now ninety years of age, retained
his enthusiasm for the cause of Jerusalem. Many
of the higher clergy did, or appeared to do, the
same; and the supreme Pontiff, conceiving it his
duty to call the slumbering princes to arms, and
confiding in the strength of his exhortations, sent
letters to all the bishops and archbishops, desiring them to preach immediately on the duty of
again wrenching the Holy City from the power of
the infidel. Though the veneration for Jerusalem, however, still existed in the mind of Celestine, and might yet exercise some influence over
the hearts of the devout, these sentiments retained little hold on the minds of the people at large.
A century is far too long a period for the prosperity of any cause which depends for its success on
popular passion. Society is never stationary in its
governing principles or interests; and the objects,
consequently, which may at one period be effected
by a word, it will require at another all the arts of
the politician and the wealth of kingdoms to bring
into notice. Had no other causes, therefore, existed, but the simple change which had taken place
in the state of the popular mind, the recovery of
Jerusalem would have been listened to at this period with a far different temper to that in which its
preachers had been formerly received. But the

miseries which had followed the expeditions undertaken for that purpose, though not sufficiently, regarded at first to prevent crowds of enthusiasts
from following those who perished, could not be
remembered without a thrill of horror ; and a feeling of this kind gains strength, in proportion as the
period recedes in which the enthusiasm or the
cause of the suffering existed. It was, however,
not so much the recollection of the thousands who
had fallen by the sword of the Moslem which produced this effect, as the deep sense of injury with
which the people groaned under the arbitrary taxes
which had been imposed by their monarchs to provide means for the crusades. All the sober or selfish feelings of the people were by this means called into action, to oppose those of enthusiasm or
devotion ; and though the former will be some time
in gaining the complete ascendency, they will be
sure to do so at last. Popular sentiment had already passed the first stage of its progress towards
this change ; and as trade and increasing information on subjects connected with social rights, were
beginning to cast a glimmering light over the states
of Europe, every day added strength to the common sense decision of prudence and interest.

Such were some of the difficulties with which
Celestine had to contend, when he published a New
Crusade ; and he soon found, that not only the people had considerably changed their opinions on the
subject, but that the monarchs, who had formerly
been his great support, could be no longer moved
by his persuasions. Richard had not laid aside
the badge of a crusader ; and the Pontiff for some
time hoped, that his arguments, and those of the
English bishops, would reach the heart of the lion-

hearted King, and persuade him again to cross the
sea for Palestine. But Richard had suffered too
much already by his adventures, and was now too
busily occupied with the disturbed affairs of his
dominions, to listen to the suggestions of his spiritual advisers. Another reason is also mentioned
as a probable one for his resisting all arguments of
the kind. The power and jealousy of his rival
Philip were greatly to be dreaded, and had been
more than once in action against his authority.
Had his captivity been longer continued, there appeared to be no doubt that the machinations of the
French King would not have ceased, till he had
possessed himself of a part of the English dominions; and it was equally probable, that if Richard
again left them unprotected, these attempts would
be renewed.

Finding his endeavours produce little effect on
the King of England, the Pope next turned his
attention to Philip; but the fear which the former
monarch had of his Gallic rival was shared by the
latter in respect to himself; and neither of these
devout and chivalrous Kings, therefore, dared a
second time adventure the recovery of Palestine,
lest, in so doing, his former associate in the holy
enterprise might attempt the seizure of his territory.

Thus disappointed in his expectations of reani-
mating the fire of devotion, which had burnt so
brightly in the hearts of Richard and Philip, Celestine determined on addressing the Emperor
Henry VI., who, though excommunicated the preceding year, he thought might be prevailed upon
to take up arms at the call of the church. Henry
was well calculated, as affairs then stood, to be the

willing instrument of the Pope's designs. He was proud and ambitious, and desirous of extending his authority by any means which might present themselves. The ban of the church, though not to be so much dreaded as its aggression, was an obstacle to his plans, which he was desirous of removing the first opportunity; and the message of the Pontiff was, therefore, listened to with the most respectful attention. Henry then summoned a diet at Worms; and, declaring his intention to proceed to Palestine, made an eloquent appeal to his auditors on the duty of restoring that sacred land to the faithful. The zeal of the monarch, his personal addresses as a preacher of the crusade to his people, and the eloquence which he displayed in these addresses, made a lively impression throughout Germany; and in a short time the principal noblemen of the empire assumed the cross, and determined to follow their monarch to Syria. Among these were Frederic, son of Leopold, Duke of Austria; Henry, Duke of Brabant; Conrade, Marquis of Moravia; and the Bishops of Wurtzbourg, Bremen, Verden, Halberstadt, Passau, and Ratisbonne.

The real designs of Henry were far from being the recovery of the Holy Land. That ambitious prince had, it appears, fixed his eyes on Sicily, of which he anxiously desired to make himself master, not only on account of the value of the island itself, but for the passage which it would secure him to the Greek Empire. He had, in observing the weak state of the Byzantine Court, suffered himself to conceive the idea of reuniting the Eastern division of the Roman Empire to that of the West. The possession of Sicily, and of the maritime

Italian provinces, would, he was aware, be the first necessary step to such a gigantic undertaking; and having obtained the alliance of the Venetians and Genoese, by promises of giving them a share in the spoil, he hoped easily to effect the conquest of Sicily, and that circumstances would speedily occur to render him the master of his new allies.

It had all along been the professed intention of the Emperor to proceed himself at the head of the crusaders; but motives of policy allowed him to be persuaded to remain in Europe, and direct the measures of the enterprise while safely seated on his imperial throne. The expedition, therefore, of which we are about to trace the events, assumes an aspect strikingly different to that of the former crusades. Policy might, in some measure, enter into the views of the princes and nobles engaged in the earlier expeditions; but it was not the prime mover of their undertakings, and it acted a very secondary part even in the last great enterprise, carried on by two powerful and ambitious monarchs. We have now, however, to regard the crusades as political, rather than religious wars; as begun and supported for political purposes; and as leading to important political changes in the condition of the world.

Few portions of history are fraught with more interest than the one before us. The character of Henry, living when he did, and compared with that of cotemporary monarchs, is worthy of observation, for the extensive schemes which entered into his mind, the resolution with which he pursued his purposes, and the talent which he evinced in bringing them to perfection. The subjection of the Greek empire to the Latins, is also one of the most memorable events of modern times. It formed the commencement of a new period in history—of a period cut short by the revolution which followed, and which again turned the stream of events into another course—but yet equally worthy of attention, as the result of circumstances which operated in an unforeseen manner, and at putting the world into a state, with regard to the several relations of its political divisions, which tended to the complete subversion of its former condition.

Having finished his preparations, and determined on the conduct of the war, Henry gathered around him a choice army of forty thousand men, destined for the intended attack on Sicily. The remaining number of the crusaders, who were allowed to proceed on the proper purposes of the expedition to which they had devoted themselves, were divided into two parts, one of which was placed under the command of the Dukes of Saxony and Brabant, and embarked from different ports of the Baltic; and the other, under that of the Archbishop of Mayence, and Valeran of Limbourg, with whom was also Queen Margaret of Hungary, sister of Philip Augustus, who, having lost her husband, took the vows of a crusader, and now led an army of her subjects to fight with the infidels. This division of the imperial armament having passed the Danube, took the route towards Constantinople, where a fleet had been prepared by the Greek Emperor, Isaac, to carry it to Ptolemais.

It was with some degree of surprise the Christians of Syria beheld the approach of their Western brethren in hostile array. The truce which had been formed between Richard and Saladin, though not productive of all the good which they had at first been led to expect, was yet so far acceptable to them, that they had no inclination to change the comparative security it afforded for a renewal of their former sufferings. It also appears, that corrupt and licentious as they had become, they had retained so much of their Christian truth, as not to dream of preparing for a regular attack on the Saracens so long as the truce bound them to peace. On the arrival, therefore, of the Archbishop of Mayence and the other chiefs of this division of the army, Henry of Champagne, the late king of Jerusalem, and the principal barons who had remained in Syria, employed their urgent endeavours to dissuade them from any sudden violation of the treaty. They represented the evils which hostilities might produce, and the little advantage which could be gained by any present attack on the Moslems; and desired them, if they should finally determine on war, at least to wait the arrival of the remainder of the forces under the Dukes of Saxony and Brabant.

Whether this advice sprang from indifference to the declining cause of the Christian authority in the East, or from a real apprehension that it might be greatly injured by the hasty measures of the new crusaders, it was that which the wisest counsellors would have given on the occasion, and merited the most serious attention of those to whom it was offered. But the Germans had left Europe full of a high enthusiasm for the cause in which they were embarked; they had experienced nothing on their route to damp their ardour; and

the object of their hopes and wishes seemed now
within their grasp. The opinions, therefore, of their
Syrian brethren were listened to with doubt, and
some mixture of indignation. These feelings at
last broke out in expressions of rage and contempt;
and they were answered, by the other party, with
the observation, that they were better acquainted
than strangers to the Holy Land with its true situation ; that they had neither solicited nor desired
the assistance of the German warriors ; and that,
as they had hitherto been able to meet the perils
with which they were menaced, they trusted they
should still be capable of doing so without foreign
assistance.   But this reply served only to increase
the anger and zeal of the crusaders, and they immediately separated themselves from the Syrians,
to pursue measures better suited to their feelings
than those advised by their more prudent brethren.

CHAPTER VII.

THE FOURTH CRUSADE AND ITS INGLORIOUS TERMINATION.—
PREPARATIONS FOR A NEW CRUSADE.

THE impetuous Germans having resisted, as has been detailed, the unwarlike opinions of Henry of Champagne and his barons, immediately took arms, and, marching out to Ptolemais, began the war of the Fourth Crusade. Their first operations consisted in ravaging the lands of the enemy; but they had not carried on this predatory warfare long, when Malek-al-Adel summoned his chiefs around him, and laid siege to Joppa. The vigour and promptitude with which this experienced Saracen prepared to repel the approach of the invaders, had the effect of rousing those of the Christians who had hitherto evinced themselves backward in assuming a hostile position. The proud bands of consecrated knights, in whose ranks were to be found the bravest as well as haughtiest warriors of Christendom, prepared themselves for the conflict. Henry of Champagne resigned himself to the necessity of the case, and his barons followed his example. A considerable force was, therefore, soon ready to cooperate with the Germans. But just as they were preparing to set forth on their march, their plans were put a stop to by the sudden and melancholy death of Henry. The unfortunate prince had stepped out into a balcony of one of the windows of the palace, when it gave way, and he was precipitated to the earth. The accident was ascribed by the Germans to the anger of God, who thus, they asserted punished, the indifference of the Count to his cause. In the midst of the confusion which this disastrous event created, news was brought, that Joppa had fallen into the hands of the Saracens, and that twenty thousand Christians had been put to death by the conquerors.

The arrival of the other division of the army, under the Dukes of Saxony and Brabant, was now anxiously expected by the Christians; and they were at length comforted with the sight of the fleet in which were their brave companions. As soon as a union had been effected between the forces, they were hastily led to the siege of Berytus, a town important both for its station between Jerusalem and Tripoli, for the safety and size of its harbour, and for the honour which had been conferred on it, by its being the city chosen for the coronation of the Moslem princes. On the banks of the river Eleutherus, between the cities of Tyre and Sidon, the Christian army was met by that of Malek-al-Adel. A battle was immediately commenced; and for a long time it was doubtful whether victory would decide in favour of the Christians or Moslems. At length, the determined bravery of the former prevailed. Malek-al-Adel was wounded, and obliged to save himself by flight, and his whole army was dispersed. The conquerors proceeded without delay on their vic-

. torious route to Berytus, which they took, and not only became masters of the immense wealth which that place contained, but had also the gratification of delivering nine thousand Christian prisoners who had been confined there by the Saracens.

The Emperor Henry had, in the mean time, been equally successful in his attempts on Naples and Sicily; and, though his flagitious conduct was worthy of the greatest detestation, he still gloried in being the first promoter of the crusade, and as furthering the purposes of the sacred expedition by these projects of his own ambition. Being now, however, able to spare a further portion of his forces, he sent a large body of his men to join their brethren in Syria, under Conrade, Bishop of Hidelsheim, and Chancellor of the Empire. The arrival of this additional force, together with their late capture of Berytus, Sidon, and Giblet, inspired the Christians with the highest confidence in the power of their arms; and it was not till after a warm debate, that many of the chiefs could be persuaded not to march directly to Jerusalem.

As the winter was approaching, this project was deferred to the following year. But Thoron, an almost impregnable fortress on the sea-coast, and the only one which now remained to the Saracens from Antioch to Ascalon, excited the cupidity of the Christians, and the siege was immediately commenced. The strength of the fortifications, and the skill and bravery of the garrison, set the arts of the besiegers for some time at defiance; but nothing could resist their final success. There were men in the army who had passed their lives in working the mines of Germany, and these were set to excavate the mountain on which the fortress was built. By this means, and by the constant employment of their engines against the walls, the barriers were at length shaken to the foundation; and the besieged, finding any further resistance vain, sent deputies with an offer to capitulate, the only condition demanded being the preservation of their life and liberty. Violent contentions existed about this time in the Christian camp; and when it was debated whether the garrison of Thoron should be admitted to the terms proposed or not, no one appeared to have sufficient power or influence to determine the matter. Most of the chiefs were on the side of mercy and the justice of war, and decided in favour of the besieged. But there were others who declared, that no agreement ought to be entered into with the infidel, and were guilty of the base conduct of both urging the unfortunate garrison to continue their defence, and inflaming the minds of their own soldiers with the desire of taking vengeance on them for their obstinacy. In the midst, however, of this confusion the capitulation was signed by several of the chiefs, among whom was the Bishop of Hidelsheim; and one part of the army assumed an attitude of peace, while the other retained its warlike array.

The deputies returned to the anxious garrison. They described what they had seen and heard; the fury which had manifested itself in the minds and countenances of several of the Christian leaders; the bloody sentiments which evidently inspired their measures; and the preparations which still existed for pursuing their destruction. This address was received with that indignation which gives strength and resolution to despair. Enraged

at the base and savage feelings of their enemies,
they seemed to derive, from the barbarity of the
Christians, a new motive for continuing their defence.
This feeling was followed by an instant determination to die rather than yield ; and the besiegers,
who were every instant expecting the arrival of the
hostages in the camp, were suddenly surprised
with the reappearance of the Moslems in an attitude of defiance. The siege was, therefore, again
commenced. But the crusaders in vain attempted
to regain their former position. The garrison
promptly repaired the walls, and, employing the
mines which had been dug by the enemy to aid
them in their defence, numbers of Christians perished in the subterranean passages, or were drag-
ged into the fortress, and there put to a miserable
death by the infuriated Moslems.

This state of things had continued for some
time, when intelligence was brought the chiefs
that Malek-al-Adel was advancing by rapid marches
towards Thoron. The gross licentiousness in
which the Christians had lately indulged, had considerably weakened their resolution and martial
energy ; and the news of the enemy's approach
filled them with alarm. Not daring, however, to
confess their sentiments to the army in general,
the imbecile leaders taxed their invention to cover
the disgrace of their cowardice. During the festival
of the Purification, the heralds proclaimed that an
assault was the next day to be made by the whole
force. The night was passed by the soldiers in preparing themselves for the expected battle ; but at
the dawn of day, and when they were listening for
the signal of assault, intelligence was brought them

that Conrade and most of the other chiefs had left
the camp, and fled towards Tyre.

The disorder which reigned through the army,
when this became generally known, was terrible.
The soldiers, not waiting to form themselves
into any order for effecting their retreat, rushed tumultuously from their tents, some with their
arms, and others without ; while in their precipitate flight they were followed at a distance
by the sick and wounded, many of whom, obliged to stop before they had scarcely left the
camp, fell into the hands of the enemy ; and
others sunk overpowered, and perished by the
way. A violent storm of thunder and lightning
added to the terror of the fugitives ; and when the
remnant of the proud army which had besieged
Thoron appeared before Tyre, the Christians of
that place beheld only a wretched rabble, exhausted by fear and fatigue, and bearing no resemblance
to the hardy bands which had boasted of being able
to re-conquer Jerusalem.

The disgrace of this event was not followed by
any improvement in the manners or counsels of
the Christians. The jealousies which had arisen
on the first arrival of the Germans, were every
day carried to a higher pitch of animosity ; and
the faithful mutually accused each other of accepting the bribes of their enemies, or bringing down
destruction by indifference to the holy cause. A
battle which the Germans won about this time,
by increasing their pride, added to the causes of
hatred between them and the Syrians. The Dukes
of Saxony and Austria, two of the principal leaders, also fell in this engagement ; and nothing presented itself but distrust and anarchy.

·Henry of Champagne, though he had refused to retain the name of King, without any means of vindicating his right, was regarded by the Syrian Christians as their chief; and though his authority also was a mere shadow, it had saved the people from that utter licentiousness into which they were now thrown. Isabel, his widow, was yet living, and was regarded as having the right of disposing of the crown as she thought fit. In the bad state of affairs, therefore, which now existed, it was the advice of the principal prelates and barons, that she should again give her hand and the crown of Jerusalem to some prince, who might be both able and willing to support their cause. Amaury, the successor of Guy of Lusignan on the throne of Cyprus, was chosen for this honour by the Queen and her counsellors; and the marriage was celebrated with great festivity at Ptolemais. But the death of the Emperor Henry, which occurred at this time, gave another turn to the course of affairs. That monarch, having been the author of the crusade, was also, throughout, its great supporter. He had been unremitting in supplying the army with stores and recruits, and prevented, by this means, most of those evils which had cut off so manythousands in the former expeditions. The real state of the army was seen, as soon as his support was withdrawn. Having no enthusiasm but that which had been inspired by the persuasions or the gold of Henry, the chiefs, on receiving intelligence of his death, resolved on immediately returning to Europe; and neither the exhortations of the Pope, nor those of the Syrian Christians, could induce any of them, except the Queen of Hungary, to delay their departure.

Thus ended this short and inglorious crusade, which would hardly deserve to be ranked among the expeditions known by that name, but for its being the commencement of a series of events which are presently to engage our attention, and which have an importance equal, if not superior, to any of those already recounted. It is with the commencement of the fourth crusade we discover the beginning of that change which marks the difference between the middle and modern ages of the world. The impassioned enthusiasm, the untiring devotion, the imaginative belief, which gave life and spirit to inanimate things, and a visible form and body to the fleeting visions of the mind—these were now fast giving way to the more selfish principles of action. Instead of being carried out of themselves, and moved to seek consolation in the vague but not less certain sources of pleasure, men began to value only the positive goods of life ; and as this feeling became more and more prevalent, the requisition of wealth was more eagerly sought for, and social liberty was a blessing better understood, and more highly prized. Both kings and people participated in this change ; and the wars of the one were gradually assuming an entirely political character, while the latter employed their growing energies in working out, one after the other, the rights which were to be the pillars of future constitutions.

It is in this respect that the crusade, undertaken by the Emperor Henry VI., is most worthy of attention ; and the careful reader of history will take pleasure in oberving the difference between the character of that monarch, the means which he employed to carry on his designs, and the general events of the enterprise, and the same kind of objects, as they offer themselves to inquiry, in the expeditions before described.

A. D. 1198. On the departure of the German crusaders, a truce for three years was concluded between Malek-al-Adel and the Count de Montfort, who had lately arrived from France with several other chevaliers of the same country. But little trust was to be placed in a treaty, for the strict observance of which the Christians themselves had set so bad an example. The worst miseries were, therefore, hourly apprehended; and they turned with a supplicating aspect towards their brethren in the West. They had, in the late crusade, hastily rejected their proferred cooperation, but they were now obliged to solicit it; and for this purpose, the bishop of Ptolemais, with several noblemen, embarked for Europe; but they were shipwrecked on the coast, and most of them perished in the waves. Fortunately, however, for the believers in Syria, Innocent III. had just mounted the Papal throne, a man whose talents and ambition rendered him capable of conceiving and undertaking the boldest projects. He eagerly seized, therefore, upon the opportunity, which the situation of the church in the East afforded, of increasing his influence and authority. He addressed a pathetic letter to the people and clergy of France, Hungary, Sicily, and England, in which he deplored the fall of Jerusalem, the indignities to which the disciples of the Lord were subject; and, above all, the licentiousness and faithlessness of those who ought to have offered their lives in defence of the sacred places. " If God died for man, will man fear to die for God? Shall he refuse to give his short life and perishable possessions to him who opens to us the treasures of eternal life? "

The usual means were employed for persuading both high and low to engage in the enterprise, and the Pope himself set an example for contributing largely of worldly possessions to the design. Commanding that vessels only of wood or earthen-ware should be placed upon his table, during the continuance of the crusade, he had the gold and silver-plate of his household melted down, to supply money for the armament. But what the zeal and resolution of Innocent might have effected, if they had been employed on their proper object, his pride and ambition destroyed almost as soon as he had commenced his plans. The monarchs of Europe had for some time been growing more independent of the church; and though the Popes might still effect much by the ancient reverence rendered to their names, and the impression it had left on the opinions of mankind, they could now only govern the world, as they employed a superior policy, and as men were willing of themselves to pay them homage. But the state of Europe, at this period, presented a tempting prospect to a pontiff of Innocent's character. Germany was troubled by the contentions of two powerful parties for the crown, to one of which he attached himself, and declared his right to dispose of the empire according to his sacred will. By this exposure, however, of his ambitious designs, he not only raised against him many formidable enemies, but lengthened a controversy, which, while it lasted, stopped all proceedings which regarded the crusade. France was at the same time labouring under many evils from the interdict incurred by Philip Augustus, against whom Innocent had fulminated a bull of excommunication, on account of his repudiating Queen Ingeburge, in order to marry Agnes de Méranie. This circumstance put a barrier to the progress of any efforts in favour of the Eastern Christians in that nation; and thus, two of the principal states in Christendom were put as it were *hors de combat* by the ill-timed pride or severity of the Pontiff. Richard yet remained faithful to his first intentions of attempting the final recovery of Palestine; but his wars with France, and the disturbed state of his dominions, hindered from time to time his prosecuting the chivalrous plans he had formed; and he died before he could effect any thing further for the cause of the Holy Sepulchre.

A.D. 1199. Notwithstanding, therefore, all the efforts of Innocent, the preparations for the crusade made small progress; and they would probably have ceased altogether, but for the appearance of one of those singular men on the scene of action, whose characters form so interesting an object of speculation in the history of these events. Foulque, curate of Neuilly-sur-Marne, was a man distinguished neither for learning nor any remarkable ability. When he began to preach abroad, either his manner, or the style of his discourses, was so little engaging, that he was not unfrequently subjected to the ridicule and abuse of his auditors. But he was thoroughly imbued with devotion to the cause which employed his mind, and was serious and unaffected in his piety. These were mighty aids to success; and as he proceeded on his mission, his audiences increased, and he was every day listened to with more attention and earnestness. It is not improbable that the religious gloom which pervaded France at this time, assisted the impression which the simple eloquence of the curate of Neuilly was calculated to make. Since the publication of the interdict, the ceremonies of the church had been suspended, the bells even had ceased to sound, and the offices of charity been refused the dead. The voice of a plain and energetic preacher at such a time must have been heard with deep emotion. Men, in general, value nothing so much as religion, when either its exercise is prohibited, or they meet with any obstacle to its profession. Foulque at last gathered such crowds around him, that the clergy and nobles began to regard him as worthy of attention; and he was in a short time listened to with the reverence due to an apostle.

A. D. 1200. Intelligence was quickly conveyed to Innocent respecting the excitement occasioned by the preaching of this extraordinary man, and the Pontiff was not slow in perceiving how useful such a labourer might be in his favourite project. He accordingly put Foulque at the head of the preachers of the crusade, all of whom were chosen either for their eloquence or station in the church, and they began their work supported by the whole influence of the pontifical authority. It was not long before Foulque had an opportunity of exercising his zeal to the most useful purpose. At a tourney which was held in Champagne, and at which many of the most distinguished chevaliers of France were present, he proclaimed the crusade, and, struck by the power of his appeal, the knights forsook the lists to assume the vows and badge of pilgrims. Thibaut, Count of Champagne,

Louis, Count of Chartres and Blois, both allied to the Kings of England and France, the Count of Saint Paul, Simon de Montfort, whom we have already seen in Syria, and the historian of this crusade, Geoffrey de Villehardouin, Marechal of Champagne. Several other French noblemen, and many of the most powerful Knights of Flanders, followed the example thus set them; and a large army was speedily formed, the command of which was given, in a Council of Barons, to the Count of Champagne.

The manner in which the preparations for this expedition were carried on, will strike the reader as not a little different to that in which the earlier enterprises were commenced. A considerable time had now passed since Innocent first published his intentions respecting the Holy War; and the barons who engaged themselves in the undertaking, set about the preliminaries with politic caution. To secure the safe transport of the troops to Syria, they sent deputies to the celebrated Dandolo, Doge of Venice, of whom they required a sufficient number of vessels for the passage of four thousand five hundred knights, twenty thousand foot soldiers, and provisions for the whole army for nine months. The Venetian's demand for this supply was eighty-five thousand silver marks; and in return for fifty gallies, which the Doge offered to send without payment, it was stipulated, that half the places which might fall to the Christian army should be ceded to Venice.

To ratify the agreement thus made between the crusaders and Dandolo, a general assembly of the republic was called; and the Marechal of Champagne addressed the Venetians in terms which prove both his own earnestness in the cause, and the high degree of power and wealth to which the state had at this period arisen. " The most high and potent Seigneurs and Barons of France," said he, " have sent us to beseech you, in the name of God, to take pity on Jerusalem, which is in bondage to the Turks. They claim your mercy, and supplicate you to accompany them to avenge the contumely of Jesus Christ. They have made choice of you, because they know that no maritime nation has so great power as the Venetians. They have desired us to throw ourselves at your feet, and not to rise till you have granted our demand, and taken pity on the Holy Land." ·

Many were the tears and exclamations of emotion which accompanied this address. The assembled people burst out at its conclusion, into one loud declaration of consent ; and from the place of Saint Mark, to the extremities of the city, nothing was to be heard but the expressions of devout thankfulness with which the multitude filled the air. On the day following, the Marechal and the rest of the deputies reassembled in the palace of Saint Mark, to take an oath that they would, on their parts, fulfil the stipulations of the agreement. The treaty having been thus ratified, it was forthwith despatched to the Pope to receive his approbation ; and the French deputies took farewell of their new allies with many protestations of fidelity and affection. * From Venice they repaired to the maritime states of Pisa, and Genoa ; but their proceedings at Venice had offended the pride of those cities, and but a cold re-

* Villehardouin.

ception was given their offers of alliance. One
or two other noblemen, however, were added to
the list of the crusaders, before Villehardouin and his
companions returned to Champagne; and their arrival would have been greeted with unmixed pleasure, had not the dangerous sickness of Thibaut
spread despondency among the crusaders. The
death of that prince, celebrated for his deep piety
and enthusiastic devotion to the cause of Jerusalem, rendered the choice of another leader necessary. Two noblemen, the Count of Bar and the
Duke of Burgundy, successively refused to accept
the distinction; and Boniface, Marquis of Montferrat, and brother to the renowned Conrade, was
elected general of the Christian army.

CHAPTER VII.

DEPARTURE OF THE FOURTH CRUSADE.—ALLIANCE WITH THE VENETIANS.—SIEGE AND CAPTURE OF ZARA.—CONQUEST OF CONSTANTINOPLE, AND RESTORATION OF ISAAC AND ALEXIS.

A.D. 1202. EARLY in the spring of this year, the French forces began their march; and having taken the route to Venice, they were shortly after joined by the Marquis of Montferrat, at the head of his army, composed of Lombards, Piedmontese and Savoyards, and by a small band of Germans, who were led by the bishops of Halberstadt and Martinlitz. Their march to the place of rendezvous was accomplished without difficulty; and, on their arrival, they found the fleet appointed to convey them to Syria ready for setting sail. Thus far success had attended the slow but prudent measures of the crusaders; and every thing seemed to promise a prosperous issue to the design, the preparations for which were thus cautiously pursued. But an unexpected difficulty now arose, and one which was as disgraceful to some of the parties engaged, as it was unpropitious to the enterprise. Of the vast number of barons who had taken the cross, and agreed to assemble at Venice, for the purpose of embarking in the fleet which they had engaged by their deputies, only a very few were arrived; and after anxiously expecting them, the Marquis of Montferrat had the misfortune to learn that they had taken a different route, and embarked at other ports. Great confusion followed this announcement. The Venetians, who were eager for the fulfilment of the treaty which they had made with the deputies, demanded the payment of the price stipulated for the fleet and provisions. As the sum was a considerable one, and could only be raised by the equal contributions of all the parties who took a share in the enterprise, the barons who had arrived in Venice, and were desirous of honourably fulfilling the agreement, were struck with consternation at their situation. They wore neither able to raise the money required, nor willing either to break the treaty so solemnly signed, or stoop to solicit the indulgence of the republic; but while they were in this dilemma, a proposition was made by the Doge, which it was thought would deliver them out of the difficulty. The city of Zara, over which the Venetians claimed sovereign authority, had revolted, and put itself under the protection of the King of Hungary. To reduce it again to its allegiance, was an object greatly desired by the republic; and the crusaders were invited to lend their arms for that purpose, being offered, as a reward for their services, such an indemnity with regard to the late agreement, as would free them from all further distress. This proposition was joyfully acceded to; but doubts arose in the minds of some of the knights as to the lawfulness of their employing those arms against a Christian city which had been consecrated for fighting with the enemies of the cross; and the

Pope himself sent a message by his legate, forbidding the Venetians to prosecute their design. The determination, however, of the haughty republicans was not to be easily controlled; and the Doge, in order to secure the co-operation of the crusaders, and remove their scruples, assumed the cross, and proclaimed his intention of accompanying them in their expedition. A fleet of four hundred and eighty vessels transported a formidable army of forty thousand men to Trieste, and other maritime towns of Istria, which yielded to the Venetians and their allies; and the forces arrived before Zara on the tenth of November, the eve of Saint Martin. The situation of this city, which stands on the Oriental side of the Adriatic, the strength of its fortifications, and the assistance rendered it by the King of Hungary, who himself had taken the cross, threw a damp at first upon the ardour of the besiegers. The citizens, however, alarmed by the preparations made for the attack, sent deputies to offer their submission to the Venetians; but when they arrived in the camp, dissension and faction had destroyed all union between the different parties engaged in the siege; and the deputies heard, with astonishment, the question, " Why are you willing thus to surrender your city ? " *

The Count de Montfort, the Abbé de Vaux-de-Cernay, and a few others among the crusaders, at last had the sense to discover, and the good conscience to feel, that they were not performing their duty, as vowed soldiers of the cross, by employing their arms in destroying the liberty of a Christian state. This sentiment, it is likely, would have earlier

* Villehardouin.

prevailed, had it not been for their desire to fulfil the treaty with the Venetians, the eagerness
with which some of their brethren urged them to
the enterprise, and the politic conduct of the
Doge. They now found it impossible to resist
the determination of the opposite party to continue
the siege; and the citizens of Zara were reduced
to employ whatever means the arts of either piety
or war could invent to resist the assault. But
though they fought with valour, and crowded the
walls with crosses, as signs of their brotherhood
and common faith, they could not succeed in warding off the threatened evil beyond the fiftieth day
of the siege, when they opened their gates to the
combined forces.

The booty found in the city was divided between the French and Venetians; but in a few
days after the army had taken up its quarters for
the remainder of the winter, symptoms of dislike
and rivalry between the allies broke out with fresh
violence; and bloody combats ensued, which were
badly recompensed by the subjection of Zara. The
Pope, in the mean time, sent fresh messages, to
warn the crusaders of the peril they would be incurring, by persisting in a design so foreign to their
proper engagement; and such an effect had these
admonitions on the minds of the French, that most
of them professed submission to the will of the
Pontiff, and, with many demonstrations of repentance, began to prepare for the prosecution of the
crusade against the common enemy of Christendom.

There was every appearance, therefore, that,
having achieved the conquest of Zara, the French
crusaders would pursue their original intentions

without farther delay, and be contented with having done thus much towards honourably fulfilling their agreement with the Venetians. But during their preparations for departure, circumstances occurred which once more disturbed their pious designs, and contributed to warn them that a new order of things was about to engage the warriors of Europe. Previous to the sailing of the armament, ambassadors had arrived from Constantinople to desire the assistance of Venice and her allies in favour of the Emperor Isaac, whose throne was usurped by his brother Alexis, while he himself had been deprived of his sight and thrown into a dungeon. The son of the unfortunate monarch, also named Alexis, who had just escaped from sharing the captivity of his father, pleaded the cause of his parent with great fervour and eloquence ; but as Zara was the object immediately before the Venetians, the consideration of the Emperor's misfortunes was deferred till the rebellious city should be forced back to its allegiance. That design having been effected, and the ambassadors of Isaac again appearing to solicit the aid of the crusaders, the business was considered with more seriousness, and the different parties engaged employed their most strenuous efforts, as they felt inclined, to attempt the subjection of Constantinople to the Emperor, or the restoration of Palestine to Christendom and the church.

The dispute was carried on with great warmth on both sides. The Doge, the Marquis of Montferrat, and Philip of Swabia, King of the Romans, embraced the cause of the dethroned monarch, and seconded his son in all the appeals which that young prince made to the feelings or avarice of the crusaders. Their influence was also increased by that of the Counts of Flanders, Blois, and St Paul, who joined the imperial party; and the promises which Isaac made by his ambassadors, were listened to with eagerness by the greater portion of the army. They deprecated the idea of hindering the soldiers of the cross from finally pursuing the real object of their sacred enterprise; shewed them how great a duty they would be performing by dethroning a tyrant who would prove even a worse enemy to their cause than the treacherous emperors of former days, and proceeded to enumerate the further advantages that would accrue by their uniting with Isaac. " If you restore the lawful sovereign to his just rights, " said the young prince, " the son of Isaac promises, by the most sacred oaths, to support your fleet and army for a year, and to pay two hundred thousand marks of silver for the expenses of the war. He also promises to accompany you in person to Syria and Egypt; to lend you, at his expense, ten thousand men; and support, during the whole of his reign, five hundred chevaliers in the Holy Land. He moreover engages, and this should be sufficient to determine the intentions of Christian warriors, to put an end to the heresies which exist in the Greek empire, and to submit the Greek church to that of Rome." Neither these promises, however, nor the pathetic appeals with which they were mixed up, were sufficient to determine the chiefs and barons in favour of the Emperor, till after many boisterous debates. A strong party in the assembly, whose ideas were more pious than politic, could not be persuaded to turn their thoughts from the recovery of Palestine to a war with Constantinople, the emperors of which, whether friendly or hostile, had proved such hinderancies to the success of the former expeditions. The Pope, also, who was inimical to all projects which were either started by the Venetians, or were likely to benefit them, had shown himself unfavourable to the design, which must not only greatly retard the progress of the crusade, but would serve to increase the pride and freedom of the republicans; while those who were not affected by these considerations, alleged the known strength of Constantinople, and the resources of the usurper, as reasons for their dissent. But the Venetians and the party who agreed with them, were too powerful to be stopped in their designs ; and the rivalship of the former with the Pisans, who had entered into a mercantile treaty with Constantinople, and their private enmity against the Greeks, were additional motives for their prosecuting the war. The fleet, accordingly, at length set sail; having on board a strong and well-accoutred force, and the flower of French, German, and Italian chivalry. The son of Isaac had arrived at Zara shortly before the embarkation of the troops ; and his presence among them greatly contributed to animate both French and Venetians with resolution. Employing all the arts which could render himself or his cause popular in the minds of the crusaders, he proceeded through the camp, accompanied by the barons, who supported his claims; everywhere addressing himself to the feelings which he had already been so successful in awakening by his eloquence. Nothing was thenceforward talked of but his filial piety, the misfortunes of his father, or the good which would result from the reign of a prince whose youth was marked by the possession of so many virtues and talents. These feelings, fortunately for the deposed Emperor, sup-. plied the place of those with which the crusaders had left their homes ; and under the idea of following an affectionate son, to rescue his father from a dungeon, they silenced their consciences, which had at first reproached them with abandoning their duty to the Saviour and his church.

April 1203. Our limits will not allow us to pause in describing the voyage of the splendid armament which crowded the bosom of the Adriatic ; but it was one of those magnificent spectacles which so frequently passed across the great stage of events in those days. On the morning after Easter, the ships were laden, the Venetians engaged themselves in destroying the city, together with its walls and fortifications ; and the pilgrims took up their station on the shore, to be ready for the first signal of departure. But shortly before the embarkation commenced, Simon de Montfort, who held so high a situation in the army, abandoned the camp, and entered into confederacy with the King of Hungary. He was accompanied in his retreat by his brother, Guy de Montfort, the Abbot de Vaux, and several of the noblemen who had originally protested against any change in the expedition. This event, however, was not permitted to occasion any delay in the proceedings of the rest ; and the fleet was immediately manned, and set sail for Durazzo, of which the inhabitants freely swore fealty to the prince, and surrendered the city into his hands. Corfu was the next stage of their voyage, where a part of the army had already arrived, and was encamped. The intelligence that the son of the Emperor was on board

the fleet, produced the most lively sensation of
joy throughout the camp; and a large party of
the chevaliers mounted their horses, and having
received him with great respect as he reached the
shore, conducted him in procession to his tent.

It will have been remarked by the reader, that
many evils were suffered in almost every crusade of
which we have given an account, from the delay
which the leaders allowed to take place in the progress of their enterprises. At Corfu the fleet anchored ; and the troops being disembarked, were allowed for several weeks to enjoy the luxurious scenes
and productions of that delicious island. But the disorders which had, a short time since, so nearly destroyed the expedition, broke out afresh; and several of the knights whose ardour for Palestine was
not yet diminished, expressed their intention of
separating from their brethren, and proceeding direct to the Holy Land. By the entreaties, however, of the Marquis of Montferrat, the Doge and
others, they were persuaded to forego this intention ; and a promise being given, that they should
be furnished in the autumn with vessels to carry
them to Syria, they agreed to defer their departure till that time. The forces were, therefore,
again embarked ; and on the eve of Pentecost, all
the galleys, palandars, * and other ships of war, together with the merchant vessels which accompanied them, weighed anchor. The day was
bright and clear ; soft gentle winds filled the sails;
and never, says the chronicler, was a more glorious spectacle witnessed. The armament seemed fit to conquer the world ; for, as far as the eye

* Flat-bottomed boats, provided with small moveable
bridges.

could reach, the sails of ships and galleys covered
the waves. Sailing along the open sea, they arrived at Cape Malea, in Laconia; and here they
met with two vessels, which had on board a
number of pilgrims, knights, and sergeants, who
were leaving Palestine, but the sight of the fleet
made them repent of their desertion; and one of
the sergeants leaped into a barge in order to join
the crusaders, declaring that he would follow them,
for that it seemed certain they would conquer the
earth. They then sailed to Negropont, and having
made a descent on Andros, entered the passage of
Abydos, and cast anchor before that island. Here
another division of the armament awaited them,
in order that the whole of the fleet might have
time to assemble before proceeding up the Hellespont. When they set sail from Abydos, their
hearts were filled with joy at the magnificent sight
of so many ships, galleys and palandars, sailing
proudly to the conquest of an empire; but when,
after a short passage, they reached the Abbey of
Saint Stephen, situated within three leagues of Constantinople, their eyes were charmed with a different spectacle. The imperial city was now within sight. Its extensive walls, the lofty towers
which surrounded it, its splendid palaces and tow-
ering churches, which seemed to be innumerable,
rose before them; and while they were mute with
astonishment at the imposing prospect, many of
them trembled at the idea of attacking a city so
extensive and so nobly defended.

The counts and barons, together with the Doge,
having landed at the Abbey, held a council to determine on the measures next to be pursued.
Many different sentiments prevailed on the occa-

sion; but the Doge concluded the debate by a speech, to which his experience and knowledge secured attention. "I know more of this country and of its customs than most of you," said he, "for I have been here before. You have undertaken as perilous an enterprise as men ever attempted, and it is, therefore, necessary that we should proceed with caution. You are to consider, that if we land on the continent, which is far extended, our people will be tempted, by the want of provisions, to disperse themselves about, and may, to our great loss, fall a sacrifice to the numerous inhabitants. But there are islands within sight, both well peopled, and fruitful in corn and other productions. Let us proceed thither, and provide ourselves well with corn, and whatever stores may be necessary, after which we will advance against the city, and do that which our Lord shall seem to direct." *

This advice being received with approbation, the next morning, the feast of Saint John the Baptist, the vessels were prepared for setting sail, the banners and standards were elevated, and a strong fence raised along the sides of the decks, composed of the shields and bucklers of the warriors, while every one looked to his arms as now standing in full need of their aid. A favourable wind carried the fleet so close under the walls of Constantinople, which were crowded with the affrighted population, that many missiles struck the vessels; and, instead of pursuing the intention of landing on one of the islands, the chiefs ordered anchor to be cast before Chalcedon, which is situ-

* Villehardouin.

ated on the Asiatic side of the Bosphorus, opposite Constantinople, and about ten miles distant
from that city. The knights and barons, with all
their horses and followers, and the other pilgrims,
went on shore, a part of them taking up their
lodging in the magnificent palace, which had been
long consecrated to imperial luxury; while the rest
pitched their tents in the surrounding gardens, or
found quarters in the city. Leaving the ships
of burden still at anchor before Chalcedon, the
chiefs assembled their followers on the third day
from their landing, and sailed to Scutari, which is
within about a league's distance from Constantinople, and where the forces were again landed.

The Emperor, who had hitherto remained im-
mersed in pleasure, and indifferent to the affairs of
his government, now began to perceive the real
danger of his situation, and would willingly have
protected himself from the impending evil by negotiation. But the ambassador whom he sent to
the chiefs of the invading army, was received with
haughty contempt. He expressed the astonishment of his master that they should invade a
Christian empire; and they replied, that the empire did not belong to him, but to the prince whose
cause they had espoused. He declared that it was
the wish of the Emperor to concur with them
in their pious design; and, at the same time, his
determination immediately to take arms in defence of the state, if his offers were not complied
with; and to these remarks they answered, that
he was a usurper, and consequently the enemy of
all princes—a tyrant, and therefore the enemy of
the human race. "He who has sent you hither,"
continued they, "has but one means of escaping

the just vengeance of man and heaven—it is to
restore to his brother and nephew the crown of
which he has despoiled them, and to implore mercy
of those princes to whom he has shown himself so
unmerciful.   Let him do this, and we promise to
unite our prayers with his, and to obtain his pardon, and a provision for the rest of his days, spent
in quiet and security,—a state far superior to a
false and usurped glory.   But if he cannot be persuaded to act with justice—if he remain inaccessi-
ble to repentance—tell him that we disdain both
his threats and his promises, and that we have no
time to attend to his ambassadors." *

The condition of the Greek empire under the
usurper was miserable in the extreme ; but not
worse than it was in the reigns of many of its former sovereigns.   The only difference appears to
have been, that the evils were now of longer
standing ; and the mere continuance of evil,
without decrease, is equivalent to its being
greatly multiplied.   It is only in proportion, however, as a people enjoy peace and freedom under
their legitimate monarchs, that they hate a usurper
for his injustice ; and the tyrant Alexis, therefore,
though detested by his subjects for the oppression and misery which they suffered, cared little
about the manner in which he had raised himself
to the throne.   The Franks, conceiving that the
people, on seeing the son of their lawful sovereign,
would at once rise in his cause, carried him in a
galley, to the walls of the capital, the Doge and
the Marquis of Montferrat supporting him between
them, while a herald exclaimed, as they past in

* Villehardouin.

sight of the people, " Behold the heir to the throne!—acknowledge your sovereign;—have pity on him, and on yourselves." But the address was heard in silence; no emotion was evinced by which the chiefs could hope that their project had been attended with success; and shortly after a tumult took place, in which the Greeks attacked the Latin inhabitants of the city with great fury, and plainly declared themselves on the side of Alexis. This circumstance was followed by an attack which a party of the usurper's troops made on the crusaders; but they were instantly put to flight; and the eighty knights to whom the honour of the victory belonged, compared them to timid stags, not fit to join in combat with men who merited the name of exterminating angels or statues of brass, which diffused terror and death. *

The opinion was now general that the siege should be no longer delayed. An assembly, or parliament as it is called, was held in the open plain, the knights and barons who composed it appearing mounted on their richly caparisoned chargers, and deliberating respecting the measures to be pursued, as if already prepared for the on-set. It was decided that the forces should immediately be transported across the strait, and encamped under the walls of the city. On this determination being made known to the army, the bishops and clergy exhorted the warriors to prepare for the conflict, by shriving themselves and making their wills, which pious advice was devoutly attended to; and the rites of religion having been performed, no time was lost in embarking for the

* Nicetas.

opposite shore. The knights went on board the
palandars with their war-steeds, and armed from
head to foot, with helmets laced, and lance in
hand, and their horses saddled and covered with
superb housings. They were followed by the
sergeants * and warriors of inferior rank, and
the numerous bands of bowmen and other troops
who were embarked in the larger vessels, to
each of which was attached a light galley to
quicken its passage. The forces thus embarked
were divided into six battalions, the first being led
by the Count of Flanders, who obtained that honourable post from his being followed by a brave
and more numerous band of archers than the other
chiefs. His brother Henry led the second division ; the Counts of St Paul and Blois the third
and fourth ; Matthew of Montmorency the fifth, in
which, among many other noble knights, was the
historian Villehardouin ; and the Marquis of Montferrat the sixth. The Venetians were to remain
in their ships, as being more likely to assist the
army by their naval skill, than in any other mode
of action.

The current of the Bosphorus is frequently rapid
and dangerous ; but on this memorable day the
heavens were clear, the sun shone with great brilliancy, and the warlike fleet bore gallantly from the
shore. The opposite bank was quickly reached ;
and the imperial troops, forming an army of seventy thousand horse and foot, were seen ranged a-
long the beach. The clarions of the crusaders now
resounded from every vessel. The palandars and
galleys drove impetuously towards the shore ; every

---

* The common name given to horsemen not knights.

warrior was pressing to be foremost; and before they could reach the land, many of the knights leaped into the sea, which reached to their baldrics, and rushed with their lances against the enemy. The sergeants, archers and balastriers, imitated their valour; the bridges attached to the palandars were let down, and the horses landed; when the whole army began to form in order of battle. But Alexis had fled; his troops, without waiting for the attack of the Latins, readily obeyed his summons to retreat, and the bloodless victory put the conquerors in possession of the imperial camp.

Pursuing their success, the crusaders proceeded early next morning to attack the fortress of Galata, which commanded the port of Constantinople; and while the army was thus engaged, the Venetians approached with the fleet, and began to destroy the boom, which was thrown from the tower of Galata to the opposite shore. Both parties succeeded in their bold enterprises. The fortress was stormed and taken by the French; and the Venetians, having totally vanquished the Grecian fleet, cut asunder, by means of an enormous machine, the iron links of the boom. Having obtained these important advantages over the enemy, a council of chiefs was called to decide on the manner in which the siege was to be prosecuted. In this assembly the Venetians strongly advised that the assault should be commenced from the sea; but the other Italians, and the French and Germans, opposed this proposition, observing, that they were unaccustomed to naval warfare, and only knew how to fight on their good steeds, and with their knightly weapons. The dispute was speedily terminated, by its being agreed that the Venetians should attack the city by sea, while the army assailed it on the land. The forces were then led towards the upper part of the harbour, where the river Barbyses falls into the gulf. The bridge over this river had been destroyed by the Greeks on the approach of the crusaders, and the latter employed the day on which they reached this spot, and the following night, in repairing it against their passage. This work they were suffered to perform without hinderance, and the next day they took up their position under the walls of the city. The fleet also ascended the gulf in fighting order, and anchored in a broad basin about three bow-shots distant from the station of the land forces.

An attempt was again made to interest the Greeks in favour of Isaac, but fruitlessly; and the siege was begun by the crusaders with the most determined courage. The small number of their forces, when all were united, rendered the success of the enterprise extremely doubtful. The circuit of the walls was estimated to measure three leagues in extent; and while their army consisted of only twenty thousand men, Constantinople was supposed to have within its barriers above four hundred thousand inhabitants capable of bearing arms. The line of the besiegers extended along a very small portion of the walls, and was terminated by the gate of Gyrolimne on the one end, and the castle of Bohemond on the other. From each of these points the Greeks made continual sallies; and the crusaders, having provisions only for three weeks, and exposed to the constant danger of being surrounded and besieged in their camp, resolved, after

ten days of incessant toil and peril, to attempt a
nearer and more general assault of the city.

On the seventeenth of July, the signal being
given, the forces began the attack both by land
and sea. A breach was at length made, and a
knight and two squires instantly appeared with
scaling-ladders and the standard of the cross, which
fifteen of the bravest warriors of the army exposed
themselves to almost instant death to place on the
ramparts. Only two of these devoted soldiers escaped destruction, and they were carried captive
before Alexis, who, it is reported, rejoiced at the
sight, as if it had been the sure harbinger of victory. The Greeks continued to defend themselves with unlooked for bravery; being supported by Constantinus Lascaris, a young and distinguished warrior, and related to Alexis. A
band of Danish and English guards, styled Varan-
gians, was also employed by the Emperor in the
defence of his throne and capital; and the Latins
were repulsed, every charge they made, with considerable loss.

But while the besiegers were thus waging an
unequal contest by land, the Venetians, from their
ships, had cast terror into the city by the valour
and rapidity with which they repeated their desperate charges. The fleet was drawn up before
the walls in two lines, of which the first was formed by the light galleys, having on board the archers, and the second by the heavy vessels, on the
decks of which platforms and turrets were erected,
and the huge engines intended for battering the
ramparts. The conflict had been thus carried
on, from the beginning of the day, with unceasing
fury, when the Doge, who, though blind and aged,

was foremost among the assailants, gave the command for his people to land. His orders, issued as he stood in full armour on the poop of his vessel, were backed by the threat, that he would kill the first man who delayed to obey the summons. Some of his followers, taking the heroic old man in their arms, bore him immediately to shore; and the standard of Saint Mark being carried before him, announced his bravery to the rest of the fleet. A rumour of applause now ran through the multitude; and every galley and vessel was quickly seen moving towards the shore. While the greater body of the warriors hastened to the support of the Doge, the rest remained on board the ships, which were formed into a close line against the ramparts. The bridges with which they were furnished were then turned out, and the lofty towers of the city shook under the strength of the assailants. The soldiers, in the mean time, who had landed, fixed numerous engines and scaling-ladders on other parts of the walls, when suddenly the lordly banner of Saint Mark was seen displayed on one of the highest towers, no one being able to tell how or by what hand it was placed there. Fighting, as they believed, under the protection of their Saint, twenty-five towers fell at once into the hands of the Venetians. Some of the Greeks attempted to oppose their progress, but were instantly overthrown; and the victors rushed into the city, driving all before them, and setting fire to the streets through which they passed. The squares and avenues were filled with the inhabitants, who fled tremblingly from their houses. Every instant the conflagration spread wider and wider, enveloping one whole side of the city in flame; while the wind, which blew freshly from the opposite quarter, drove the dense masses of smoke and ashes into the interior, and presented a barrier to the soldiers of the Greeks, which effectually prevented their offering any resistance to the enemy.

While the old Venetian was thus leading his people to victory, the French and their confederates were closely pressed by the troops of Alexis. The usurper, compelled into action by the murmurs of both his subjects and army, had gathered round him the best of his troops; and, at the head of his host, which consisted of sixty battalions, he hastened to offer them battle. But at the moment when the latter were in the greatest danger of being overpowered by numbers, the Venetians appeared with the Doge at their head, to share the peril. Alexis, terrified at seeing them thus reinforced, took flight, without waiting the issue of a battle; his immense army followed the example of their pusillanimous leader, and the Franks were left sole masters of the field.

The camp of the crusaders, after this unexpected victory, exhibited a scene of unwonted festivity. The soldiers, who had been long threatened with the want of provisions, found on the field large quantities of stores, and, laying aside their arms, they passed the night in refreshing their exhausted bodies. The morning, however, was expected with anxiety. Alexis, though driven from his position, had yet an immense force at his command; and they might at any time be surrounded, and cut off by his sixty battalions, any one of which was more numerous than the largest of their divisions. But while the crusaders were occupied with these

thoughts, the usurper was preparing his flight from
the city. On returning to the imperial palace, after
his disgraceful retreat, he collected together ten
thousand pounds of gold, and a quantity of jewels,
which he put into a boat, and, in the first watch of
the night, secretly escaped from the city, leaving
both his wife and his throne in the power of the
besiegers.

The greatest confusion prevailed in Constantinople, when the flight of the Emperor became
known. The people, no longer fearing his vengeance, accused him of bringing them to destruction, and called down curses upon his head; while
the troops, left without a leader, instead of resuming their arms, remained motionless in their
quarters. While all was thus terror and confusion,
some courtiers flew to the dungeon, where the
blind and miserable Isaac had suffered a long captivity. Opening the door of his prison, and freeing him from his fetters, they brought him to the
palace of Blaquernes, and, there seating him on
the imperial throne, summoned the people to acknowledge again their lawful sovereign. This was
all effected in the first hour of the day; and, as
the Franks were preparing for the dreaded attack
of the enemy, they were surprised by the appearance of several Greeks in the camp, who informed them of what had taken place. A council was
hastily called, on this strange intelligence being
communicated, and the devout warriors returned
thanks to Heaven for their unhoped for success.
Some doubt, however, was still entertained as to
the truth of the report; and more than one of the
chiefs apprehended that it might conceal some
plot to ruin them. These apprehensions were

dissipated by the arrival of other Greeks, who came to pay homage to the son of Isaac; and a deputation, composed of Matthew of Montmorency, the historian Villehardouin, and two Venetian noblemen, was sent into the city to receive a confirmation of the news. On their arrival at the palace of Blaquernes, they were conducted through a double row of the Varangian guards and numerous bands of armed troops, and, in the royal presence-chamber, they beheld the blind Emperor and his consort, clothed in the most splendid apparel, and surrounded by a brilliant court, as if the unfortunate monarch had never known a different condition. Villehardouin being permitted to declare the object of the mission, he said, " You see, most gracious Sire, how the crusaders have fulfilled their promises, and what good service we have rendered your son. He cannot, however, come hither, till you have, on your part, agreed to the conditions of the treaty, to which he has given his pledge for the fulfilment. He, therefore, dutifully beseeches you his father, through us, fully to ratify this agreement which he has made with the Doge of Venice, and the barons of the crusaders." Villehardouin then detailed the several particulars of the treaty which the prince had signed; and the Emperor, having heard him to the end, replied, "The conditions of this agreement are heavy, and I can hardly see how they are to be performed; but you have so greatly served me and my son, that you would merit it were we to give you the whole empire." *
The treaty then received the imperial seal and

* Villehardouin.

signature; and the deputies, highly praising the monarch for his good faith, returned to the camp.

Nothing now remained to be done but to conduct the young prince in triumph to his father, whom he had thus delivered from a dungeon, and restored to his throne.   Accompanied by the Doge of Venice, all the knights and barons of the army in full armour, and the clergy in their most splendid robes, the son of Isaac proceeded towards the palace of Blaquernes.   As he advanced, crowds of people saluted him from all quarters of the city with the loudest acclamations of delight.   Hymns of thanksgiving and triumphant songs filled the air; but when he entered the palace, and fell into the arms of his father, the clamours were changed into expressions of deep sympathy; and those who beheld the meeting wept with joy at the spectacle, and thanked Heaven that the father and son were thus happily restored to each other.

The inhabitants of Constantinople united with the Franks in celebrating these events; but as soon as the first transports were over, the Emperor requested the chiefs of the crusaders to remove their forces to the other side of the strait, in order to avoid the danger of any dispute between them and his people.   This desire was immediately acceded to, and the next day the troops formed their camp on the opposite shore of the harbour.   The most friendly intercourse was kept up between the Franks and the people of Constantinople.   The former were permitted freely to resort to the city, and delight themselves with visiting its magnificent buildings, and partaking in the luxuries it afforded, while the latter brought goods and provisions to the camp, and kept up a constant traffic with the soldiers. The innumerable relics also contained in the imperial city, formed a fruitful source of trade between the Greeks and crusaders. Constantinople was said to possess more of these sacred commodities than all the rest of Christendom together, while no less than five hundred abbeys and monasteries rendered every part of its neighbourhood sacred to the saints. The pleasures which the crusaders derived from these sources were enhanced by the courteous conduct of the Emperor, who invited the chiefs to his table, and continually consulted them on the affairs of his government. A still greater satisfaction was afforded them, in their being able to inform their brethren in the West, that they had succeeded, by their triumph over the usurper, in restoring the unity of the church; that the Greeks would henceforth acknowledge the Pope as their head; and that the Patriarch of Constantinople would, like other archbishops, receive his pall from the apostolical chief of Christendom.

The coronation of the young prince, which took place a few days after the crusaders had removed to their new encampment, was an additional security for their safety and the fulfilment of the treaty. Sharing the throne with his father, he manifested, by every means in his power, a grateful remembrance of the services which had been rendered him, and paid two hundred thousand silver marks, or a large part of that sum, as one of the stipulations in the treaty. The harmony which thus reigned between the Greeks and the crusaders, led to a reconcilation of the Venetians with the Pisans, between whom there had long existed the most violent enmity. But the situation

of Isaac and his son was still precarious. They
had been obliged to have recourse to unpopular
measures for raising the money paid to the crusaders, and the provinces had as yet given few proofs
of allegiance. It was to the arms of the crusaders,
and not to the patriotism or affection of any of
their own people, they owed their present enjoyment of the empire; and nothing had occurred, if
we except the first popular expression of opinion,
to let them suppose that they were properly established in the affections of their subjects. It
was with no little apprehension, therefore, they a-
waited the departure of the crusaders. The success which had attended their arms inspired the
latter with new zeal for the prosecution of their
designs against the Saracens. The letters which
they despatched to Europe were filled with assurances of submission to the Pope, and of anxiety
to fulfil his intentions; and heralds were sent to
Cairo and Damascus, with formal declarations of
war against the sultans of those states, unless they
surrendered, without delay, their possessions in
Palestine.

But as the time drew near for the prosecution
of their march to Syria, the Emperors became every
day more convinced of the hazardous situation in
which they would be placed by the absence of the
Franks. At length they resolved to make known
these apprehensions to their allies, and the young
Cæsar proceeded to the camp, where a council of
the chiefs being assembled, he besought them, in
the most urgent manner, to continue their support
to himself and his father. " You have restored to
me life, honour, and empire," said he; " I ought to
desire but one thing more, the power, namely, of

fulfilling all my promises. But if you abandon me now, to proceed to Syria, it is impossible that I should furnish you with either the money, the troops, or the vessels which I have promised. The people of Constantinople have received me with many demonstrations of joy, but they love me not the more for that; and the revolutions to which they have been accustomed have destroyed the habit of obedience. Faction reigns both in the capital and in the provinces; and neither the laws, nor the majesty of the empire, are any longer respected. I am hated by the Greeks, because you have restored me to my heritage. If you should forsake me, my life or throne would probably fall a sacrifice to my enemies. I implore you, therefore, to defer your departure till the month of March next year, and I will promise, in return, not only to provide your army with all necessary supplies till Easter, but also to engage the Venetians to support you with their fleet till Michaelmas." This offer was followed by further entreaties; and the chiefs replied, that they would consider the propositions, and inform him of the decision when they had sufficient time to consult the rest of the chevaliers. Great difference of opinion prevailed among the crusaders respecting the affair thus brought before them. The contentions which had occurred at Corfu, were once more revived; and the party which had so strenuously opposed the diversion of the expedition from its immediate progress to the Holy Land, was strengthened by many cogent reasons, which could not be so powerfully urged in the earlier stages of the enterprise. In the council, therefore, which was convened for the purpose of deciding on the answer to be returned to the Emperors, it

was with considerable difficulty that those who
supported their cause could obtain a decision in
their favour.   This, however, being effected, the
Emperors manifested their gratitude, not only by
expressions of thankfulness, but by paying large
sums of money to their allies, which they obtained
either by enormous levies on the people, or by
seizing the treasures of the church, which they thus
employed to the great scandal of their subjects.

The Marquis of Mountferrat, the Count of St
Paul, and some other noblemen, hesitated not to
approve themselves worthy of the confidence which
Isaac and his son had placed in their assistance.
In company with the latter, these brave knights
set forth on an expedition, with the intention of
chasing the usurper Alexis, who still retained
some authority in Thrace, from his retreat.   Not
daring to meet any part of an army which had conquered him at the head of the whole force of the
empire, he fled immediately on the news of their
approach, and the provinces yielded submissively
to the authority of the legitimate sovereign.

But while the son of Isaac was thus pursuing
a course of victory through his disturbed dominions, affairs in the capital, and the provinces adjoin-
ing, were every day assuming a gloomier aspect.
The necessities of the weak and unpopular monarchs had already precipitated them into the adop-
tion of measures which would have shaken a long
established throne.   Groaning under the weight
of taxes which they knew were to furnish the pay
of their conquerors, the people became every day
louder in their expressions of discontent ; but
when they saw the churches robbed of their shrines

and ornaments, and heard it rumoured that this act of sacrilege was but a prelude to the general change of their ancient religion, these murmurs became wild and furious indications of sedition, and the state was daily threatened with destruction. Things were in this condition, when the rude fanaticism, or intoxication, of a few Flemish crusaders, who were followed by some Pisans and Venetians, occasioned an event which doubled the horror and confusion that prevailed. A mosque, which had been erected at Constantinople a few years before the death of Saladin at the request of that pious Moslem, was still kept open, as a house of prayer for the followers of Mahomet. The Flemings and their companions, having approached the part of the town in which the mosque was situated, speedily provoked a quarrel with the inmates, and as speedily punished them for defending their temple, by setting it on fire. Many of the neighbouring inhabitants immediately flew to arms, and joined the Moslems against the aggressors. The fire, in the meantime, spread from the mosque to other adjacent buildings. As the night set in, the wind, which had till then blown from the south, driving the flames before it, became northerly, and, suddenly meeting the conflagration, it seemed to fling the whole broad sheet of flame over the other quarter of the city. During the whole of the night the fire continued to gather strength; and when the morning broke, every corner of the heavens was covered with a dense black cloud of smoke, from which streams of flame were every instant bursting, some enveloping the tops of buildings still standing, and others flickering among the crumbling ruins. Whole streets were soon reduced to ashes;

and churches, palaces, and public monuments, shared the same fate, their places being only to be discovered by the thicker masses of flame which covered them. Day after day the conflagration continued to spread. The wretched and bewildered
people felt themselves doomed to destruction;
thousands had been rendered houseless; and where-
ever they turned for refuge the same wild scene
of devastation presented itself. As they rushed
along the streets, the pavement of which was covered with burning ashes, they were terrified at every
step with the falling of the ruins, or were barri-
caded by the huge timbers that lay smouldering a-
bout them. Eight days were passed in this awful manner; and from the eastern extremity of the
city to the western, the track of the conflagration
was marked by one long black unbroken line of
desolation. Such, at one time, was the force of
the wind, that a vessel in the port was set on fire by
the driving flames; and even the sea appeared to
be no longer a security from the appalling danger.

From their camp on the heights of Galata, the
crusaders beheld the capital of the East thus falling a prey to the flames. To save it was utterly
out of their power; and they had the miserable reflection, that the catastrophe had its origin among
themselves. To increase their confusion, above fifteen thousand of the Latin inhabitants of Constantinople fled to the camp for protection against the
infuriated Greeks; and the greatest consternation
prevailed, as every day brought intelligence of the
increasing calamity.

While the unfortunate Greeks were uttering, at
one time, the most mournful lamentations at the
loss of their homes and property, and at another

their curses upon the two Emperors and their hated allies, the young Alexis returned, with Boniface and the other barons who had accompanied him, into the provinces. He entered Constantinople in triumph; but a melancholy silence prevailed as he passed along the public avenues. He was accompanied to the palace of Blaquernes by a few of his courtiers, and some of the Latin chiefs; but the populace every where exhibited the greatest disgust at his presence. The disposition which was thus manifested on his first return to the capital, appeared in a still stronger manner shortly after. The treaty he had made with the Franks, and the odious change proposed in the national religion, operated with full force upon their minds. The late disastrous events contributed still further to rouse their passions; and when the Emperors and their ministers saw no means of protection, but in paying the crusaders still larger sums for their assistance, the rage of the people was no longer to be restrained, and the young Emperor fled to the camp of his allies, with whom he continued to pass his time, either in satisfying their rapacity; sharing in their sports and feasts, or in humbling himself to endure patiently the liberties with which they ventured to insult him. Snatching the jewelled crown from his head, the Venetians covered him, in its place, with the linen cap of their common sailors; and unless he had been willing never to recover his diadem, he dared not resent the affront.

CHAPTER VIII.

RUPTURE BETWEEN THE CRUSADERS AND THE EMPERORS.—
TREACHERY OF THE GREEKS.—MOURZOUFLE.—MURDER OF
THE EMPERORS.—SECOND CONQUEST OF CONSTANTINOPLE.

A.D. 1204.   At length the son of Isaac began to grow weary of the ignominious situation to which he had reduced himself.   He became less frequent in his attendance at the camp, neglected to pay court to the chiefs, and ventured to be remiss in discharging the immense debts he had incurred by his liberal gratitude for their support.   The barons immediately discovered this alteration in the disposition of the Emperor.   They were by no means insensible to their own merit in restoring him and his father to the throne, and they loudly vented their reproaches of his ingratitude.   Every day the discontent of the crusaders increased; and the Emperor, urged on by a few of his courtiers to resist their demands, grew equally determined in his opposition.   While things were in this state, deputies arrived in the camp from the Christians of Palestine, giving an account of the miseries which they had suffered, and imploring the speedy succour of their brethren.

This was an additional motive for the crusaders to be urgent in coming to a conclusion respecting the conduct of their imperial ally.   A council of the chiefs was accordingly called, and deputies were appointed to carry the decision of the assembly to the palace of Blaquernes. The ambassadors were six in number; Conon of Bethune, the Mareschal Villehardouin, and Milo of Provence, together with three Venetian councillors, chosen by the Doge. Girding on their swords, the deputies rode out of the camp, and proceeded to the city, which they entered, while the populace were breathing only vengeance against the whole army of the Franks. They reached, however, the palace in safety, and were conducted into the magnificent hall, where the two Emperors, and the young and lovely consort of the aged Isaac, sat throned, and surrounded by all the pomp and splendour of their court. Conon of Bethune then addressed the younger of the monarchs in these terms:—" We come, gracious Sire, by the command of the Barons of the army, and of the Doge of Venice. They desire to remind you of the service which, as is known to all the world, they have rendered you, and to prevent any cause of contention from destroying the alliance which has existed between them and the Emperor. They beg you, therefore, to consider the treaty which both you and your father have, without cause, neglected to fulfil. They have already often desired you to perform your duty in this respect; and we again this once give you the same counsel. If you receive this warning, they will be content; but if you reject it, know, that they will no longer recognise you, either as the Emperor, or as their friend. They thus openly declare their sentiments and intentions, for it is not the custom in our land to attack an enemy before proclaiming war. You have now heard what we had to say—do your will."

This address was heard by the monarchs and
their courtiers with astonishment and indignation.
Loud and threatening murmurs rose from every
one present; but the haughty bearing of the deputies screened them from the pusillanimous Greeks;
and they strode proudly out of the hall, mounted
their horses, and, dashing through the angry multitudes which filled the streets, gained the camp in
safety.

War was immediately commenced; the Greeks
using all their endeavours to destroy the Venetian
fleet; the latter laying waste the coast, and
burning whatever churches or other buildings
lay within their reach. But all at once, and in
the middle of the night, the camp was illuminated
by a flame that covered both sea and land. As
they looked towards the quarter where the fire
seemed most to rage, seventeen of the largest vessels in the port were seen enveloped at the same
moment in a strong and lurid light. Watching the
opportunity, the Emperors had dexterously filled
some ships with Greek fire; a violent wind had
arisen from the south to aid their design, by driving them against the enemy; and the destruction
of every Venetian vessel in the harbour seemed inevitable. The walls of Constantinople and the
shore were, in the mean time, covered with people,
who loudly expressed their joy at the spectacle,
while the alarm-signal resounded through the camp,
and the crusaders pressed tumultuously towards
the coast. But while they were uttering horrible
imprecations against the treacherous enemy, and
the latter continued their cries of triumph, the
flaming vessels moved slowly from their position;

and the Venetian sailors were seen, with almost miraculous courage, manning the decks, and plying their oars, till, having for some time grappled with the fire-ships, they turned them afloat, steered their fleet, burning as it was, out of port, and rode safe from the reach of the Greeks. By the continued exertions of the mariners, the fire was got under, and only one ship, and that belonging to the Pisans, was lost. The people of Constantinople set up a cry of terror, when they saw the fleet sail away unharmed, and turned in despair to defend themselves, as they best might, against their still powerful adversaries.

We must pass rapidly over the events which followed this circumstance. The crusaders and their associates were now fired with indignation at the treacherous conduct of the Greeks; and the Emperors, terrified at the probable consequences of their temerity, thought of nothing but how to appease the rage of their powerful adversaries. In the midst of the distress and confusion which reigned both in the palace and the city, a personage presented himself who had lately gained the confidence of Isaac and his son, by the boldness with which he had counselled them to reject the offers of their allies. This was the celebrated Alexis Ducas, or Mourzoufle, as he was commonly called, in order to signify the union of his remarkably large and black eyebrows. To a fierce and courageous disposition, he added subtlety and ambition. The situation of the empire, the little talent or spirit that existed among the officers of government, and the influence he enjoyed among the people, as well as at court, gave him ample encouragement to pursue the most ambitious designs; and the hour now seemed to have arrived, in which he might safely put them into execution. While he artfully pretended to negotiate for Isaac with the crusaders, he took care to disseminate through the city an account of all that had passed between them and the young Emperor. A violent commotion followed this measure; and the people, assembling tumultuously in the streets, proclaimed their determination to be no longer governed by monarchs so incapable of defending their subjects. The few citizens, who were willing to use caution on the occasion, in vain endeavoured to moderate the tumult; and, in the church of Saint Sophia, the multitude invested a weak and obscure youth, named Canabus, with the imperial purple. The young Emperor being informed of this event, shut himself up in his palace, and sent messengers to the Marquis of Montferrat, imploring his immediate assistance. With a small body of men, and in the middle of the night, Boniface hastened to the relief of the distressed prince; but Mourzoufle had artfully warned Alexis not to hold any further communication with the Latins; and, too alarmed not to hearken to any advice which had the appearance of reason, the Emperor refused to admit Boniface to his presence. In the meantime, the treacherous Ducas gave it out in all parts of the city, that the Latins were in the palace, and preparing to assail them in their houses. The Marquis of Montferrat narrowly escaped the hands of the populace, who rapidly assembled to interrupt his retreat; but the unfortunate son of Isaac, terrified by the clamours which he heard in the streets, allowed Mourzoufle to lead him from his apartment, to

conduct him, as he supposed, to a place of safety.
No sooner, however, had he left his retreat, when
he found that it was to be immured in a prison,
and treated with the severity of a criminal.

Mourzoufle having effected thus much of his
scheme, hastened to acquaint the populace that he
had secured them from the machinations of their
monarch, by holding him captive till their will,
might be known. The name of Alexis Ducas,
was instantly repeated by a thousand voices, as
alone worthy of being united with the title of
Emperor. The sentiment was echoed by a thousand other tongues; and he was borne to the cathedral, where, without any regard to the election
of Canabus, he was invested with the insignia of
royalty. From the church of Saint Sophia he returned to the prison of his captive; and, with his
own hands, strangled him to death. The aged Isaac,
being informed of his son's murder, died shortly after; and the usurper thus became the sole possessor
of the title of Emperor. The Latin chiefs were for,
some time kept ignorant of these events; and Mourzoufle hoped, by inviting them into the city, to
cut off at once the only enemies he dreaded. But
his treachery was discovered; and the crusaders
immediately took arms to avenge the death of.
their former ally. Vigilance and resolution were
not wanting on the part of the usurper. He
put the city in a posture of defence; and, by.
his example, gave new spirit to the troops. A
nocturnal attempt, which was made by Henry
of Hainault to surprise the city, nearly proved
fatal to that nobleman and his followers, by the
boldness with which Mourzoufle rushed upon
them from his ambush. After a desperate con-

flict, however, the Franks succeeded in driving
him back; and they were left masters of the
standard of the Virgin, in which the Greeks
placed great hopes of safety, and of the sword
and shield of the usurper, which he lost in his
flight.

Mourzoufle was too well acquainted with the
temper of the Greeks, not to be aware that he
could with difficulty resist, for any length of
time, the attacks of the crusaders. Not trusting,
therefore, either to the courage of his soldiers or
to the strength of the fortifications, he offered to
enter into negotiation with his enemies; and the
Doge of Venice persuaded the allied chiefs to receive his propositions. The preliminaries of peace
were discussed by Dandolo and Mourzoufle, the
one standing at the head of a galley rowed near
the shore, and the other sitting on his charger,
each being surrounded by large numbers of their
people. After the debate had continued for some
time, the negotiation was broken off, by the usurper's refusing to admit any change in the national
religion; thereby showing himself either more
conscientious than the legitimate sovereigns, or
more politic; for they had probably lost their
throne, from the unpopularity of such a measure.

The confidence which reigned throughout the
ranks of the crusaders, though at first in some degree diminished by the activity of Mourzoufle,
rose at length to such a height, that the chiefs
drew up a set of regulations, by which they were
to divide and govern the empire, as soon as it fell
into their hands. Preparations were then made
for a general assault; and, by the advice of the

Venetians, it was agreed that it should commence on the side next the sea. The line of vessels, drawn up in order of battle, extended for half a league, and the walls were crowded with troops, and multitudes of the inhabitants anxiously waiting the commencement of the conflict. Mourzoufle himself was posted on the heights, and his magnificent tent, formed an object on which the eyes both of Greeks and Franks were frequently fixed. At length the battle began. The air was darkened by the showers of missiles flung from the machines of the besieged. The crusaders rushed on, reckless of danger or death; and the walls were assailed, at the same moment, by a thousand spears, swords, and battle-axes, while the Venetians continued to labour incessantly at the heavy engines on board their vessels. But the strength of the fortifications resisted every effort of bravery, and the Franks were obliged to retire with considerable loss. The greatest joy prevailed in the city, on the retreat of the besiegers; the people proceeded to the churches to offer up thanksgivings for the victory, and seemed to believe that their foes were entirely overthrown. The crusaders, in the mean time, held a council, to deliberate on the best method of repairing the loss they had sustained. The most ardent of the chiefs observed, that though they had been this once defeated, they ought not to have the less confidence in their valour, and in the justice of their cause; that the Greeks were fighting on the part of usurpation and parricide; and that God would certainly assist those who contended against such a corrupt people. These observations had their due effect; and after some little opposition, another assault was decided upon, and to be made in the same direction as the former. No precaution was omitted which might serve to promote the success of the enterprise ; and two days were spent in repairing the ships which had suffered in the last engagement. Every thing being arranged on the morning of the 12th of April, the crusaders were in arms, and ready for battle.

The Venetian fleet advanced against the ramparts, while the army prepared to second their attack on land. The ships, which were grappled two and two together, were then formed into a line, and the combat soon became general. From the early part of the morning till noon, the battle was continued without any decisive success on either side. But at length the wind suddenly blew from the north, and drove two of the grappled ships upon the shore. It was a singular circumstance, that the names of those vessels were the Pilgrim and the Paradise, and that they were commanded by the Bishops of Troy and Soissons. The moment that a landing was effected, the banners of the cross were floating on one of the towers ; the crusaders, animated with the sight, instantly made for the part of the walls where the prelates fought. Four towers and three of the gates were soon left without defenders. Mourzoufle fled almost alone from the field, and the conquerors entered the city without resistance : the carnage which followed was unlimited by regard to either sex or age ; and before they sought for places where to repose themselves, they set fire to that quarter of the city of which they had taken possession, again threatening the inhabitants with the destruction of their devoted capital.

As soon as the flight of Mourzoufle was made known in Constantinople, the people turned, in the midst of their agitation, to elect a new emperor. Theodore Ducas and Theodore Lascaris were the two candidates for the dangerous honour; and the last, owing to the support he received from the clergy, fell in favour of the latter. On receiving this new dignity, the Emperor besought his subjects to defend their country with vigour, assuring them that they might speedily drive from the coasts a set of men who fought neither for their religion, country, possessions nor families, for all of which the Greeks felt they were contending in this war. "If you are Romans," said he, "victory is easy. Twenty thousand barbarians have attempted to enclose you within your walls; fortune delivers them into your power." In the same manner he addressed his guards; but neither the soldiers nor the people replied to his enthusiasm, and when the signal was given for battle, he found himself without subjects, without guards, and deprived of all means of defence but a rapid flight. While these events were taking place, the conflagration of the city continued to rage with the most frightful violence, and more houses were burnt, it is said, than were contained in the three best cities of France.[*] Not content with this, or with the pillage of the houses and public buildings into which they could hastily penetrate, the crusaders showed an equal contempt for the sacred objects of religious worship. "Alas!" says an eye-witness of these events, "How did they stamp under their feet the images of the saints! How did they throw the relics of

* Villehardouin.

T 2

martyrs into vile and filthy places! A thing was
then to be seen which it is horrible to bear—the
precious body and blood of Christ was poured out
and cast upon the ground." The receptacles of
the sacred things were broken open, and the ornaments stolen; while the vessels which were consecrated to the service of the church, were used for
the common purposes of eating and drinking. "Verily," says the venerable chronicler, "Jesus Christ
was unclothed and mocked by this cursed nation,
as he was anciently, and they cast lots upon his
garment; only they pierced not his side with a
lance, to make streams of blood flow from it."

The great church of Saint Sophia was the glory
of the Greeks for its sanctity, the magnificence of
the building, and the wealth which it contained in
plate, jewels, and the ornaments of the altars. To
this splendid temple of worship the conquerors
hastened unsatiated with the spoil they had already
secured. The chief altar of the church was formed
of a variety of precious stones, which, when united,
had the brilliancy of fire. This beautiful monument of antiquity was immediately destroyed by
the soldiers, who divided its fragments among
themselves. The gold and silver vessels, and the
ornaments with which different parts of the building was richly covered, were seized in the same
manner; and the admirable mosaic pavement,
which, it is said, irritated the barbarians by its ex-
quisitely polished and slippery surface, was defiled
by their mules and other beasts which they ordered to be brought in for that purpose, and some of
which they killed, that their blood might spread
and clot over the sacred floor. Not satisfied with
this, they placed a wretched and abandoned pros-

titute on the throne of the patriarch, addressing
her with songs, and advancing before her to manifest their contempt of the place.†

While the holy asylums of religion were thus
despoiled of their riches, the people, driven from
their homes, and dreading either death, or evils
worse than death, were traversing the streets, uttering the wildest lamentations. Never was a
spectacle of more human misery witnessed. " O
eternal God, " exclaims Nicetas, calling to recollection the sight of his countrymen thus flying
before their pursuers, " What misery ! what poverty ! Why, and how is it, that these evils were
not predicted by some overflowing of the sea, some
eclipse of the sun, some bloody apparition of the
moon, or some comet? Verily have we seen the
abomination of desolation in the holy place ! " It
must not be forgotten either, that the ruthless barbarity with which the Franks thus destroyed whatever was venerable in the eyes of the vanquished
people, extended to the destruction of all the noble
monuments of antiquity with which the capital of
the Greek empire abounded. Several statues, celebrated for their exquisite beauty, the work of
Phidias and Praxiteles, were battered to pieces,
while others, of bronze, were afterwards melted
down, and converted into money. But besides
treasures of this kind, Constantinople contained
others of a different species, and of which the
crusaders were better able to appreciate the value.
The wax relics hoarded up by the clergy of the
capital, were not only more numerous than what
were to be found in any other city of Christendom,

Nicetas.

but were also of the most valuable description.
The bones of Saint John the Baptist, a piece of the
true cross, an arm of Saint James, and so on,
were the reputed possession of one church ; and
others, it appears, were equally rich in the same
venerable articles. No corner was left unsearched
in which it was suspected any relics might be deposited, and very few, it may be reasonably concluded, escaped the devout vigilance of the active
conquerors.

The spoil of every kind which was thus collected, is said to have been the richest that ever fell
into the hands of a victorious host. Immense
stores of all the most valuable articles of Eastern
merchandise,—silks, gems, and spices,—as well as
the booty derived from the churches and public
buildings, composed the splendid prize, which, by
the order of the chiefs, was deposited in three of
the churches, till it should be divided justly among
the forces. The severest punishment was de-
nounced against every one who might be guilty of
a breach of the regulations ; and a knight, who had
concealed something from the knowledge of the
barons, was hung in his armour, by the command
of the Count of Saint Paul.

Success had thus attended the arms of the Latins beyond their most flattering hopes ; and if
the wealth of which they had become masters
may be estimated as greater than what had fallen
to the lot of previous conquerors, the misery which
they had inflicted will come up to the same proportion. The historian Nicetas, who has left
such a melancholy lament over the fallen empire,
has also detailed, in the same volume, the personal afflictions of himself and his family. He

was one of the senators under the Imperial government, and, in the days of his prosperity, inhabited a superb palace, which was reduced to
ashes in one of the conflagrations of the city. He
then removed his family to a small house near the
church of St Sophia, where he resided when the
capital was taken. When the crusaders were pursuing the work of spoliation through every quarter
of the city, a party appeared in the neighbourhood
of the senator's retreat, and he dreaded every instant to see his wife and children in the arms of
the brutal soldiers. In this distress, however, a
Venetian merchant, whom he had saved, when in
power, from the Greeks, presented himself at his
house, and promised to protect him. For a long
time he succeeded in keeping the barbarians from
entering; and he had hopes that, by his wearing
the habit of a crusader, and constantly affirming
that the house was his prize, he should succeed
in his purpose. But seeing, at last, that he could
no longer defend the objects of his anxiety by
these artifices, he warned Nicetas of the danger in
which he stood, and led forth the senator and his
family into the public way. Walking before them
with his sword in his hand, the soldiers, whom
they continually met, believed they were his prisoners, and suffered them to pass unmolested.
One young girl only was in danger of being lost
from the party, owing to her beauty, having attracted the attention of a crusader; but she was
saved by the courage or eloquence of Nicetas, and
they reached the extremity of the city in safety,
when they bade adieu for ever to their protector
and their native home.

But though the fugitives had thus succeeded in

escaping the danger of being taken by the enemy,
they had still hardships to encounter which they
were ill prepared to meet. Nicetas had been
joined, before he left the city, by several friends
and relations; and a number of children, carried
in the arms of their anxious mothers, were part-
ners of their want and fatigue. To increase the
distress of the party, unprovided with the common necessaries of life, it was the depth of winter when they had to undertake this melancholy
journey; and they travelled for forty miles on foot,
laden with baggage, and exposed to a thousand
insults from the peasantry, before they reached a
place of safety. The Patriarch, whom they passed on the road, was fleeing from the enemy in an
equally pitiable condition. He was riding on an
ass; his apparel was scarcely sufficient to cover
him; and his attendants accompanied him in his
exile.

The wretched condition to which those were
reduced of whom we have these memorials, was,
there is no doubt, shared by hundreds besides
themselves; few of them, perhaps, having the good
fortune to end their days so tranquilly as the historian.

CHAPTER IX.

PARTITION OF THE EASTERN EMPIRE.—REIGNS OF BALDWIN
AND HENRY.

THE first turbulent exultations which had followed the taking of the city being subsided, the chiefs
of the crusaders determined to proceed with the
division of the booty. It was at the conclusion
of Lent that they began this important business;
and for the time it lasted, it fully engaged the attention of the army. According to an agreement
which had been previously made, the fourth part
of the spoil was set apart for whoever should be
elected to the imperial throne. The other three
parts were to be equally divided between the
French and Venetians. In a secondary division
which took place, in order that each crusader
might receive his share of the wealth which he
had contributed to gain, a sergeant received a portion of double the value of a foot-soldier, and a
knight one of twice the value of a sergeant. The
barons and higher officers in the army were rewarded with shares proportioned to their rank;
and every one, by this equitable arrangement, had
such a portion of the booty as his situation and
services entitled him to expect. The whole value

of the spoil thus divided amounted to about eleven hundred thousand marks of silver, which is, however, supposed not to have been half the real value of the property which fell into the hands of the crusaders, much of it having been wasted, and a large part being concealed by such of the warriors as were not to be daunted by the threats of the chiefs. When the several divisions of the army had received their respective shares, the French finally settled with the Venetians for their grant of the vessels and stores which they had originally engaged of the republic. Fifty thousand marks were deducted from the sum due to the French for this purpose ; and the portion which remained to them after this deduction, was four hundred thousand marks, estimated by Gibbon at about eight hundred thousand pounds Sterling.

These transactions being concluded, the attention of the crusaders was next called to a business of equal interest and importance. The Emperor still preserved the shadow of royalty among the miserable Greeks ; and with their conquest the Latins became at once the undisputed masters of the nation. Their contempt for the people whom they had subdued was too great to let them think for a moment of giving them a successor to their native princes ; and, even had they been willing to show so much generosity, they would have found it difficult to fix on any of the obscure descendants of the royal races worthy or capable of reigning. But no consideration of this kind weighed with the European chiefs. They understood nothing but the rules of war, and the rights of conquest ; and they had but one plan to pursue, whether it was a city or an empire which they conquered. To choose, therefore, from among themselves, a successor to the Cæsars, was the immediate object of concern; and twelve electors were appointed, with whom the decision was to rest. Of these, six were French, all churchmen, the bishops of Soissons, Halberstadt, Troyes, Bethlehem; the Archbishop of Acre, or Ptolemais, and the Abbot of Loces. The other six were Venetians, the noblest in the army. These representatives of the two nations, one of which was to give a western prince to the Grecian empire assembled in the palace of Bucoleon; and having each sworn to be guided in their choice solely by the merits and virtue of the candidates, they proceeded to the election.

Among the many distinguished noblemen who had taken part in this conquest, there were three only on whom the decision of the assembly could long remain doubtful. These were the venerable Doge of Venice, the Marquis of Montferrat, and Baldwin, Count of Flanders. The aged Dandolo had himself given birth to the enterprise which terminated so gloriously; he had, through a long life, given proofs of the highest wisdom, and the greatest capacity for government. In the present war, he had evinced a courage equal to his wisdom, and had more than once been the first to charge the enemy. These circumstances rendered him as honourable in the eyes of the warriors who accompanied him, as he was dear to his citizens for his moderation and prudence. At first, therefore, the opinion of the electors seemed decided, that the Doge of Venice should he raised to the Imperial throne. But the qualities which had made him the father of his people, and rendered him worthy of the noblest honours, were of too great a value in the eyes of the Venetians to be shared between themselves and the abject and slavish Greeks. While no opposition, therefore, was made to the choice of the Doge by the other electors, the republicans themselves decided against him, observing, with every expression of regard and veneration for their prince, that Henry Dandolo could not be at the same time the head of a republic, and Emperor of the East.

The prize, therefore, now lay between the Marquis of Montferrat and the Count of Flanders. The character of the former was dignified and popular; the Greeks themselves were desirous of having him for their monarch; and the part he had taken in the present expedition, had rendered him a favourite with the army. But the Venetians were opposed to his election, from motives which it is not easy exactly to determine. . The neighbourhood of his possessions, however, to the republic, is generally supposed to have principally influenced these jealous citizens; and when it was remembered by the electors, that against the Count of Flanders no objection of this kind existed, that he was a descendant from the most antient monarchs of France, that his territories gave him command over the best soldiers in Europe, and that he was young, brave and virtuous, their votes were speedily given in his favour, and Baldwin was unanimously nominated to the vacant dignity. It was midnight before the assembly had come to this conclusion of their debate; but as soon as the choice was decided, the Bishop of Soissons, and the other electors, went to the vestibule of the chapel, where the candidates and many other noblemen were waiting to receive their determination. With a loud voice the prelate said, " Noble Lords, we have, through the grace of God, made choice of our Emperor; and you have severally sworn to recognise and obey him as Emperor, on whom our choice should fall. We now, therefore, in this solemn hour in which Christ was born, proclaim your Emperor. It is the Count Baldwin of Flanders and Hainault."

The decision of the electors was received with great applause, and the assembled knights and barons immediately elevated the new Cæsar on a buckler, and carried him in triumph to the cathedral, the generous Marquis of Montferrat being among the first to render the honours of an Emperor to his successful rival. In the church of St Sophia, Baldwin was invested with the purple buskins, the emblem of royalty; and the Greeks, as well as Latins, loudly expressed their satisfaction at the accession of the chief to their ancient monarchy.

The most prudent measures had been taken by the barons, before proceeding to the election, to prevent any evil consequences from the rivalry or disappointment of the candidates. The portions of the conquered territory, which were to belong to the several chiefs, were clearly defined; and, by the regulations agreed to, the Emperor was to possess a fourth part of the whole monarchy, with all the rights which appertained to his dignity. The remainder was to be shared between Venice and the French barons; but, with the exception of the Doge, every possessor of any part of the territory was to be regarded as the feudatory of the Emperor. As the coronation of Baldwin was deferred for three weeks, the intervening period was occupied with the distribution of lands and honours to the different claimants.   The Marquis of Montferrat, who married the widow of the Emperor Isaac, received the Island of Candia, and the country beyond the Bosphorus, which he changed for the province of Thessalonica, and sold Candia to the Venetians for thirty pounds weight of gold. Villehardouin was honoured with the title of Marechal of Romania; and the several dignities of the empire were distributed among the most meritorious chevaliers.   The Doge was made despot, or Prince of Romania; and, as the representative of Venice at Constantinople, he had the possession and command of half that capital.

The coronation of Baldwin was celebrated with great pomp in the church of Saint Sophia.   The Count of Saint Paul, as marechal, carried before him the imperial sword; and the sceptre was borne by the Marquis of Montferrat, as chamberlain. Amid the imposing and solemn worship of the church, the new Emperor, clad in robes that were resplendent with gold and precious stones, was placed by the bishops on the throne, and crowned by the Legate of the Pope. Boniface and the Count of Blois then rendered him homage.   A crowd of knights and nobles, conspicuous for the splendour of their habits, immediately gathered round the monarch; and the long aisles of the cathedral resounded with the loud responses of the multitude to the words of the clergy:—" He is worthy to reign!—He is worthy to reign!"

As soon as the ceremony was concluded, Baldwin was conducted to the palace of Bucoleon. The streets, covered with rich carpets and drapery, were

filled with people, all expressing their delight at
the accession of the Emperor; and, for several
days, nothing was to be seen in the city, but signs
of merriment and content. Several Christians
from the Holy Land arrived at Constantinople, in
order to be present on this occasion. The events
which had occurred seemed to promise an important change in the affairs of Palestine; and while
the ambitious barons and their followers were
occupied with dreams of ambition, the sincere
champions of the sepulchre only saw, in the circumstances which had taken place, the hand of
Providence stretched out to effect their delivery
from the infidel.

Shortly after the coronation of the Emperor, the
crusaders proceeded to make choice of a patriarch.
It was one of the articles of the agreement which
had been entered into by the French and Venetians, that from whichever party the monarch was
elected, the choice of the patriarch should be left
to the other. The Venetians, therefore, having
the right of election, chose Thomas Morosini, an
ecclesiastic of great reputation; and his elevation,
though at first opposed by the Pope, as an infringement of the pontifical authority, at last obtained
his sanction. All the benefices and riches of the
Greek church were forthwith distributed among
the French and Venetian clergy. The Romish
formulary was thus established in every part of the
country, and the natives, exhibiting an instance of
complete subjection, rarely witnessed even in a
conquered nation, as tamely submitted to this
change in religion as to the alteration in the line
of their emperors.

But though the caution and prudent measures

of the principal persons engaged in the settlement of the empire had prevented any interruption to their designs, there were difficulties to meet which it required yet greater caution to overcome. Three of the pretenders to the throne of Constantinople were still in existence; and though exiles, and without wealth or forces, they were regarded in the provinces with far less dislike than the Latin chiefs. But before the crusaders experienced any difficulty from these fugitives, they were assailed with the menaces of a far more dangerous and powerful adversary. Innocent III. had, it will be remembered, opposed from the first the proceedings into which the Venetians had led the soldiers of the cross. The brilliant success which attended their arms produced little alteration in the mind of the Pontiff, and at the conclusion of their enterprise, they had reason to dread that the power of the church would be employed against them to its full extent. In the present state of things, this was to be avoided as the most dangerous circumstance which could occur, and Baldwin, the Marquis of Montferrat, and even the Doge himself, saw the necessity of seeking to avert the evils by a timely submission. In addressing the Pontiff, they all united in professing their most profound devotion to his will; declared that their chief cause of triumph in the conquest of Constantinople, was that they were now in a better condition to execute his commands; reminded him that they had submitted the Eastern church to his apostolical authority; and offered, whenever he chose, to employ their acquisitions in the recovery of Jerusalem. By urging these, and other topics, of a similar nature on his attention, they hoped to remove the ban which he had inflicted on them for their disobedience: But at first the answers which he sent to their petitions were only filled with severe rebukes. He reproached them with having not merely resisted his sacred authority, but violated, in their victories, every principle of humanity. The debaucheries of the soldiers at the taking of the city, the horrible enormities they committed against the wretched inhabitants, and their sacrilegious destruction of altars, were all brought to recollection in the letter of Innocent. He ascribed the victory they had gained to the providence of God, which, notwithstanding their sins, had made them instruments to fulfil his purposes; and he left them a hope that, if they continued faithful to their promises of repentance, proved themselves obedient to the church, and ready to perform their duty in respect to the Holy Land, they might humbly hope to obtain the pardon of their former offences, and reconciliation with their spiritual father. This encouragement was followed by still plainer indications of his readiness to receive them into favour. The absolution which the importunities of the Venetians had obtained from the Cardinal of Capua, was ratified by the Pope; the Doge obtained his full pardon; Baldwin was confirmed in his right to the throne, having declared himself the chevalier of the Holy See; and the reconciled Pontiff sent letters to the different princes of Europe, desiring them to lend their assistance to the Emperor, and offering to those who should willingly take arms in defence of his dominions, the indulgences promised originally to the crusaders.

Every thing thus seemed to assure to the conquerors the permanent enjoyment of their new

possessions; and the faithful were daily looking
forward to measures being taken for the assistance
of the Christians of Palestine. But the prosperity of the empire was of short duration; and the
change in the triumphant prospects of the conquerors, was introduced by a misfortune which
only affected the private feelings of Baldwin.. The
wife of this distinguished man was Margaret of
Flanders, a woman who, still in the bloom of
youth, was as celebrated for her virtues as her
beauty. On setting out for the Holy Land, the
Count had found it necessary to leave her behind
him; but, too impatient of his absence to await
his return, she embarked in a vessel bound for
Ptolemais, with the intention of following him to
whatever part of Syria he might be in. On arriving, however, at the above city, worn with fatigue and anxiety, she learnt that her husband had
never proceeded farther than Constantinople, and
that he had been raised to the throne of the empire. But the intelligence came too late for the
unfortunate Margaret to participate in his glory.
She died shortly after the information was brought
her, and her remains were conveyed to Constantinople, where the afflicted Baldwin received them
with the last honours which belong to royalty.

This event, which cast a sudden gloom over the
fortunes of the Emperor, was followed by another,
which produced worse evils to the state. The
Marquis of Montferrat, having received the territory of Thessalonica in lieu of that originally granted him, together with the title of King, left Constantinople to take possession of his dominions.
Baldwin, who was making the tour of the provinces at the same time, proposed to enter the ter-

ritory of the Marquis with his numerous followers. Boniface resisted this intention, as dangerous to his independence; while the Emperor, as obstinate in asserting his right to proceed, proclaimed his determination to follow the line of march he had marked out. Both, therefore, flew to arms, and the country was threatened with a civil war; but the Doge of Venice, the Marechal of Champagne, and the other peers of the empire, by appealing first to the prudence and moderation of Boniface, and then to the generosity of Baldwin, succeeded at length in subduing their resentment; and they embraced each other, with many protestations of renewed amity.

It would have been happy for the empire, if the chiefs could have now entered upon the peaceable possession of the provinces. But Mourzoufle and the elder Alexis had to be subdued, before this could be effected with security. These deposed usurpers, however, by their hatred of each other, and their dissimulation, rendered themselves easy victims to their enemies. Mourzoufle, having entered into alliance with the brother of Isaac, was, while bathing, suddenly assailed by his supposed friend; his eyes were torn out, and he was sent to wander, alone and helpless, through the country. It was not long that he could escape, in this condition, the watchfulness of his pursuers. He was accordingly taken; and being carried to Constantinople, was flung headlong from a lofty column, and dashed to pieces on the earth. Alexis himself, after wandering about for some time in the most miserable condition, was taken prisoner by Boniface; but having escaped his keepers, he fled into Asia, and, after suffering various evils, died, despised and forgotten, in a monastery. Theodore Lascaris, who appears to have been more worthy of respect than the other fugitives, had fled to Anatolia, when the base and trembling Greeks refused to follow him to the field. Success had attended him, as he marched at the head of a small band of warriors, whom he had the good fortune to assemble, and he founded an empire, of which Nice was the capital, and which could boast of embracing the cities of Smyrna, Ephesus, and Philadelphia.

But a worse enemy than any of the former pretenders to the throne, was preparing to assail the Latins, and with better means for carrying on a war. The Bulgarians had, some time before the restoration of Isaac and his son, thrown off their allegiance to the empire; and Joanice, or Calo-John, as he is variously called, having professed his obedience to the See of Rome, obtained the confirmation of his authority, and the title of King. The son of Isaac, when he accompanied the crusaders into the provinces, threatened Joanice with an attack, but in the end left him to pursue his schemes of ambition undisturbed. When the Emperor Baldwin ascended the throne, the ambassadors of the Bulgarian King were among the first to offer him friendship and alliance; but they were repulsed by the haughty demeanour of the new monarch, who required the humble submission of their master as his vassal. The bold and subtile barbarian dissembled his rage at this affront, and patiently waited for an opportunity to take revenge on the hated Latins. This was not long wanted. The bad government of the different chiefs who had obtained parts of the empire;

the dissensions which existed among them, preventing their co-operation in any useful design;
the weakness of the Emperor, who could not mus-
ter above twenty thousand men to defend the vast
extent of his territory, surrounded on every side
by active enemies, were all destructive of the
means required for the establishment of the Latin
power in the East. We may add to these considerations, that the feudal system was, under the
particular circumstances of the empire, ill calculated
to promote the objects of Baldwin or his associates.
The principal reason of this, it may be reasonably
conjectured, was the conditions under which the
present monarchy was established. The feudal
system, though favourable in reality to the freedom
of the nobility, contained many outward signs of
despotism. When a king or a chieftain, whose
superiority had been previously acknowledged,
conquered a country, the whole warriors who accompanied him, would not unwillingly continue to
obey him as their leader, or refuse to receive their
lands as his tenants. The homage and other feudal services which they rendered him in token of
vassalage, they had been prepared to give by the
nature of their previous service; and though they
would have haughtily repelled any infringement of
their liberty in other respects, they were content
to be ready at the warlike summons of a ruler
whom they had before obeyed as a chief. But it
will be at once seen, that in the case of Baldwin,
the circumstances were very different from what they
were in the old feudal monarchies. The princes
who founded them were preeminently superior in
rank to their followers, and the power or wealth they

already possessed, entitled them, beyond question, to the kingdoms they had conquered. Baldwin, on the contrary, was only one nobleman among many, and a chief who, though great and valorous, was accompanied by chiefs whose greatness and valour were not at all inferior. His appointment to the throne was by election,—a mode of settling a government which might suit either a republic, or a state composed of warriors always seeking for war, but one altogether opposed to the nature and principles of feudalism. The acknowledgement which the holders of fiefs made of the sovereign authority, was as entire and decided as if he had been in all respects an absolute monarch ; it was an assemblage of rites, which could hardly, with consistency, be performed, except when the liege-lord possessed an authority which was of vast extent, and rendered venerable by antiquity. Nothing, therefore, could be less likely, than that a feudal government would prosper, when the head owed his superiority solely to the will of his compeers; or that he could be long secure of the obedience of vassals, who, in reality, felt themselves his equals. From this and similar causes, the empire of the Latins in Constantinople was never firmly settled, and the reign of Baldwin was early disturbed by the evils to which his situation was thus exposed. Had it not been, however, for an enemy more to be dreaded, than these internal causes of weakness, the Latins might probably have warded off for sometime the worst of their domestic troubles, and supported their authority in the East, till time had given additional power to the reigning dynasty.

A. D. 1205.   To the courage and resentment,

therefore, of Calo-John, may be ascribed the fatal shock which the empire received in the first era of its establishment. That hardy chieftain, planning his measures with the most politic skill, watched every motion of the Latin chiefs, and took immediate advantage of the discontents which were prevalent in the provinces. The expedition of Henry of Hainault, the Emperor's brother, into the country beyond the Bosphorus, was the signal for the Greeks to run to arms. He carried with him a large part of the forces, on the constant union of which the safety of the state depended. The insurrection of the natives began at Demotica and Adrianople, of which the garrisons were expelled after their numbers had been frightfully thinned by slaughter; and the principal part, Thrace, was almost instantly overrun by the Bulgarians and the Comans, a barbarous horde of Tartars, with whom Joanice had formed an alliance. The news of this insurrection was received at Constantinople with fearful forebodings of its consequences; and Baldwin sent messengers to his brother to hasten back to the defence of the empire, instead of employing his forces in the pursuit of new acquisitions. In the meantime, he assembled the little army which formed the sole support of his throne, and which, when united to that of the Venetians, amounted only to about sixteen thousand men. Prudence dictated the necessity of awaiting the return of Henry, before any attempt was made to subdue the insurgents and their allies; but the impatience of the Emperor, and the bravery of the knights, rejected all cautious measures; and Baldwin, followed by the Doge, set out for Adrianople.

The situation of the provinces was deplorable.

Surrounded on all sides by enemies, the garrisons of the different towns and villages were unable to gain any information of each other's fate, or to concert measures of mutual defence. When Baldwin arrived at Adrianople, he was joined by numbers of the French or Venetians, who had with difficulty escaped the sword of the Greeks or Bulgarians; but the want of provisions was sore felt in the camp; and the troops had to ravage the neighbouring territory for the common means of support. Scarcely were they disposed about the walls of the city, when the Tartars appeared in sight, and began their desultory attacks. An order was issued, that, on a signal being given, the knights and their followers should mount, and be in readiness for charging the enemy; but that no one should pass the intrenchments till a further signal was given for a general onset. The reason for this caution, was the mode of fighting employed by the Tartars, and who, it was suspected, had received directions from Joanice to affect a flight, in order to draw the Latins from their camp into the open field. Notwithstanding the orders which had been issued by the chiefs, the policy of the Barbarians was successful. At almost the first appearance of the enemy, the Count of Blois, who commanded the main body of the troops, rushed from the intrenchments, and, after a short conflict, the Comans turned their horses and fled. Heated by success, the Franks pursued them at the full speed of their chargers. For two leagues the flight and pursuit were kept up with equal velocity; when the Tartars suddenly wheeled round, and encountered the Franks as they came up, overpowered and breathless with fatigue. The attack was supported by the knights with a bravery far superior to their prudence, or present power of defence; but, while they were boldly defending themselves against the Comans, Joanice joined the latter with his forces, and the Latins, surrounded and assailed by the superior numbers of the enemy, strewed the ground with their corpses. The Count of Blois, to whose fatal valour the catastrophe was owing, continued to fight, though covered with wounds, and sinking from loss of blood. When one of his followers besought him to leave the field, he answered him, by praying to God that he might never be known to flee in battle; and he, and the knight who had followed him into the midst of the fray, were a few minutes after both slain. Baldwin, in the meantime, had brought up his troops to the encounter, and fought in a manner befitting an emperor and the character he had formerly gained; but after a useless conflict, which he continued to support when left alone on the field, he was taken prisoner, loaded with irons, and carried into captivity, from which he was doomed never to return.

Calo-John, with more wisdom than chiefs of greater renown have at all times shown, lost no time in following up the success he had thus obtained over his haughty foe. By the skill of the Marechal of Champagne and Romania, however, the retreat of the discomfited and diminished army was protected against his attacks. The siege of Adrianople was raised; and, after a hasty march, during every moment of which they were in danger of destruction, the Franks reached Rodosto, where they met the brother of Baldwin returned from his expedition into the Asiatic provinces. The chiefs then held a council to deliberate on the melancholy

condition of their affairs, and Henry was appointed Regent; and most of the chevaliers expressed
themselves eager to return against the enemy, and
attempt the delivery of Baldwin. But their enthusiasm was not general. A great number of the
knights bade adieu to Constantinople, and returned
to their own countries; while the Greeks became
every day more inclined to revolt, and Joanice pursued his career without any effectual opposition.
At last the Latins bethought themselves of soliciting the aid of other European nobles and princes;
and the Pope himself added his exhortations to
their requests, and summoned them to the aid of
their distressed brethren. He wrote, moreover, to
Joanice, desiring him, on the strength of his long
professed obedience to the Holy See, to restore
Baldwin to liberty. In neither the one instance
nor the other, however, was he successful in his
applications. The princes of Europe were unmoved by either enthusiasm or ambition to undertake an expedition to Constantinople; and the
Bulgarian chiefs returned for answer, that the Emperor had died in prison. Several romantic accounts are given of the circumstances which attended the unfortunate Baldwin's captivity; such
as, his having received an offer of freedom from the
Queen of Bulgaria, who was enamoured of his
person, but whose addresses he virtuously rejected. They are, however, usually treated as fables;
and the only fact which appears to be well ascertained, is his death while in the power of Joanice.

A. D. 1206. When this circumstance was certainly known in Constantinople, Henry of Hainault was
proclaimed successor to the throne. He obtained
the Imperial power when it was reduced to its

lowest degree, and it appeared impossible that it
should be much longer preserved to the Latins,
Henry was left without any of the distinguished
men who had founded the empire, to support him
in his elevation.   The venerable Doge of Venice,
to whom it was owing that the Franks ever gave
laws to the Greek empire, died about this time.
The Marquis of Montferrat, who, after a slight
dispute with Henry, had given him his daughter
in marriage, was soon after killed in a battle with
the Bulgarians, and his head carried as a trophy.
of victory to their chief.   The excellent Villehardouin also, it is observed by Gibbon, ceases to
pursue his history with the events of this period,
and " his voice seems to drop, or to expire."
Four of the first men, therefore, among the Franks,
and those whose rank and capacity were alone sufficient to keep the rest together, were thus lost at
almost the same time.   Baldwin, Dandolo, Boniface of Montferrat, and the Marechal of Champagne, are conspicuous throughout the history of
this period, as the only characters worthy of attention.   They were bold and politic ; in many
instances they exhibited the talents of able generals ; and when the mass of their followers were
inclined to the most pernicious violence, they employed all their power and authority to diminish
the evil they had produced.   The generous patriotism of Boniface was more than once manifested in his conduct towards his successful rival.
The Emperor was ready, on all occasions, to defend
his followers at the risk of his own life, and is described by his cotemporaries as not being more
courageous than he was kind-hearted and virtuous.
Villehardouin appears to have united, in his person,

more valour and prudence, together with great
descriptive powers, than could be found combined
in any other man among the crusaders, excepting
the Doge.   That celebrated republican was worthy
of the respect which the powerful state over which
he presided rendered him ; and in saying this, we
give him the praise which best indicate his virtues
and talents.   Henry Dandolo had the chivalrous
heroism of the monarchs of his age, and the noble
port of a sovereign, with the moderation, the cool,
cautious wisdom, and the sternness of principle
and manners, which belong to a republican.

The brother of Baldwin, when he mounted the
throne, thus saw himself the last of the heroes
who had inspired a small army of Latins with sufficient confidence, to attempt the conquest of a
vast empire.   But he possessed a large portion of
the talents and excellent qualities which distinguished the great men of whom we have been
speaking ; and he supported an arduous struggle
against his enemies, when a sovereign of less ability would have been obliged at once to yield up
his throne, or would have fallen an early victim to
his temerity.   Fortunately for him, Joanice, by
his cruelty to the Greeks, drove them into a coun-
ter rebellion, and they voluntarily submitted themselves to the new Emperor.   The Bulgarians next
entered into an alliance with Lascaris, whose establishment at Nice has been already mentioned ;
and who seemed again in a condition to contest
the prize with Henry.   But Lascaris was hated as
much by many of his followers as by his enemies ; and, while encamped before Thessalonica,
to which city he had laid siege, he was stabbed
one night in his tent.

Henry succeeded in making peace with Lascaris and the descendants of Joanice, by which means he secured himself leisure to attend to the internal affairs of his dominions. The policy which he employed to appease the angry feelings of the Greeks, has been greatly and deservedly praised. He justly attributed much of the misery, which had been experienced in the reign of his brother, to the oppression which the people had suffered on account of their religion. Refusing to be instigated by the narrow and selfish views of the Romish clergy, he distributed justice with an equal hand among all classes of his subjects. The distinction also of Frank and Greek, as regarded the enjoyment of public offices and emoluments, was no longer kept up; and by these, and other wise measures of a similar kind, he raised his authority to the highest degree of security it was capable of attaining. His reign, which lasted for only ten years, forms a subject well worthy of study; but, to pursue this branch of history any further, would lead us from the immediate object of the work, and we must return to the account of the affairs of Syria.

Before, however, concluding the brief detail which has been given of the above events, it may be worth remarking, that they furnish an excellent index to the manners and state of feeling which then prevailed in Europe. The power of the Pope, it may be learnt from the recital given, was greatly diminished, not only in Italy, but in other countries. With regard to the maritime cities of the former, they are seen defying his authority, and pursuing measures in direct opposition to the policy of the Roman Sea. This would be less worthy of a particular observation, were it not for one circumstance which merits especial attention, namely : that the states, which, before the thirteenth century, thus resisted the power of the Pope, and in a great measure threw off their allegiance, were republics.   Instances had occurred in much earlier times of this opposition to Papal despotism ; but they were the result of great pride, licentiousness, or ambition in monarchs, and were as manifestations of what the people thought, or how they were disposed to resist the great head of the church. It appears indeed certain, that no such disposition even existed among the populace, till the republics of Italy set the example.   The independence of those free states, as it resulted from the growing intelligence of the community, so was it exhibited in all the acts of the government ; and the resolution with which the Doge pursued his designs, notwithstanding the threats and prohibitions of the Pope, represented the true feeling of the people in regard to the Pontiff's power.   Their neglect of his threats was the effect of cool, sober deliberation—the triumph of freedom and intelligence over popular superstition and its promoters. The readiness with which the Venetians united with the French and the other crusaders, in deprecating the wrath of the Pope, after they had completed their designs, was dictated by sound policy, and bore no marks of either fear or enthusiasm. The Pontiff was still regarded by their allies with the deepest veneration ; and it would have been imprudent and useless to awaken their dislike, when no further object was to be attained by opposition.

Learning had not yet spread sufficient light over the states of Europe, to make men see the benefits which would result from the cultivation of the arts; or the superior value of riches produced by the regular and wealthy exertion of national strength, to the most splendid conquests made in warlike expeditions. The thorough contempt of the Franks for learning was indicated at Constantinople, by their making the supposed erudition of the Greeks an object of constant ridicule. The little notion which the princes and barons had of improving their resources or rank, by the improvement of their territories, is still further manifest by the promptness with which they forsook them at the call of avarice or ambition. The most certain sign of barbarism in such princes being the facility with which they can be persuaded to pursue the first prize that is held out to them, at the risk of ruining their subjects, and draining their possessions of all the resources they enjoy.

Of the general state of morals at this period, we have a lamentable picture, in the circumstances which followed the taking of Constantinople. The violences which were then committed, exceeded in horror the frightful scenes of the earlier crusades, and could only have been perpetrated by men prepared for the commission of the darkest crimes. At no period either was the resistance of the Greeks sufficiently obstinate to provoke this fury in their conquerors. They were pusillanimous, and soon beaten; and the destruction of their homes, therefore, and the slaughter of themselves after the battle was won, were unjustifiable even by the maxims of warfare. To increase the horror, also, of these transactions, we are re-

minded, throughout the detail, that they occurred
in a war of Christians with Christians, and during
an expedition which had been commenced for the
delivery of Christians from oppression and distress.
The only excuse which these warriors of the cross
could make for their barbarous excesses, was, that
though their victims were Christians, they hallowed a Patriarch instead of a Pope. This, in fact,
was the strongest plea which most of the leaders
set up to justify their invasion of the country; and
the independence of the Greek church made its
unfortunate members as heathen men in their sight.
What are we to think of a system which could
thus colour the most horrid barbarities with a pretended sanctity, and suffer its disciples to suppose,
that, in propagating it, they might employ the
worst passions that can inflame the heart? The
Pope, it is true, in the present instance, deprecated the measures of the crusaders; but it appears
that the opposition resulted from his anger against
the Venetians; and even if we allow it to have
proceeded from the purest motives, the system itself appears in equal deformity—its corruption not
being the less, because it sometimes occasioned
more evil than its promoters were willing to justify.

The effects which the possession of Constantinople produced on the manners and opinions of
Europe, were at first but slightly felt, and, it is
probable, were less beneficial than hurtful. The
conquerors had so little veneration for the noble
monuments of art which fell into their hands, that
they had given most of them up to destruction;
and their authority was assailed by so many dangers, that they had no time for cultivating the ad-

vantages which their new empire offered for awakening a love of literature and the sciences. Those of the Latins, therefore, who returned to their own countries in the early years of the conquest, bore with them no new lights, or increased means for the dissemination of the truth. They had revelled for a time in gross, intoxicating luxury; but they had learnt none of those refined and softening arts which, if they sometimes minister to sensuality, always subdue barbarism, or lessen its fierceness. The licentiousness which the events of the war had encouraged, was thus transplanted in the West, and tended much more to the corruption of the people, than the enlarged possessions of the barons did to their authority.

If we are to look, therefore, for any important results from this conquest of the Latins, it must be in their subsequent history, when the empire, having been some years established, opened a wide field for commercial speculation; and a settled intercourse was carried on between Europe and the East, not for adventure, but for profit or information. If the Greek Emperors had been inclined to peace, and had suffered the Latins to hold free intercourse with their dominions, all the advantages which resulted from this war would have been secured at a much earlier period; and Europe might have been enlightened with Grecian literature, and enriched by Eastern wealth, while the empire stood firm, and remained an insurmountable barrier to Mahometanism. But the weakness and ignorance of the Emperors seem to have forbidden this profitable intercourse; and the conquest, therefore, of Constantinople by the Latins, was the only means by which it could be secured.

Looking at the events which have been related, in this light they occupy an important place in the general history of Europe. Modern civilization is the product of a long and complicated series of circumstances. To trace them to their origin, and estimate their respective influence, is one of the highest and most useful employments of the understanding. The causes which produce the amelioration of our race are not always, perhaps are rarely, those which first attract attention ; and it therefore often happens, that an importance is attached to events which they, in reality, do not possess. The stream may be troubled, without its course being changed ; and its fountain may be made sweet or bitter, without any difference being perceptible on its surface. When this is the case, the careless observer reaps only error from his inquiry. Fortunately, however, there are certain great events, which form land-marks in these investigations, or divide the great volume of human history into chapters. The subjection of the Greek empire to the Latins may be considered as one of these occurrences, and as having powerfully operated on the civilization of Europe.

CHAPTER X.

JOHN OF BRIENNE ELECTED KING OF JERUSALEM.—INVASION OF EGYPT.—CONQUEST OF DAMIETTA—FREDERIC II. AND THE FIFTH CRUSADE.—IRRUPTION OF MOGUL TARTARS.—FALL OF JERUSALEM.

A. D. 1215. THE events which occurred between the accession of Henry to the throne of Constantinople, and the period at which we resume the thread of our narrative, form a fitting link to the two epochs. Before proceeding, therefore, to detail the final measures of Innocent to accomplish another crusade, it will be proper to give a brief account of the circumstances under which he undertook this arduous enterprise.

The minds of men had undergone a great and wonderful change since the first crusades; and, amid the constant struggles for freedom, the eager endeavours after wealth, and the growth of commerce which marked this period, enthusiasm had less nourishment, and was more unnatural in its operations. It may be remarked, perhaps, without error, that both superstition and enthusiasm, when they appear in times comparatively enlightened or civilized, are always far wilder, more dangerous, or baser, than in ages of more general darkness. Certain it is, that some of the occurrences which preceded the crusade we are about

to describe, were hardly equalled by those which
we regard with most astonishment in the narrative
of the former.

Innocent continued to exert himself with undiminished fervour in the cause of Palestine, notwithstanding the failure of his original project.
The heaviest sins were atoned for, in the judgment of the church, by the promise of a pilgrimage; monarchs had an opportunity of securing the
support of the whole pontifical authority by the
same means; and the arms of the Holy Father were
extended in affection towards all, whatever might
be their station or character, who were ready
to unite with the Christians of Syria. But, unfortunately for the success of the undertaking,
the situation of the great European States prevented their princes from attending to the application
of the Pontiff. France was employed continually
in defending herself against the attacks of England, or the allies of this country; and Philip Augustus, who was the most politic monarch of his
times, had too many projects for aggrandizing his
kingdom, to engage in a crusade. Germany was
at the same time distracted by the contentions of
the Emperor Otho, whom the Pope pursued with
his weightest maledictions, and Frederick II.,
whom he at length succeeded in seating on the
throne. Causes equally important kept England
out of the field. It was the momentous birth-day
of her liberties; and while John had neither the
means nor sufficient enthusiasm for engaging in
the designs of the church, the barons of England
had all their ardour and resolution fully employed
in the contest for their great charter.

The East presented a very different spectacle to

this of Europe. In the latter, we see only the objects to which the ambition of princes, or men's natural love of freedom, give constant life and activity. The former terrifies the mind with unusual and supernatural appearances, and terrible signals of Divine anger. Both Egypt and Syria had, of late, been subjected to the most awful visitations of famine and pestilence. The regular overflowings of the Nile having been interrupted, the land had every where the appearance of a dry and sterile wilderness. The corn and all other productions of the earth were burnt up by the sun, and nothing remained on the ground but a little withered grass, or parched stubble. Even this refuse of the fields was speedily exhausted by the wretched multitudes that thronged the country. In vain they traversed plain after plain in search of the coarsest production of nature. The same dry and burning air every where prevailed; not a strip of land could be discovered that retained the smallest signs of fertility; and the earth became daily more unfit for supporting life.

The despair which pursued the famishing crowds from one corner of the land to the other, was converted into a fiendish madness as their strength decayed. Some, rushing to the depositaries of the dead, tore the corpses to pieces, and satisfied their hunger with the fragments; others flew upon the companions of their misery, and, murdering them, devoured their remains. Women, in the same manner, slaughtered their infants; and in one day, thirty miserable females were convicted at Cairo of having killed and eaten children. These violations of nature increased the horror of the period. Cannibalism had become so common, that

the practice was regarded with indifference; till
a raging pestilence began to assail the victims, and
hasten their fate. As they wandered about, hundreds
perished in the streets and roads; and the cities
of Egypt were filled with heaps of bodies, which
lay corrupting on the ground for want of burial.
More than a million of people perished before this
calamitous famine ceased; and the misery which
it produced extended itself through Syria, threatening both the Christian and Mussulman provinces with devastation. To complete the melancholy picture, we have only to mention, that a
destructive earthquake followed close upon these
miseries, and in its ravages overthrew and en-
gulfed whole cities. The strongest fortresses were
shaken to the ground; and the walls and towers
of Balbec, Ptolemais and Damascus, crumbled beneath its scourge.

The distresses occasioned by these convulsions
of nature were amply sufficient to place the Syrian Christians in the most deplorable situation.
But to these causes of misery, they added others
of their own producing. The rivalry which had
long existed between the two great orders of chivalry, manifested itself in open acts of hostility; and, in the contentions which took place between the chiefs of the different provinces, they
espoused opposite sides, and fought against each
other with as much fury as against the infidels. The
truce, also, which had been made with the Saracens,
was near its termination, and was now so badly
kept, that engagements were continually taking
place between the two people. The death of the
titular King of Jerusalem increased the confusion
which prevailed, and rendered it necessary for the

common safety that measures should be taken for
putting affairs into a better order. To this object
the principal barons and knights were at length
induced to devote their attention; and they proceeded to the choice of a successor to Amaury.

The crown of Jerusalem had descended by inheritance to the daughter of the late King and
Isabella. This princess, however, was unfitted,
both by age and sex, for the station to which her
birth elevated her; and it was the prudent determination of the barons to espouse her to some
warrior, who might be able to defend the little
remnant of their conquests. Either mistrusting
their own courage, or fearing to excite a spirit of
jealousy, they agreed to leave the choice of their
king to Philip Augustus; and ambassadors were
shortly after despatched to France, to make their
desires known to that monarch. Chivalry was
no longer dependent for its support on religious
enthusiasm; and the observer of its progress, and
of its effects on society, will find it useful to
mark the change which had thus occurred in
its character. The age of deep, imaginative, in-
tense devotion, was, as we have seen, rapidly passing away. Most of the feelings which
it had for a time rendered natural to the heart,
were declining with it; and if chivalry had not
been gradually strengthening its connection with
royalty, and all the pomp and glory of princely courts, it would have vanished long before
its most splendid eras. But as it lost some of
its graver and more impressive characteristics, it
daily acquired greater external brilliancy; and the
magnificence which was diffused over the whole
institution, entirely supplied at last the place of

its devotional features. Every age gave some fresh indication of this alteration in the character of chivalry; and the circumstance we are relating serves to illustrate the opinion now advanced. The Christians of Syria had no champion sufficiently distinguished or meritorious among the rich bands of their own Templars or Hospitallers—no noble presented himself, led only by the sanctity of his knighthood, as the devoted chief of the faithful and they had to seek for a King of the Holy City among the gay and ambitious courtiers of France!

The choice of Philip, to whom the deputies had entirely referred the election, fell on John of Brienne, whose brother had gained great glory, but lost his life in the conquest of Naples. John himself was one of the most valiant knights of Christendom, and eagerly bent on any adventure which might increase either his fortune or reputation. He had been originally intended for the church; but his fiery disposition rejected the idea of living in idleness and tranquillity, and he was allowed to follow his natural inclination. The offer of a crown was as splendid a testimony to his worth, as it was flattering to his imagination. It associated him with the pious heroes whose memory was hallowed throughout the world; it seemed to promise him a renown equally wide and lasting as theirs; and the difficulties with which he might have to contend, were such as it befitted a knight always to meet undaunted. That the prize of royalty was to be given him by a young princess, whom romance might fairly invest with all the charms of beauty, added not a little to his enthusiasm; and John of Brienne accepted the boon, with many declarations of devotedness to the cause of Jerusalem and its Queen.

Had the new champion of the Sepulchre been able to accomplish his design of proceeding to Syria at the head of an army, he might have produced a considerable change in the situation of his oppressed subjects. The Saracens, surprised at the confidence which the Christians seemed to place in their expected monarch, offered to lengthen the truce; but, notwithstanding the persuasions of the Hospitallers, and the indefensible condition of the faithful, the proposition was proudly rejected; and the arrival of John of Brienne was the signal for commencing hostilities. Instead, however, of appearing at the head of a numerous host, he was followed by only three hundred knights; and the festivities of his marriage and coronation were scarcely concluded, before he had to defend himself against the formidable attacks of the enemy. The Saracens fought with all the advantages of numbers and good supplies on their side; and Christian valour was obliged to yield to these powerful auxiliaries. In a short time, the dominions of John were reduced to the single city of Ptolemais; and there was no reason to hope that this last resort of the believers could hold out long against the Moslem. Deputies were therefore sent to Europe to implore succours of the princes who still pretended to reverence the land of Palestine. The final ruin of the Christian territory there, must evidently shortly follow, if this aid were denied; and if it were ever a duty of believers to fight for the sacred birth-land of their Saviour, it was especially so now, when it appeared ready to fall for ever into the hands of the infidel.

But Europe was, at the same time, violently
agitated both by religious and civil contentions.
The ruthless persecutions of the Albigenses, which
were just commenced, filled the south of France
with dismay and ruin. Ignorance, superstition,
and ecclesiastical tyranny, formed the triple scourge
of reformers in those days; and they who ventured to turn their eyes to the day-spring of truth,
were doomed to destruction, the moment they
confessed themselves enlightened. Had we room
to enter into details not immediately connected
with the crusades in Syria, the wars carried on
against the early opposers of papal corruption
would serve so well to illustrate the character of
the age, that we should with difficulty refrain
from digressing into their history. The principles,
however, in which these persecutions had their
rise, the mingled fanaticism and corruption by
which they were nurtured, may be sufficiently understood from a memorable circumstance which
occurred about this time.

While Innocent was urgently pursuing his measures for raising an armament, and had so far succeeded in his attempts, that many thousands of
the people were roused to the highest pitch of excitement, the feeling which had descended from
the pontiff to the multitude, was thence trans-
ferred into the hearts of children, who were allowed to receive it as a Divine inspiration. It
seems scarcely credible, but it is a well-attested
historical fact, that no less than fifty thousand
children of France and Germany assumed the
cross, and set forth for Palestine. The origin of
this strange crusade is differently described by the
authors who have given any account of the occur-

renée." By some it is said, that the young enthusiasts had no instigator but their own crude
imaginations; but others, who appear to have gained the greater credit; assert, that in France they
assembled at the call of two ecclesiastics who had
lately returned from captivity in the East. These
priests recovered their liberty, it is said, by promising to furnish the Old Man of the Mountains,
who held them in bondage, a certain number of
European youths, to be trained up in his service.
In Germany, the seven thousand children who
prepared themselves for the same exploit, were
headed by one Nicholas, by some writers mentioned as also a priest, by others as only a youth,
not much superior in either age or sense to the
rest. The honour with which he was treated by
his followers elevated him beyond measure. Having seated him on a sort of triumphal car, they
pressed around his person, as if it deserved the
most reverential care; and he was nearly overwhelmed by the numbers who sought to possess
themselves of some fragment of his garments, or
of any thing which he had rendered sacred by pos-
sessing.*

Whatever was the immediate motive which induced fanaticism or imposture to prepare these
victims for destruction, the design, in a certain
sense, succeeded. Traversing Saxony, and making
their way through the toilsome passes of the Alps,
the Germans arrived at Genoa, where their presence excited the most lively astonishment. The
French, in the mean time, were collected near
Paris, whence they set out for Marseilles, and

* Matthew Paris.

reached that city without any diminution of their ardour. The route of the young crusaders, was marked by tumultuous expressions of devotion and confidence in supernatural support. " O Lord Jesus Christ! restore to us thy cross," was their constant cry. When they were asked respecting the intention of their journey, " To visit the Holy Land," was their reply; and if any of them were detained by their friends or parents from pursuing the design, they employed every art till they succeeded in rejoining their companions. Notwithstanding, however, the resolution with which they had borne the fatigues of the journey, they presented a miserable spectacle to the inhabitants of Genoa and Marseilles, when they assembled under the walls of those cities. Several dissolute wretches of both sexes had joined the bands on the way; and the greater part of the children were despoiled of their clothing, and whatever little stores they possessed. Some of them had strayed from the beaten track, and wandered about till they perished with fatigue or hunger; and the others had undergone so much privation and misery, that they all seemed equally doomed to an untimely end.

The spirits of the unfortunate children had been kept up to this period, by the expectation that miracles of the most extraordinary kind would be wrought in their favour. It was their confident belief, that, when they arrived on the shores of the Mediterranean, they should find the waters dried up, and a path made for them through the bed of the sea. On discovering that the waves had not changed their course, the hopes of the crusaders received a considerable check; and at

Genoa they were thrown into still greater consternation, by the Senate's issuing an order for their departure from the city. A very few had the good fortune to interest some of the inhabitants in their favour; and they are said to have been the ancestors of some of the noblest families in Italy. The rest suffered the same miseries, in endeavouring to retreat to their homes, as they had undergone in their previous journey. In the villages through which they passed, they were derided as idiots; and when asked what had induced them to leave their country, they replied, they could not tell what. Hunger and fatigue spared few of these victims to the barbarous errors of the age; and they perished either in the woods, or passes of the mountains through which they endeavoured to find their way.

The troop which had arrived at Marseilles shared a similar fate. Their expectations had been the same with regard to the drying up of the sea; and the miracle failing, they had no means of prosecuting their design. A number of them yielded to the disappointment, and returned home; but the greater part remained anxiously looking for any opportunity of passing the sea to Syria. In this situation they were found by two merchants of the city, whose names are not inapplicable to their characters. Hugh Ferrens and William Porcus carried on a considerable trade with the Saracens, and found no article of commerce more profitable than European youths. The opportunity now offered them, of entering largely into a speculation of this kind, was not to be neglected; and they proposed to the deluded children, to convey them in vessels of their own to the place of destination. Devotion was the sole motive which these wretches professed to have in view; and their plan succeeded to admiration. The crusaders accepted their offer with many expressions of gratitude. The miracle, in one sense, seemed accomplished; and they joyfully embarked in the seven vessels prepared for their reception. At the close of the second day a violent storm arose, and the fleet, which had approached the island of St Pierre, was threatened with instant destruction. Two of the ships were swallowed up by the waves, and all on board perished. The other five managed to outlive the storm, and were carried into the ports of Alexandria and Bugi, where the crusaders were landed, and immediately sold for slaves. The Caliph of Egypt bought forty, who are said to have been all in holy orders, by which, however, we are not to understand that they were older than the rest, the church of Rome conferring consecration at a very early age. These young clerks were brought up by their master with the greatest care, but if we are to believe the common report of the chroniclers, not one of the captives could be prevailed on to renounce his religion. Of the remainder, twelve perished as martyrs to their faith; and the few who succeeded in reaching Ptolemais, amazed the Christians of that city with their melancholy recital. Accustomed as the faithful had been to miracles and prodigies, they could not account for this strange expedition; and it is worthy of observation, that they considered it as a terrible proof that the nations of Europe were in a state of dissolution, and were left without laws or government either human or divine.

Many questions arise in the mind on the simplest consideration of this recital. What was the condition of the people in general, if so many thousand children could be permitted to congregate, and devote themselves to almost certain destruction? and if the parents or friends of these young devotees opposed, but in vain, their expedition, to what circumstance are we to attribute the extreme weakness of parental authority in those times?—Was it that nature had then less power than now, or was it that the priesthood had usurped the rights of domestic rule, and by that means put the whole beautiful economy of human life and its relations in constant peril? The strongest feeling of disgust at the concern, appears to have been manifested in Genoa. Is not this another indication of the superior intelligence of the maritime cities of Italy to the other European States? And, lastly, how are we to regard the character of Innocent, or estimate the condition of the Church, when we find him expressing no horror at the wretched folly of these children, and only remarking, when informed of their miseries, "They reproach us for being plunged in sleep, while they fly to the defence of the Holy Land."* We might add to these questions; but the above are sufficient to indicate the curious nature of the subject, and how it may serve to illustrate the state of things when the Pontiff employed the powers of the Church against the Albigenses.

- A signal victory obtained about this period over the Moors, who had long established their dominion in Spain, added considerably to the re-

* Albert de Stadt.

solution with which Innocent published the new
crusade. Hitherto, his efforts had been attended
with little success, and he saw no prospect of
awakening the slumbering warriors, unless by some
measure which should excite the attention of the
whole Christian world. To this end, therefore,
he determined on calling a general council at
Rome ; and in the letters which he circulated for
that purpose, he strongly appealed to the feelings
and consciences of all the princes, barons and
knights, who acknowledged his spiritual sovereignty. He also encouraged the faithful of all ranks
to join the standard of the cross, as the surest method of obtaining the full remission of their sins ;
and inflamed their hopes of victory, by declaring
that the final doom of the false prophet and his
followers was at hand, and that the Moslem territories were about to be added to Christendom.
Churchmen of distinction were exhorted to furnish
a certain number of soldiers, and to contribute
their wealth to the enterprise. Towns and villages received the same directions; and the princes
or barons who could not give their personal services, were summoned to assist, by donations fitted
to their rank and possessions. Preachers of the
crusade were chosen from the most eloquent of the
clergy, among whom were the Cardinal de Courçou, the Pope's legate in France, and several bishops. Not content with thus exerting himself
among the faithful of Europe, Innocent sent letters
and ambassadors to the East, charging the Christians there to employ all their energy in seconding
his designs for their delivery. At the same time,
he tried the effect of his eloquence on the Saracen
princes, whom he endeavoured to convince of their

injustice in retaining the Holy Land from the Christians, its rightful possessors; and to alarm, by assuring them, that the Lord was ready to receive again his disciples into favour, and restore them to their heritage.

The Cardinal de Courçon, and the celebrated James de Vitri, succeeded in gaining the most respectful attention to their exhortations. While the people expressed their reverence for these distinguished preachers, by receiving the cross at their hands, the princes promised to devote a part of their revenues to the enterprise; and the King of France extended his piety and liberality to the fortieth part of the income derived from his domaine. These successes assured Innocent that he should finally establish the great object of his reign; and after every preparation had been made to render the assembly as splendid as possible, the council met in the Lateran; where having decided upon the ruin of the Albigenses, the Count of Thoulouse who had aided them, and all others engaged in the same cause, decrees were passed for prosecuting the Syrian crusade with all possible despatch. The pulpits again resounded with the energetic appeals of the bishops, and the Christian world seemed once more prepared to follow the dictates of its sovereign; but before the design, which had occupied so many years of his life, could be executed, Innocent was taken ill and expired.

A. D. 1216. This Pontiff was succeeded by Honorius III., who, the day after his elevation, wrote to the King of Jerusalem, to acquaint him with his resolution to follow the counsels of his predecessor. The wars of England and France, and, in fact, the political condition of all Europe, still proved a formidable obstacle to the crusade; and but for the zeal of Frederic of Germany, and several of the bishops and princes of that nation, it is a question whether it would have ever taken place. The persuasions of the Emperor, who, however, had no present means for prosecuting the expedition, induced the Dukes of Austria, Brabant, Moravia, and Limbourg; the Archbishop of Mayence; the Bishops of Passau, Bamberg, Strasbourg, Munster, and Utrecht, with many other of their powerful countrymen, to depart, without farther delay, for Syria. Before these embarked, they were joined by Andrew II. King of Hungary, who appeared at the head of a numerous army, to fulfil the vow which his dying father had imposed upon him, to fight for the restoration of Jerusalem.

The North was at this period in a singular state of agitation. The feeling which had induced the church and the King of France to persecute the Albigenses, afforded an ample plea for the Teutonic Knights and their confederates to attack and exterminate the Prussians. There was something more worldly, perhaps, in the outward appearance of the latter, the ambition of warriors' being less easily concealed than that of corrupt churchmen; but the guilt of both these bloody massacres had its origin in the same corruptions—the same wilful perversion of the truth, and its divine, humanizing doctrines. But, leaving their countrymen to convert the barbarians of Prussia as they best might, the crusaders proceeded to Spoletro. Thence sailed to Cyprus, where they were met by deputies from the King of Jerusalem, and the different orders of knights. A number of Italian and French crusaders also joined them here; and Lusignan, king of the island, professed his determination to accompany them in their expedition.

The army, thus reinforced, shortly after set sail for Palestine, and arrived without accident at Ptolemais. But famine, that constant scourge of the European armaments, speedily stopped the triumphs with which their arrival had been greeted; and they were obliged to remove without delay into those parts of the country possessed by the Saracens. Malek-Adel, who had abdicated the throne in favour of his sons, had counselled them not to encounter the Christians in the field, but to leave them to disperse, which they were likely soon to do, either from want of supplies or from the dissensions which had ruined so many other expeditions. The crusaders, therefore, advanced without interruption, and reached the banks of the Jordan, in the sacred waters of which they bathed, and then traversed the plains of Jericho and the shores of the Lake Gennezareth. On their return to Ptolemais, after this bloodless expedition, the chiefs, either ashamed of such a useless campaign, or fearful of suffering their soldiers to remain inactive, resolved to attack the strong fortresses of Mount Tabor. The passes of this rocky eminence were defended by the Moslems with great skill and bravery; but the crusaders drove them from their defences, and were on the point of entering the fortress, when they were seized with a sudden panic, and commenced a hasty retreat. Whatever was the cause of this circumstance, it produced the greatest discontent among the Christians of Ptolemais. The Patriarch, who had accompanied the army, bearing a fragment of the true cross, expressed himself disgusted at the conduct of the warriors, and refused any longer to encourage them by his presence. An expedition into Phœnicia was productive of no better effects than those above mentioned; and a separation of the forces being agreed upon, the campaign ended as uselessly as it had begun. The death of the King of Cyprus, and the retreat of the Hungarian monarch, tended still further to dispirit the Syrian Christians; and the prophecy of Malek-Adel seemed on the point of being accomplished.

A. D. 1218. There was far less unity among the later crusaders than among their predecessors; and the reason of this was, that the powerful and pervading enthusiasm which inspired the former, no longer existed to agitate the whole of Christendom by one simultaneous electric shock. In the present instance, this was so far fortunate, that the Christians of Palestine had still champions in reserve; and had only lost, by the discomfiture and separation of the late armament, a small portion of their defenders. Shortly after the departure of Andrew, Ptolemais was crowded with a large body of French, Italian, and German crusaders, who, having vanquished the Moors in Portugal, came to reap fresh glory in the Holy Land.

The conquest of Egypt was a project which had long possessed the minds of the faithful, both in Europe and the East; and the time now appeared to have arrived when that design might be carried into execution. The Duke of Austria, the Count of Holland, and the King of Jerusalem, accordingly united their respective forces; and, embarking at Ptolemais, sailed up the Nile to Damietta, a strong fortress on the western bank of the river. This city,

surrounded by a triple wall, was also defended by
a double rampart on the side of the Nile, and by a
tower built in the middle of the stream, across
which a huge iron chain was suspended, extending
from the tower to the batteries. The country, at
the time the crusaders pitched their tents before
Damietta, was smiling in all the luxuriousness of an
Egyptian spring. The orange and citron groves
were in full bloom; palm-trees, jasmines, syca-
mores, and a variety of odoriferous shrubs, hung
their graceful foliage along the banks of the stream;
and the wide and level plains beyond were covered
with rich harvests of rice.

The delicious scenes which every where met
the gaze of the crusaders, served not a little to
inflame their desire to possess themselves of the
country. The tower in the river was first attacked, but the assailants were driven back with loss.
They next attempted it on another side, broke the
bridge which connected it with the city, and prepared an immense tower, which they contrived to
build on two ships, bound together with heavy
beams and chains. The Duke of Austria had the
command of this machine; and, on the day appointed, three hundred warriors mounted it in full
armour. The vessels then moved slowly to the
point of attack. The battle was carried on by
darts and javelins on the one side, and by Greek
fire on the other. At length, and in the very heat
of the conflict, the tower of the Christians appeared in flames; the standard of the chief was
seen floating down the river; and the terrified believers, who watched the battle from the shore,
fell prostrate upon the earth, imploring the mercy
of heaven. Their prayers seemed to be heard;

for instantly the flames died away, the crusaders renewed the assault, and the Moslems speedily threw down their arms and surrendered. The prisoners, when led into the camp, required, it is said, to see the men clothed in white, and bearing white arms, who had conquered them; but no such persons were to be found among the warriors; and the crusaders then knew, it is further added, that the Lord Jesus Christ had sent his angels to attack the tower.

The prosperous termination of this encounter gave the Christians an important advantage over the enemy; and the death of Malek-Adel, which occurred at the same time, contributed still further to open a prospect of success. That veteran chief, though he had resigned the reins of government, continued to be regarded by the Saracens as their protector in all times of difficulty. His united piety and valour had obtained him the appellation of the " Sword of Religion;" and his moderation, the simplicity of his manners, and the wisdom with which he directed the affairs of the states he governed, are represented as having been equal to his valour. We must allow something for Oriental exaggeration, in the pictures which are drawn of this prince by Saracen historians; and it is also to be remembered, that he acquired the sovereignty, by usurping the rights of his brother's children; but the above accounts seem to approach much nearer the truth, than the prejudiced abuses of his enemies; and, with regard to the manner in which he acquired the throne, he probably justified the usurpation, both in his own eyes, and in those of his subjects, by the ruinous dissensions which prevailed among the young princes, by their imbecillity, and his own capability of restoring the nation to its former prosperous condition—a justification which would not be valid in these days, but which hardly left the idea of usurpation, when inheritance by immediate descent was not fully established, and thrones were commonly disposed of more by force or merit than by law.

Instead of taking immediate advantage of their present prosperity, the crusaders, by some unaccountable fatality, resigned themselves to sloth and inactivity, and neglected any measures either for pursuing their conquests, or rendering useful that which they had obtained. The Saracens, after the death of Malek-Adel, were thrown into the greatest disorder, by the incapacity of his sons. But the crusaders made no attempt at interfering with their government; and several thousands of them departed for Europe, but were lost in the passage. Others soon supplied their places in the camp. Henry II. of England sent out several of his bravest knights, who now arrived at Damietta, and the crusaders were encouraged by the arrival, about the same time, of the Cardinal de Courçou, and the Cardinal Pelagius; the former being distinguished by his piety and eloquence; the latter by the treasures which he brought with him, as the contributions of the faithful, as also by his ambition and his arrogance. A slight victory which the troops gained under his guidance, increased the presumption of this haughty prelate, and the Cardinal de Courçou dying soon after, he subjected every one to his authority. The winter season now brought with it a variety of sufferings. Want of food and shelter greatly weakened the troops, and some

defeats which they met with in their constant encounters with the enemy, threw them into despair.

A. D. 1219.   There is little to interest in this
period of the crusades.   The energy of the Christians was wasted in partial encounters with the
enemy, and their enthusiasm became every day
less visible.   One battle, however, may be mentioned, as the defeat which the faithful sustained
was predicted, according to his own account, by
the celebrated Francis d'Assisse.   That remarkable baron had lately arrived from Europe, and
had traversed sea and land, to proclaim his doctrines among infidels as well as Christians.   In
his youth he united, to a strong imagination, a
deep veneration for all things connected with religion ; and one day hearing that passage of scrip-
ture, in which it is said, " Carry neither gold, nor
silver, nor money, in your scrip, nor sandals nor
stores, " he took the directions as applying literal-
ly to those who heard it, and thenceforth devoted
himself to a life of poverty and privation.   He
met with little success in Egypt, though he armed himself with the sanctity of a prophet, and had
the boldness to present himself before the Sultan,
to persuade him to embrace the gospel.   On returning to Europe, he established the order of
Minor Friars, celebrated as well for the strong and
heroic piety of some of its early members, as for
the corruption into which it subsequently fell.

Both armies remained in anxious suspense as to
the final issue of the struggle.   At length Malek-
kamel, the Sultan of Cairo, offered the Christians
peace, and on terms which it might be imagined
would be immediately accepted by the warriors of
the cross.   The delivery of Jerusalem was the

professed object of the war; and Jerusalem the Sultan now consented to yield. It is true, he had previously demolished the fortifications and walls; but the Holy City was thus within the reach of the faithful; and it only required their ceasing from a useless contest, to become again the sojourn of thousands of devout worshippers. The King of Jerusalem, and almost all the chiefs and knights in the army, were eager to accept this fair proposal of the Sultan; but the Cardinal Pelagius strenuously opposed their councils, urging, that it would be impossible to defend the city against the Saracens, whenever they should choose to recommence the war. Few of his auditors were convinced of this reasoning; but they were obliged to yield to his authority, and hostilities were renewed. The siege of Damietta was now carried on with greater vigour, and the Cardinal employed both his power and persuasion to urge the crusaders forward. The boldness and energy of his conduct were perhaps the best support which the faithful at present could have had; and the city was so closely blockaded, that no supplies of any kind could be conveyed to its relief.

The sorties of the garrison, the defiances of the warriors who crowded the ramparts, and the constant attempts made by the Saracens to relieve the town, had hitherto kept up the stir and clamour of war. But the bustle of the siege gradually subsided. No sally was attempted by the besieged; the crusaders were undisturbed by any efforts of the Moslem to aid their brethren; and not a soldier was to be seen on the walls. A gloomy and death-like silence prevailed. For some days the

Christians watched the fortifications, not knowing how to account for the tranquillity which reigned around them. At length, in the middle of a wild and stormy November night, the Cardinal Pelagius gave orders for a secret assault. The heavy roar of the tempest prevented any other sound from being heard, and a small band of the bravest men ascended the walls by means of scaling-ladders. They accomplished their purpose undisturbed; and a few Moslems whom they found on the ramparts were instantly despatched. No others appeared to arrest their progress; and the first assailants being joined by more, they took possession of a tower, and expressed their triumph by singing a hymn of thanksgiving. This was answered by the rest of the army, drawn out in order of battle at the foot of the ramparts. The Cardinal then beginning the Te Deum, the anthem was sung by all the troops; and as soon as it was finished, the gates of Damietta were torn down, and the whole army rushed into the city. The day was now near dawning; and with the first ray of light, the conquerors proceeded to secure their victory. But even yet, not an enemy appeared to resist them, and they began cautiously to traverse the silent and empty streets. No signs were to be discovered that the place was inhabited, but a fetid and suffocating smell prevailed as they penetrated into the town. When they entered the public square, the mystery was revealed. Hundreds of corpses lay exposed to the sight, exhibiting all the marks of famine. Every street and building were filled with the same melancholy objects, and the warriors shuddered with horror when they found them selves thus environed with the dead. Of the few wretched inhabitants who were still living, some were in the last agonies, and others were crying for help, which it now seemed almost fruitless to afford them. Several of those who had thus survived their fellow-sufferers were children, who kept continually crying out for bread, while others were seen hanging at the breasts of their mothers, who had died in giving them nourishment.

By the conquest of Damietta, the crusaders obtained a great and valuable spoil; but it was sometime before they could venture to inhabit it; and the Saracens who had survived, were employed in cleansing it from the impurities which covered the streets.

A. D. 1221. The important conquest which the Christians had thus obtained, filled the Mussulman chiefs with affright; but, for a time, the indetermination of the former saved them from the perils with which they were menaced. The King of Jerusalem, not able to endure the haughty demeanour of the Cardinal, separated himself from the army in disgust, and by far the greater part of the barons expressed an equal dislike to the overbearing conduct of the prelate. On the arrival of fresh forces from Europe, he prepared to attempt the capture of Caior; but he was opposed by the common voice of the warriors; and obliged to restore tranquillity, by begging the King to return to the camp. John acceded to the request; and the chief men in the army were again summoned to decide its future operations. The Cardinal opened the council, and delivered the same opinion as before respecting the attack on Cairo. He spoke with great vehemence, and urged his opinion more as the commands of a sovereign, than as the advice of an ecclesiastic to free warriors. His zeal was seconded by the other prelates; but notwithstanding his rank and impetuosity, the King of Jerusalem offered a strong opposition to the proposed undertaking, showing the extreme hazard of the design, and observing, that they had not assembled under the banner of the cross to besiege Thebes, Babylon, and Memphis, but to deliver Jerusalem, which was the proper place for the faithful to seek as an asylum from their enemies. This prudent and pious counsel was instantly adopted by most of the barons and knights who were present at the meeting; but the Cardinal replied, that it was pusillanimity, and not caution, which led to this opinion; and he also intimated, that whoever offered any further opposition to his will, would incur the danger of excommunication.

By these means the Cardinal prevailed; and the army, amounting to about seventy thousand men, began its march, a fleet laden with stores and warlike instruments proceeding at the same time up the Nile. The crusaders continued their route, without meeting an enemy, till they reached the extremity of the Delta, when they came in sight of the Saracen forces encamped on the plain of Mansoura. The most strenuous efforts had been made by the Sultan to collect a force capable of meeting the crusaders, and all Mussulman princes had contributed their support on the occasion. But he still felt himself unprepared to cope with the flower of European warriors; and preferred

suing again for peace, to risking the fate of himself
and his subjects on the issue of a battle. He,
therefore, sent ambassadors to the Christian camp,
charged with an offer of surrendering the entire
kingdom of Jerusalem, on the crusaders laying
down their arms. The King, as formerly, expressed his strong desire to accept these terms ;
but they were again rejected at the instigation of
the Cardinal. The Sultan, on receiving the answer of the crusaders, redoubled his exertions to
repel their attacks,, and the overflowing of the river
seconded his efforts. A retreat was then commenced by the discomfited Christians. Three
hundred priests perished on board the vessels in
which they sought to escape the enemy. The
main body of the forces was attacked by the Sultan with his Ethiopians, who terrified the faithful
by their black and savage forms ; the flood-gates
of the Nile were also opened, and many of the
soldiers perished in the waters, as they slept on
the ground. Throwing down their arms and baggage, such of the troops as escaped the enemy fled
in the greatest dismay ; and not even an attempt
was made to restore order. It was now the Cardinal's turn to sue for peace, and he was obliged
to offer the surrender of Damietta, for permission to
retreat unmolested to Ptolemais. The moderation
of Malek-Kamel induced that prince to listen to
these proposals ; and having sent his son to inform
the Christians of his decision, the King of Jerusalem, the Cardinal, and several of the chiefs, proceeded to the Sultan's camp to await the fulfilment of the treaty. The crusaders who had been
left in Damietta could not be prevailed on, without

many threats, to surrender ; and nothing remained
to comfort the faithful, or remove some of the
odium which the chiefs had incurred, but the a-
greement of the Saracens to restore the wood of
the true cross.' This circumstance deserves to
be remarked, not for any importance in the occurrence itself, but for the light it throws on the
state of feeling among the Moslems. A change
surely of no slight nature must have taken place
in their religious character since the titles of the
heroic and devout Saladin, who could not be persuaded, on any account, to surrender either Jerusalem or the wood of the cross, which had been
more than once offered to the Christians by his
descendants.

The evacuation of Damietta having been effected, the faithful began their melancholy retreat towards Ptolemais. Sickness prevailed to a great
extent among the troops, and the state of the
country rendered the fatigues of the march almost
insupportable. The brother of the Sultan attended them on their route, having the double office of
a spy and a guardian ; and they reached Ptolemais,
while its inhabitants were still celebrating the triumphs that had been obtained before the late defeat.

A. D. 1222. The intelligence of these re-
verses in the affairs of the crusaders produced
a lively consternation throughout Europe, but
not sufficiently disheartening to prevent either the
Pope or the Emperor of Germany from pursuing
the enterprise. Frederick II., by his rank among
the sovereigns of the West, and above all by his
close alliance with the church, was now regarded

as the great champion of Christendom. To an
accusation of the Pontiff, that the late disasters
were owing to his remissness, he replied with so
much warmth of zeal, that Honorius was obliged
to believe him sincere, and his subsequent conduct
served to confirm this opinion. In order, however,
to secure the services of Frederic, who was the
only monarch in whom the church could place
confidence, the Pope determined to connect him
by a stronger tie than that of duty, with the faithful in the East. Shortly after the fall of Damietta,
John of Brienne arrived in Europe, in order to obtain new aids for the recovery of his dominions.
With the daughter and heiress of this monarch
Honorius proposed to unite the Emperor, and
thereby afford him a prospect of one day becoming
King of Jerusalem. The marriage of Frederic and
the Princess was accordingly celebrated at Rome
with great pomp; and, for a time, the former omitted
no exertion to fulfil the oath he had taken to deliver
Palestine from the infidels. His union with the
daughter of Jean de Brienne also inspired the Syrian Christians with new hopes; most of the German, and several French and Italian nobles, professed their willingness to follow his standard;
and the Hospitallers, Templars, and Teutonic
Knights, were unanimous in their expressions of
loyalty. But Frederic soon became weary of his
consort; treated her father with indignity, and assumed the title of King of Jerusalem. It might have
been supposed, that, after so many promises to the
Pontiff, and this indication of his ambitious views
respecting the Holy Land, he would have entered
at once upon the expedition. But year after year
was suffered to pass over, to the great scandal of

the church, and large numbers of the faithful who had assumed the cross. In England, especially, the preachers of the crusade had prospered in their mission. A luminous cross, marked by the five wounds of our Saviour, is said to have appeared in the heavens, to encourage the pilgrims in their design; and above sixty thousand persons obeyed the heavenly summons. Frederic at length professed himself ready to depart; and the forces being collected in his Neapolitan States, no further obstacle was anticipated to the expedition. But, as if to deliver the Emperor from a situation in which he never appears to have willingly stood, Honorius was suddenly taken ill, and expired.

Gregory IX. succeeded to the pontificate, and far exceeded his predecessor in severity and firmness of character. Equally zealous for the prosecution of the crusade, the first measures which he adopted after his elevation, were in relation to this grand project of the church. Frederic, therefore, again found himself obliged to prepare for his pilgrimage, and he embarked with his troops, amid the prayers and benedictions of the faithful. Scarcely, however, had the fleet left the shore, when he began to repent of the step he had taken; and, if we are to credit the common report, a slight sickness, the roughness of the waves, and some discontent among his followers, contributed to lessen what little resolution he possessed, and he disembarked at Oporto. Nothing could induce the Pope to pardon this dereliction of his servant. Frederic was excommunicated; and a long contest ensued between him and Gregory, which threw all Christendom into confusion. Happily, however, for the faithful of Syria, Malek-Kamel

and the other Saracen princes were in an equal
state of dissension; and, to the astonishment, as
well as delight of the Emperor, ambassadors arrived from Egypt, to offer him the alliance of their
master, and the kingdom of Palestine as the bond
of union. This proposal was immediately accepted, and Frederic proclaimed his departure for the
East with more pomp than ever. But the Pope now
loudly protested against such a design, in one who
lay under the heaviest anathemas of the church.
The Emperor, however, regarded the prohibitions
of Gregory with as little respect as he did his
commands, and set sail with a little armament of
twenty galleys and six hundred knights. His presence in Ptolemais diffused at first great joy among
the inhabitants; but it was speedily interrupted, by
the arrival of two Franciscans, who had been sent
by the Pope to denounce him as a rebel and a re-
probate. The citizens now regarding him with the
greatest horror, he removed and encamped his
army between Cæsarea and Joppa, where he renewed his negotiations with the Sultan of Cairo,
who had already fixed his camp in the neighbourhood of Jerusalem.

Frederic and Malek-Kamel appear to have been
the most accomplished princes of their time; and
it was probably only owing to this, that the proposed treaty was ever carried into effect. Motives of policy had brought them together; but
they had scarcely time to commence their negotiations, before the more prosperous condition of
the Sultan's affairs rendered his union with Frederic unnecessary, if not dangerous. The character, however, of the Emperor, as a wise and
learned, as well as a powerful sovereign, induced

Malek-Kamel to pause before he sacrificed his friendship to a slight question of interest. Instead, therefore, of employing their time in discussing points which might lead to hostilities, they amused each other by displays of their knowledge and taste, both being skilled in all the learning of the times, and the Sultan priding himself on the skill with which he could compose verses on whatever subject came before him. To show still further their mutual regard, Frederic sent him his sword and cuirass, and Malek answered the compliment by several camels, an elephant, and some of the most valuable productions of the East. But their amity was regarded by their several partisans with a jealous eye. The faithful of both religions considered their cause betrayed by this agreement of their chiefs; and the most audacious means were employed to convince the monarchs of the contempt and hatred in which they were respectively held.

A. D. 1229. That Frederic and the Sultan were induced, by the personal respect with which they had inspired each other, to abstain from hostilities, there seems to be little doubt; but the only cause for which they could have fought, was so greatly diminished in importance, that their private reasons for peace were left without any thing to counterbalance them. Neither the one nor the other cared for Jerusalem, but in so far as it was sacred in the opinion of their followers; and absolute as they were, this was not likely to weigh much in their decisions. The negotiation, therefore, was ultimately terminated, by the establishment of a truce for ten years, five months, and forty days; the principal articles of which

were, that the Sultan should surrender Jerusalem,
Bethlehem, and all the villages between Joppa and
Ptolemais, to Frederic; and that the latter should
prevent the Franks from making war against the
Sultan, and leave the mosque of Omar in the Holy
City still open to the Moslems. To this measure
they were hastened by the plots daily formed
against their lives, and by the seditious spirit which
prevailed throughout the camp. But their arrangements were far from being followed by tranquillity.
Frederic, who had been forsaken by the Hospitallers, and the best part of his army, found himself
regarded with still greater dislike on the announcement of the truce. The permission he had granted the Saracens to continue the exercise of their
religion in the city, occasioned general indignation;
and the Bishop of Cæsarea went so far as to interdict the faithful from visiting the Sepulchre, or
bathing in the Jordan. The same feelings prevailed among the Moslems against Malek-Kamel.
The surrender of Jerusalem was lamented by the
priests and preachers of the faith, as an abandon-
ment of all that was most sacred in their eyes; and
the people assembled in crowds, at one time exclaiming against the Sultan and at another weeping over their losses.

The object for which so many Popes had laboured, for which all Europe had been called to
arms, and so many thousands left their homes and
perished, was now accomplished. Jerusalem was
again open to believers, and in the possession of a
Christian monarch. The worshippers at the Sepulchre had no longer to dread the persecutions,
or insults of the scoffing infidels, or to shake with
horror at the idea that the holy places were defiled

by their mockeries. Under the banner of the cross,
they could now approach those scenes in triumph
for which they had a short time before wept so
passionately; and the hour seemed approaching,
when bands of pious pilgrims, from all quarters
of the world, would make the hills and vallies
of Sion resound with hymns of thanksgiving.
But no such sentiments prevailed on Frederic's
entry into Jerusalem.   He was accompanied only
by the Teutonic Knights; and as he proceeded
through the city, the clergy and people fled at his
approach, manifesting the strongest aversion to his
presence.   When he entered the church of the resurrection, where the ceremony of his coronation
was to be performed, he beheld the images of the
saints and apostles clad in mourning; no priest
appeared at the altar to give him the blessing of
the church, or to offer up a prayer for his reign;
and, taking the crown into his hands, he placed it
himself upon his head, the shouts of his own knights
and barons supplying the place of religious cere-
monial.

Immediately after his coronation, Frederic announced to the Pope the triumphant conclusion of
his expedition, and set forth in lofty language the
claims he had to the regards of the church.   But
whatever he advanced was abundantly countervailed
by a letter of the Patriarch's, written about the same
time, and containing a full account of the unholy
compromise which had been made with the infidel.
The indignant father was also equally successful
in preventing the new subjects of the Emperor
from showing him any respect.   He was, therefore, quickly obliged to leave Jerusalem, and return to Ptolemais; where the same reception awaited

him as in the Holy City. The public services of religion were all suspended, or performed in a low voice, and within closed doors. No bell was to be heard; the altars were stripped of their crosses and other ornaments, and every corner of the city presented some token of the abasement which the faithful suffered.

It is difficult to say how long the monarch who had dared the malediction of the Pope would have been able to endure these contumelies unmoved; but the machinations of Gregory were now become of too dangerous a nature to be treated with contempt. Intelligence was brought to the Emperor that the Pontiff had raised a considerable army, which he had placed under the command of John of Brienne, whose hatred of Frederic added greatly to the chances of success. He, therefore, bade a hearty adieu to his conquests—the faithful celebrating his departure with expressions of triumph—and arrived in the kingdom of Naples, only in time to save either that or the empire from the grasp of his enemies. Frederic fought, and the Pope continued to hurl against him his direst anathemas; but the weapon of the warrior prevailed. The Pontiff found it necessary to submit to a negotiation; and after a few months, peace was restored between these redoubtable combatants. It was about two years after this that Gregory summoned a council at Spoleto to renew the crusade, and with the usual regard to the observance of treaties, it was determined to commence war against the Sultan without delay. Near three years more, however, were passed before any signs appeared of an army ready to combat for the East; but this interval was employed by the Pope in sending

missionaries through the different Christian states,
and the fervency and devotion which some of
these men exhibited, served to calm, for a brief
space, the discord and agitations which prevailed.
John of Vicentia was heard with the veneration
which had attended the preaching of Saint Bernard,
or Foulque of Neuilly: rival cities laid down their
arms at his voice: warriors vied with each other
in the desire of peace: and the most turbulent
passions yielded to the power and unction of his
persuasions.

A. D. 1235. France again afforded the first
band of pious knights prepared to combat for Jerusalem. Thibault, Count of Chatepagne and
King of Navarre, was one of the most celebrated
Troubadours of the age, and possessed all those
accomplishments which became the high born
knight and the minstrel of romance. But he was
ambitious of power as well as distinction; and as
Louis IX. was then a child, Thibault headed a
powerful party of the barons, ready, like him, to
contend for their independence. All at once, however, he changed his conduct, deserted from his
opposition to the government, and proclaimed his
intention of taking the cross. The reason commonly assigned for this, is his sudden and romantic
passion for the Queen mother; in deference to
whose desire he determined on a line of action
more befitting his chivalrous character. The rest
of the barons followed his example, and he employed both his power as a poet, as well as his
princely wealth and influence, to accomplish the
expedition. A council was some time after held at
Tours, in which several resolutions were entered
into, creditable to the wisdom of the assembly,

and well calculated to forward the success of the
design, but indicating how greatly the feelings
were changed which had fed the enthusiasm of the
first crusaders.

A. D. 1239. Every thing being prepared for
their departure, Thibault and his companions assembled at Lyons to consult finally on their future
measures. Before they had concluded their de-
liberations, however, a nuncio arrived from Gregory desiring them to desist from their designs, and
return to their States, that they might be in readiness to serve him, in situations where their aid
was at present more requisite than in Syria. The
enemies who had been raised against the Pope by the
increasing license of thought, and the gradual advance of civil liberty, were numerous and powerful. He required, therefore, all the friends whom
he could rally around him to preserve his authority
over Christendom entire; and it was only by the
skilfullest management of those who remained faithful to him, that he could hope to succeed. The
age was gone in which pontiffs could rule by spiritual weapons; and the period had commenced in
which they were compelled to change them for
those well-tempered and polished instruments of
political craft, which they wielded so long and
with such admirable skill.

Gregory had also another plea for desiring the
crusaders to pause in their expedition to Palestine.
Constantinople, after suffering the most deplorable
calamities, had received John of Brienne as its monarch, and, though greatly advanced in age, the Ex-
King of Jerusalem proved himself worthy of the
distinction he enjoyed. For some time he successfully resisted the attacks of the allied Greeks and

Bulgarians; but, before he died he saw himself left without the power of longer defending his illfated dominions. His son-in-law and successor, Baldwin, no sooner obtained the crown, than he was obliged to seek in Europe the means for making a last struggle against his enemies. There were many motives to induce the Pontiff to engage in the defence of Constantinople. It was his duty to assist a monarch who so humbly sought the aid of the church as Baldwin. The faithful of that empire were in as perilous a situation as those of Syria; and, above all, the times were still within recollection when Constantinople was felt to be the only barrier against the innumerable hordes of barbarians who threatened Christendom with devastation. But the entreaties of Gregory were little regarded, and the French chevaliers embarked forthwith at Marseilles. They left Europe, violently agitated by religious and civil dissentions; and Thibault, it is recorded, condemned an hundred and eighty of his vassals to the flames before his departure, on an accusation of heresy. The disputes between the Emperor Frederic and the Pope broke out at the same time with greater violence than ever; and the Christian world was scandalised by seeing the head of the church besieged in his own capital.

When the crusaders arrived in Syria, they found the Christians in the lowest state of depression, and the whole country impoverished and desolated by the conflicts of the Moslem princes, as well with each other as with the faithful. The knights began their campaign, by ravaging the territory of Damascus and Gaza; but their expedition into the latter province had nearly proved fatal to the party who undertook it. Having travelled several leagues through a strange country, they at length came to a narrow defile, formed by barren sand hills. Here they resolved to repose and refresh themselves; but in the midst of their carousal, the heights around them were covered with archers; thousands of Saracens were seen rushing from all quarters; and the wild ravine in which the Christians were confined, and which till now had been as silent as the grave, re-echoed with the mingled shouts of the multitude and the shrill peals of the Syrian war-music. The crusaders, attacked on all sides, seemed evidently doomed to destruction; and the Duke of Burgundy and the Count of Joppa immediately prepared to retreat. The Counts of Bar and Montfort remained obstinately determined to await the issue of a combat. For a considerable time they repelled all the assaults of the enemy; till the latter, feigning to retreat, drew them from their position, and the two noblemen, with most of their followers, were either slain or taken prisoners. After this calamitous event, the King of Navarre remained a short time at Ascalon, and then returned to Ptolemais. No further warlike measures were proposed; and the expedition ended by the agreement of the different chiefs with the Saracen princes,—the Templars having formed a treaty with the Sultan of Damascus; and the Hospitallers, the Duke of Burgundy and others, with the Sultan of Egypt, who promised them Jerusalem in return for their alliance. These treaties were, however, on the point of being broken, by the chivalrous and devout Richard of Cornwall, brother of Henry III. of England. But the pious intention of this prince to effect the more perfect delivery of

the Holy Land, was resisted by the other Christian
knights; and he was obliged to be content with
having made a pilgrimage rather than a crusade.
Europe, in the meantime, continued to be equally
disturbed by the struggles of Frederick and Gregory; and when the latter died, he left his successor to pursue a conflict, which was as injurious
to the present peace of the church, as it was favourable to its future reformation.

Innocent IV. mounted the pontifical throne at
a time when both Europe and Asia were thrown
into the deepest alarm, by the progress of the Mogul Tartars. This barbarous people still retained
the habits of ancient times; but to the plain and
simple manners of herdsmen, they added the fierceness and savage customs of constant warfare.
While the different tribes, which composed this
vast nation, remained separated, either by the necessities of a wandering life, or the animosities to which
these necessities give rise, the iron-bound deserts of
the North were a sufficient barrier between them
and the civilized world. But there is a social
principle in humanity, which, under the first circumstances favourable to its action, attracts and
binds men together. Large families of the Tartar
races were thus united; and the desire of conquest
as well as its necessity, grew with the increasing
number of these tribes. At length, by the conquest
of Constantinople, the mighty partition-wall, under
which the nations of the East and West had slum-
bered for centuries undisturbed, fell with a frightful crash. From the bleak and immeasurable wilds,
myriads of savage warriors were soon ready armed for the conflict. Their fierce countenances,
hardy frames, and immense numbers, filled all

men with dismay; and the nations cowered under their menaces, as if they possessed no means of resisting such a people.

The terror which the Moguls occasioned, contributed greatly to preserve the peace of Palestine; and the Syrian Christians remained for some time undisturbed by any of the Saracen princes. But, unfortunately for the faithful, the Tartars, in the course of their invasions, had fallen upon the Carazmians, a people inhabiting the borders of the Caspian, and had driven them from their country. The exiles, scarcely less barbarous than their conquerors, wandered about in search of a new settlement, carrying death and devastation in their train. On approaching Syria, the discord which prevailed among the Moslems favoured their arms; and the Sultan of Cairo entered into a league with them, by which he promised to yield Jerusalem into their hands. The Holy City, unprepared for defence, was immediately abandoned by the Christians; and the Carazmians found in it only a few sick and aged people, who were unable to escape with their brethren. The greater part of the conquerors, on seeing this, retired behind the city, and those who remained, hoisted the standard of the cross on the walls and citadel, and rang the bells of the different churches. The fugitives paused in their flight at this singular occurrence. "God!" exclaimed they, "has had mercy upon us, and driven away the barbarians." Seven thousand of them immediately returned to their homes, when the Carazmians started from their retreats, re-entered the town, and slaughtered, or loaded with irons, the whole number. Their fury even extended to the dead, and they destroyed the suppened tomb of our Saviour, that of Godfrey of Bouillon, and whatever relics they could find of the saints and martyrs who were buried in the Holy City.

A. D. 1244. This melancholy event united all parties; and an army was speedily raised, composed of both Christian and Mussulman, the command of which was intrusted to the prince of Emessa, renowned for his valour and prudence. Having encamped in the plains of Ascalon, this General recommended that the forces should there await those of the enemy; but the Christians would not hear of this cautious method of proceeding, and encountered the Carazmians in the territory of Gaza. Before the engagement commenced, the forces, kneeling down, received the benedictions of the priests. Scarcely had they risen from their devotion, when the enemy advanced, and poured their arrows among the ranks of the allied troops. For a moment the assault was unresisted. The prince of Joppa, the bravest knight in the army, was under sentence of excommunication; and the patriarch of Jerusalem had sternly forbidden him to advance. But the time was too precious to be thus wasted; and the Bishop of Rama, seeing the situation of the army, flew to the prince, and exclaimed, "March! I absolve thee, in the name of the Father, and of the Son, and of the Holy Ghost."

From the rising of the sun to its setting, and throughout the greater part of the next day, the battle raged in all the horrors of slaughter; but at last, the prince of Emessa fled, and the faithful, left without his support, found it impossible to resist the strength of the enemy any longer. Of the splendid array of knights who had entered this field of blood, few remained to tell the tale of their disasters. The Templars had either all perished, or were taken prisoners, except thirty-three; of the Hospitallers only twenty-six escaped; and of the Teutonic knights only three survived. Nor was the loss of the Saracens less severe. Two thousand of the noblest Moslems were left dead on the plain, before their retreat; and altogether above thirty thousand of the allies are supposed to have fallen by the sword of the Carazmians.

Jerusalem had now again become the possession of Egypt; and the Carazmians continued their triumphant march through the neighbouring provinces. At the siege of Joppa, the heroism of other days was revived in the person of the prince of that city, who had been taken prisoner in the late battle. Placed on a cross, and threatened with instant death, if he would not desire the inhabitants to surrender, he cried to his people, " It is your duty to defend this Christian city, and mine to die for Christ." The place, however, was taken, and Gauthier of Brienne perished under the hands of a barbarous rabble. In little more than a year after this event, the Sultan of Cairo broke his engagements with the Carazmians; and the Saracen princes forming a strong junction with him against these barbarians, they were finally driven out of Syria. But the Holy City remained in the hands of the Sultan; and the loss the Christians had sustained in the battle of Gaza prevented their attempting any measures for its recovery. New tribes of Tartars, also, continued to harrass the country with their invasions, and the whole land was involved in gloom.

The distress and anxiety which depressed the states of Europe were scarcely less afflicting. The contest between the Pope and his opponents had compelled the former to seek safety in flight; and having taken refuge in Lyons, he called a general council in that city, to consider what measures should be taken for restoring peace to the Christian church. The Emperor of Constantinople, the Bishop of Berytum, and other distinguished prelates, and deputies from nearly all the princes of Europe, were present at this assembly. Previous to its being opened, a meeting was held to settle some points, preparatory to the general debate, when the representative of Frederic, assured the Pope of the determination of his master to obey all the commands of the church; and offered, as his guarantees, the Kings of England and France. But Innocent rejected with disdain, promises which had been so often broken; and at the opening of the council, he compared the miseries of Christendom to the five wounds of Christ on the cross, which he enumerated in the following order: The irruption of the Tartars; The schism of the Greeks; The invasion of the Carasmians; The progress of heresy; And the persecutions which he suffered from Frederic. Mutual recriminations now took place between the Pope and Thaddeus, the friend and eloquent representative of the Emperor; but the attention of the assembly was at length turned from this furious dispute to the situation of Jerusalem and Constantinople. The account given of the condition of these cities moved the hearts of all present, and a crusade was proclaimed in the usual manner, those who should embark in it being assured of the benedictions of the church, and of all the privileges bestowed on their predecessors in the sacred cause.

The deputies of Frederic had requested the Pontiff to allow them a fortnight to make their master acquainted with his will. At the end of that time, the council was again assembled; but the Emperor refused any farther to humble himself. Thaddeus, therefore, could only deprecate the vengeance of the Pope, till another and more numerous assembly might be called; but his proposition was unattended to, and the audience awaited in terror the resolution of Innocent. Having made some preliminary observations in a tone of paternal tenderness, his voice suddenly changed, " I am, said he, the vicar of Jesus Christ: What I bind on earth is bound in heaven; and, in conformity with the will of the church, I pronounce Frederic guilty of sacrilege and heresy; of felony and perjury; excommunicated and cast from the empire. I absolve all from their oaths who have sworn allegiance to him. I forbid them, under pain of excommunication, to obey him. I desire, also, the electors to choose a new Emperor, reserving the disposition of Sicily to myself." Terror struck the deputies of Frederic at this denunciation. " O day of wrath and evil! O terrible day!" cried Thaddeus, " Now may the heretics triumph, and the Tartars possess the world!" The council was concluded with the Te Deum; and Innocent exclaimed, " I have done my duty; but God do his will." The Emperor heard of his excommunication with the most violent indignation; and putting on his crown, bid defiance to the Pontiff and his threats.

CHAPTER XI.

A. D. 1246. THE ambition, passion, or resolution of Innocent, had thrown all Europe into agitation. Italy, Germany, and England, suffered the heaviest calamities from his fatal defence of the church ; and France owed to the piety and enthusiasm of her monarch, the privilege of accomplishing the new crusade. Louis IX., whose devotion obtained him the title of Saint, possessed by nature the noblest qualities of humanity ; and the virtues which he exhibited from the earliest period of his reign, had gained him the universal veneration of his people. A dangerous malady, which seized him a short time before the Council of Lyons, threatened his life ; and having fallen into a deep sleep, his attendants concluded that he was dead. He gradually, however, gave signs of returning animation ; and the first words he uttered were to demand the cross, and to take the vow of the crusade. His recovery was regarded as a miracle ; but when he renewed the declaration of his intentions respecting the Holy Land, his mother Blanche, the princes and prelates of the kingdom, implored him to desist from such a perilous enterprise ; and were only silenced

by his assuring them, that he had been commanded in a vision, by a Divine voice, to deliver Jerusalem. Louis then summoned a parliament, at
which several of his principal barons agreed to
follow him to Syria. His three royal brothers
were of this number; and these noblemen and
princes were joined in the vows they made by
their wives, who were persuaded to this measure
as well by the example of Queen Margaret, as by
their affection. Besides the public exertions which
Louis employed to effect his designs, he used all
his private and personal influence to the same purpose. Having to bestow, according to an ancient
custom, a peculiar kind of robe upon his courtiers, he ordered crosses to be privately embroidered on the mantles, so that when his friends received them, they found themselves invested with
a badge, which their regard for the King, and
their chivalrous ideas, would not permit them to
remove. But neither the enthusiasm nor popula-
rity of Louis could blind the eyes of his most faithful admirers to the danger of his enterprise. The
queen-mother, Blanche, continued to urge every argument with which her maternal solicitude and good
sense supplied her. Accompanied by the Bishop of
Paris and the principal personages of the court,
she made a last appeal to his feelings, and besought
him to consider the misery into which she should
be thrown by his departure, which would be to her
the same as his death; the danger his states would
incur by being left without the sovereign, and,
bursting into a passionate flood of tears, she concluded by likening his undertaking to the sacrifice
of Isaac which God saved Abraham from making.
Louis embraced his mother, and with a voice ren-

dered calm by the intensity of his devotion, he repeated his unalterable determination to fulfil his vows. The queen and her attendants now ceased to oppose his will, and the preparations for the expedition were carried on with redoubled vigour. Frederic now implored the mediation of Louis with the Pope, to effect a reconciliation, but in vain; and the disturbed state of affairs in England prevented her from assisting in the design. France was thus left to complete it by her own resources, and the devotion of her monarch had ample exercise in overcoming the obstacles which opposed themselves to his wishes. One of the most interesting of the incidents related respecting the preparations for this crusade, is that a spirit of deep humility and charity powerfully affected the principal persons engaged in the enterprise. Acts of the greatest benevolence were performed by the barons as their best preparations for the danger they were to encounter. Some who had been notorious for injustice and oppression, restored what they had gained to the rightful possessors, and others, among whom was the Sire Joinville the excellent chronicler of Saint Louis, assembled their vassals, and besought them to pardon whatever affronts or injuries they had received at their hands. Monasteries and hospitals were raised at the expense of these pious warriors, and this enthusiasm of charity was crowned by the benevolence and justice of Louis, who employed the last days preceding his departure in examining the situation of the kingdom, placing men of probity in all situations of trust, and correcting public abuses of every kind.

A. D. 1248. The most profound tranquillity reigned throughout the kingdom, and all classes of people seemed inspired with the same deep feeling of devotion. Processions were continually passing through the streets, and hymns and loud acclamations of holy joy filled the air. At the Abbey of Saint Denis, Louis received the standard of the cross from the hands of the Legate, and heard mass for the last time in the cathedral of Notre Dame, after which he bade adieu to the capital amid the prayers and lamentations of his subjects, and repaired to Corbeil, where his mother and his wife awaited him. He then gave the reins of government to Blanche, and after two days more of religious preparation, commenced his journey. At Lyons Louis received the blessing of the Pope, and again vainly endeavoured to make peace for Frederic. He next proceeded to Aigues-Mortes, where a fleet of a hundred and twenty ships awaited him, and immediately embarked, all the crusaders joining in the anthem of *Veni Creator Spiritus*, as the vessels left the shore. The French knights, unaccustomed to sea, expressed their terror at being committed to the uncertain waters; but the fleet arrived safely at Cyprus, where the King and his followers again disembarked.

Here Henry, the King of Cyprus, and lately endowed with the title of King of Jerusalem by the Pope, received Louis with great honour, and conducted him to his capital. Having already determined to proceed to Syria the following spring, he employed every argument to persuade Louis to defer his own departure till that time; to which the King, unfortunately, consented; for during the stay of the army in Cyprus, luxury and licentiousness corrupted the bravest of his companions. A pestilence, which also raged at the same time, cut off two hundred and fifty; and the barons, having exhausted their money, were now threatened with the total desertion of their followers. Joinville confesses himself to have been in this situation; but he was relieved by the liberality of Louis, who gave him eight hundred livres, to pay the sums due to his knights. Great disputes were at the same time agitated between the different parties of Templars, Hospitallers, and Italians assembled in the island; and Louis with difficulty prevented a civil war. Occurrences, however, of a different nature served to distract the attention of the disputants from mutual recrimination. An embassy, said to have been sent by a Tartar prince, declaring his own conversion and that of the great Khan to Christianity, struck all Cyprus with astonishment; but it was never fully determined, whether the whole affair was not a fabrication of some monks. The unfortunate Emperor of Constantinople also arrived in the island as a fugitive and suppliant for charity; but all other objects of attention were lost sight of, when letters were received by Louis from the Grandmasters of the Hospitallers and Templars, advising him to enter into negotiations of peace with the Sultan of Aeris. The strongest indignation was expressed, both by the King and his followers, at the mention of such a measure; and, a fleet having been again assembled, the army of Louis and the King of Cyprus embarked a few days before Pentecost. A violent storm, which drove many of the vessels on the Syrian coast, compelled Louis to put back; but the loss he had sustained by the tempest, was amply repaired by the arrival of William of Salisbury, with two hundred English knights, and other warriors from Constan inople. The sails were therefore again set; and at the end of four days, the towers of Damietta appeared in sight. The various chiefs then entered the ship on board of which was the sovereign; and having received his exhortations to unity and courage, they all embraced, and vowed to follow him to the last.

A. D. 1249. Malek-Saleh Negmeddin, the present Sultan of Cairo, had taken the wisest precaution for the defence of his dominions against the crusaders; and the fleet having been reconnoitred by four galleys, of which however only one returned, the walls of Damietta, and the whole line of coast, were quickly seen covered with troops. At the head of these forces was the celebrated warrior Takreddin, who, clad in brilliant armour, looked like the sun in his strength, * while the Nile was covered with the Saracen fleet; and the wide extent of sea and land resounded with martial music, and the mutual menaces of the two armaments. A consultation was held on board the royal vessel, as to whether the descent should be immediately attempted, or deferred till the arrival of a part of the fleet dispersed by the storm. The former measure was determined upon; and the next day, the troops began to disembark amid showers of the enemy's arrows. Louis, whom his attendants in vain endeavoured to restrain, leaped from his galley into the sea, which reached to his shoulders. Covering himself with his buckler, and with sword in hand, he rushed towards the shore, shouting "Mont Joie Saint-Denis!" He gained the land in safety, and instantly fell on his knees,

* Joinville.

and returned thanks to heaven. The troops, impatient to follow him, soon joined his standard; the two armies and fleets joined battle without delay; and victory, both by sea and land, rewarded the valour and piety of the crusaders. The death of the Sultan, who had been some time sick, was at this time reported to the vanquished Moslems. Their spirits, already subdued by defeat, were entirely broken by this intelligence. Tahreddin fled with his whole army; Damietta was also forsaken by the garrison; and the next day its deserted streets were filled by the triumphant crusaders. The Sultan, who still lived, punished many of the fugitives with death for their cowardice; and the victory of the Christians spread dismay throughout Egypt. Louis, in the mean time, divided Damietta and its territory among the three chief orders of knights; and the worship of the Saviour was again established in the churches.

Malek Saleh Negmeddin, summoning all the little strength which remained to him, removed to Mansourah, where he reviewed his forces, and endeavoured to restore discipline. While he was thus exerting himself, the Christians allowed their energy to be diminished by inaction, and the enervating influence of the climate. Disputes also, of a dangerous kind, arose respecting the division of the booty; and gaming and every species of licentiousness prevailed throughout the camp. The authority of the King was every day less respected; and, to increase the confusion, parties of Caramians and Bedouin Arabs were constantly on the watch, to surprise the crusaders who ventured out of their quarters in search of spoil. The loss of Sidon, which fell into the hands of the

Prince of Damascus, and the zeal of Negmeddin, still further affrighted the crusaders; and their prosperity seemed to be rapidly declining. At this moment, however, when the prospect of Louis was most gloomy, his spirits were restored by the arrival of his brother, the Count of Poictiers, who had been long expected, and had escaped the perils of a most tempestuous voyage, in an unhoped for manner. The reinforcement which the army thus received rendered the crusaders impatient to commence operations against the enemy; a council was therefore summoned, and, after various measures had been discussed, the dangerous measure was adopted of an immediate descent upon Cairo.

A. D. 1250. Leaving a garrison in Damietta, with the Queen and the other ladies, the army, consisting of about sixty thousand men, proceeded to Pharescour, where it encamped. Negmeddin died at this time, but his Sultana wisely cautioned the Emirs to conceal the event from both his subjects and the Christians. Her counsel was followed; but the new Sultan, mistrusting his strength, sent ambassadors to the crusaders, to offer terms of peace. They rejected the proposition, as they had done others of the same kind in the lifetime of Negmeddin, and continued their march to Massourah. Five hundred Moslems, who endeavoured to surprise the Templars during the route, fell victims to their own perfidy; and the Christians formed their encampment near the canal of Aschmoun Thenah, on the site occupied by John of Brienne, when he suffered the disastrous defeat in the previous crusade. The Saracens were encamped on the opposite side of the canal, to pass which, the Christians had to form a dike and causeway; but their labours were every hour counteracted by the vigilance of the enemy. A month was passed in these useless endeavours, and in that time they suffered greatly from the assaults of the Moslems, who, pouring their showers of Greek fire into the camp, repeatedly threatened the whole army with destruction. Takreddin was at the head of the forces thus opposed to the crusaders, and Louis began almost to despair of passing the lake. The treachery, however, of a Saracen renegade, relieved him from his doubtful situation. Under the guidance of this man, the army commenced its passage at a ford, about half a league distant from its former position; and the Count of Artois, the brother of Louis, resisting the cautions of the King, led his division at once across the stream. A party of the enemy who attempted to oppose him was speedily defeated; the Count, inflamed by success, refused to await the junction of the remaining forces, and followed the flying enemy; he reached the camp of Takreddin just as the chief had left the bath; mounting his horse almost naked, the Emir instantly led his followers into the field; but his valour was exercised in vain; the Christians rode triumphant through the camp; and he fell, after exhibiting the noblest instances of heroism.

Not content with the victory thus suddenly obtained, the Count determined to continue the pursuit of the enemy, who was rapidly fleeing towards Mansourah. The conquerors entered the town without resistance; and while a part of them pursued their route to Cairo, the rest remained to pillage the city. But suddenly the Saracens dis-

covered the smallness of the force before which
they had fled; and, rallying under the chief Bibars
Bondocdar, they flew upon the Christians, intent
on their spoil, and massacred them without mercy.
The main body of the army was in the mean time
passing the stream, which it succeeded in doing;
but on reaching the shore, the troops were assailed
by several parties of Moslems; and soon after, the
whole Saracen army appeared in sight. Louis,
clothed in magnificent armour, attracted the admiration of the forces by his majestic port, his golden
helmet, and his burnished German sword. The
skill, however, of Bondocdar, enabled his troops
to resist the impetuous charge of the Franks, who
were at length obliged to retreat towards the
canal. Louis at this moment was surrounded by six Moslem warriors; but, freeing himself from their swords, his troops again rallied, and
renewed the combat. The chevaliers, who had
hastened to the assistance of the Count of Artois, found him ready to perish amid a host of foes;
and their heroic fidelity quickly placed them in
equal peril. The battle had commenced at ten in
the morning, and it continued till three in the afternoon, when the Christians entered Mansourah;
but, before this time, the Count of Artois, the
Lord of Salisbury, and the greater part of the
Hospitallers and Templars, lay dead on the field.
The crusaders had thus dearly purchased their
triumph, and their minds were filled with gloomy
apprehensions for the future.

The defence they had made against the invaders
greatly elevated the spirits of the Saracens, who
had at first regarded them as invincible. At night
they attacked the encampment, but were repulsed.

Not depressed, however, by this slight defeat, Bondocdar prepared for a general battle, and on Ash-Wednesday the two armies were again engaged. Louis and his brothers, the Counts of Anjou and Poictiers, performed prodigies of valour in this battle; their bravery was seconded by that of the troops, and victory crowned their efforts. In writing to his friends in Europe, Louis only modestly said, " The first Wednesday in Lent, the camp was attacked by all the Mussulman forces; God declared for the French, and the infidels were repulsed." But the triumph produced little real good to the crusaders; and sickness, caused by the putrefaction of the numberless bodies left unburied, spread through the army. The pestilence, which had carried off several of the best warriors, at length seized Louis himself; and the distress, occasioned by the contagion, was increased by the constant attacks of the new Sultan Almoadam, and still more by the want of stores, which shortly added the miseries of famine to those already suffered. Louis at last consented to demand a truce; but the Sultan requiring that the King himself should be the hostage for its fulfilment, the negotiation was abruptly concluded; and no hope of safety now remained, but in attempting to repass the lake. The passage was effected, but the Christians were still exposed to the attacks of the enemy, and were too much weakened by disease to resist them. A further retreat, therefore, to Damietta was decided upon, and part of the forces began to embark in the vessels which awaited them on the Nile. Nothing, however, could persuade Louis to leave the shore, till the whole of his army should be safe from the enemy. The bishops, the chiefs,

and even the commonest of the soldiers, besought
him, with tears, to save himself without delay;
but he continued to resist their entreaties, and remained seated on his charger, though almost faint-
ing from the effects of his sickness, watching
the retreat of the troops, and retaining around
him only a few chevaliers who refused to depart.
Scarcely had the march begun, when the Saracens
were seen close in their rear; and, in the night,
great numbers of the Christians fell in the unequal
conflict. The vessels, on board of which were the rest
of the crusaders, were in the mean time attacked
by the Egyptian fleet; and these fugitives shared
the same fate as their brethren on land. Louis,
after a great many escapes, at length reached the village Minieh. The chevalier Gaucher de Chatillon
remained at his side, and fell in defending him a-
gainst the Moslems, who pursued him into the
town. The remainder of the guard, having taken
its position on a hill, resisted for some time the
approach of the assailants; but finding it impossible to defend themselves much longer, their leader
sent to request Louis to desire a truce. The King
consented, and the Moslem chief was on the point
of accepting the terms proposed, when an unfortunate expression of fear escaping one of the soldiers present, the guard threw down their arms,
and the Emir, declaring he would make no truce
with the vanquished, the Saracens rushed into Minieh, seized the pious and unfortunate Louis, and
immediately loaded him with irons. As soon as this
catastrophe was known, the crusaders, both those on
land, and those in the vessels, thought no longer
of defending themselves. Thousands fell under the
swords of the infidels, and those who were spared

were only saved to undergo the most barbarous treatment.

Our space would fail us in attempting to describe the calamities which followed these events. Lewis was conveyed down the Nile to Mansourah in triumph, and was closely confined in the house of the Sultan's secretary. Not the smallest comfort was afforded him in his prison, and the only thing he had preserved of all he possessed, was a book of psalms. With this he consoled himself in his sufferings, and no expression of either anger or impatience escaped his mouth. His resignation filled his enemies with astonishment, which was at last converted into pity. The Sultan sent him fifty splendid robes, and invited him to a feast; but these attentions were rejected. An offer of liberty was then made him on condition of his surrendering Damietta. This also was refused; and though threats of the most violent tortures were then resorted to, he remained fixed in his resolution to compromise neither his dignity nor the Christian cause. Similar offers were made to the captive warriors with like effect. Of the inferior prisoners hundreds were destroyed by drowning in the Nile, or by the sword; others saved themselves by embracing Mahometanism, and some were allowed to purchase their freedom.

We must not forget to mention, that the Queen was thrown into such deep affliction at the tidings of her husband's captivity, that it brought on premature labour. Naming the child Tristan, in memory of her grief, the only hope she now cherished was to die before the enemy could approach Damietta; but in order to secure her safety from Moslem violence, she called one of her most faith-followers to her side, and with many tears conjured him to promise that he would perform for her one solemn request. Having assured her of his readiness to execute the command, whatever it might be, she then made him swear that he would put her to death the moment the enemy should enter the town; a duty, however, which the faithful servant was never called to perform.

What no principles of mercy or justice could induce the Sultan to grant, he was compelled to offer, by the danger with which the seditious spirit of the Emirs, and the rivalry of the other Saracen princes, threatened his authority; and his wisest counsellors having persuaded him to give the King his liberty on any terms that might be safe. Louis, in the mean time, had received intelligence that Damietta must speedily surrender; he replied to the Sultan, that if the Queen would consent, he would give up the town; remarking, to the astonishment of the Moslem, that she was his wife, and that he would do nothing contrary to her will. The money which was demanded of him he also consented to give, but not for his own ransom; observing, that a King might redeem his subjects, but not himself for money. The treaty, however, was hardly agreed upon when a powerful conspiracy was formed against Almoadam, the Sultan. An interview was appointed to take place between him and Louis at Pharescour, whither he proceeded, the prisoners being at the same time conveyed thither in galleys. The day after his arrival, he gave a magnificent feast to his Emirs; when the conspirators, with an emissary of the Caliph of Bagdad at their head, fell upon him as soon as he appeared in public. Having sought refuge in a tower which was instantly set on fire, he again took to flight, but fell in the attempt to escape, imploring in vain for mercy. At last, making a violent plunge from the hands of his enemies, he rushed, all bloody from wounds, into the Nile, in the waters of which he perished; dying, it was remarked by the Arabs, by fire, by water, and the sword.

The King and his fellow-prisoners expected, in deep anxiety, the issue of this event to themselves; and it was with no little surprise and joy that they found the revolted Emirs, after the first expression of passion, disposed to treat them with respect and attention. It has been even said, that they offered to make Louis Sultan of Egypt; which, if it proves nothing else, is sufficient to indicate the feelings which they evinced in his favour. The Sultana, however, who had shown so much wisdom on the death of the former prince, was ultimately elected to the throne; and, after several debates, it was determined to act according to the principal articles of the truce already concluded with the Christians. But a strong obstacle, after every preliminary was settled, still existed to the completion of these arrangements. Louis, on being desired to swear to their fulfilment, refused to take the oath required. The Emirs, on this, again threatened him and his companions with death, or an endless captivity; and all the barons and ecclesiastics implored him to forego his scruples. But nothing could make him act in contradiction to his conscience; and after some time, the Emirs consented to receive his simple promise, observing, that he was the haughtiest Christian that had ever been seen in the East.

The greatest anxiety prevailed in Damietta during the night previous to its being surrendered;

and some of the inhabitants appeared inclined to resist the King's command. But the murmurs of the Moslems, and the persuasions of the deputies sent by Louis, induced them to retire without confusion; and the Queen, together with her attendants, and all the inhabitants, but those who were too infirm to be removed, embarked in the vessels which awaited them. The conquerors then took possession of the city, and celebrated their victory by the most barbarous treatment of the sick and aged Christians who were left behind. In the moment of exultation, they even proposed to break their faith with the King, and put him and all his followers to death. The ships were accordingly ordered back to Pharescour; but one of the Emirs representing to the rest, that they would not only be dishonouring themselves by such a measure, but would be losing the ransoms of the captives, his counsel was, after some little time, obeyed; and the prisoners being conveyed to Damietta, the stipulated sum for their freedom was paid; and the King was permitted to proceed to Ptolemais, which he reached in safety.

A. D. 1251. The misery they had endured in this disastrous campaign had reduced the crusaders to the lowest degree of wretchedness. They were emaciated in body, and broken in spirit. Without money or clothes, they were indebted to the charity of the citizens of Ptolemais for the common necessaries of life. A pestilence which broke out among them soon after, carried numbers to the grave; and others, setting out on their journey home, perished almost immediately after their departure. While things were in this deplorable condition, Louis received letters from his mother, informing him of the misery into which the news of his captivity had thrown all France, of the attempts which the King of England was making on his territories, and of the disturbed state of Europe in general; at the same time imploring him to return without delay.

Louis assembled the chiefs, to consult with them on what measures it would be right to pursue under these circumstances. His brother, and the greatest warriors present, with the exception of the Count of Joppa, and Joinville, strongly advised his return. The King having heard the opinion of each in his turn, dismissed them, and convened the assembly again on the Sunday following. He now declared his determination to continue for some time longer in Syria, but freed all who desired to return from their engagements. His brothers, and several of the barons, accepted this offer, and speedily bade him farewell, leaving him busily engaged in preparations for his better defence against the infidels. Fortunately for him, discord reigned in Egypt; the Sultana had been deposed, and the Sultan of Aleppo and Damascus offered to unite with him against Egypt. Giving, however, almost the first example among the crusaders of a religious regard to truth, in respect to treaties, he refused the proposal till he should know whether the Egyptians would fulfil their part of the arrangement. He accordingly sent an ambassador to Cairo, demanding the freedom of all the Christians still detained in captivity. Two hundred knights recovered their liberty by this resolution of the King; but several hundred still remained to bear the worst species of slavery.

A. D. 1252. The condition of affairs in Eu-

rope was such, that Louis sought in vain for succours, either from his own country, or any other
state. A few warriors joined him at different periods; and Frederic, who died about this time,
left a large sum of money to assist the expedition.
But the Pope retained his enmity against the successors of Frederic, and Christendom thus continued to be agitated in the same manner as formerly. Henry III. took the cross, but never intended to embark in the war. The only appearance of any readiness to assist Louis in his distress, was exhibited by a multitude of the lower
orders in France, who traversed the country under
the guidance of an enthusiast, named, from the
country of his birth, the Master of Hungary; but
their fervour was speedily converted into wild
licentiousness; and these shepherds or pastors, as
they called themselves, were at last pursued,
and punished as banditti. So badly was the
piety of Louis seconded, that even the knights
who were with him set an exorbitant price on
their services, and he was thus obliged to desist
from any measure of difficulty or importance. It
is worthy however of mention, that about this time
he received an embassy from the Old Man of the
Mountain. The Assassins desired to know why he
had not sent their master presents and tokens of
respect, as many of the greatest monarchs had
done before him. Louis deferred answering till
the Grand Masters of the Hospitallers and Templars were present in the council; and such, it appears, was the known power of those dignitaries,
that the deputies now behaved with the most profound respect, and their chief, shortly after, sent

him many splendid presents, together with a shirt and a ring, as tokens of his eternal friendship.[*]

The Sultan of Damascus, who had commenced war against Egypt, now sought by every means to acquire the alliance of Louis; and when the latter had visited Nazareth and other places of celebrity, he invited him to enter Jerusalem. But the barons protested against it, observing, that it would be setting an example for Christian warriors to visit the Holy City as pilgrims, when they should only enter it as conquerors. Shortly after this, the Emirs of Cairo agreed to restore all the prisoners to liberty, as the King had desired; and, as he had further stipulated, the children detained in bondage, and the heads of the faithful who had been slain in captivity. It was proposed, that as soon as the treaty was confirmed, the two armies should unite, and proceed to the attack of the other Mussulman princes. For this purpose, Louis proceeded to Joppa, where the junction was to take place. But after waiting for several months, he heard that the Caliph of Bagdad had procured the reconciliation of the Egyptian Emirs with the Sultan of Damascus, and that the forces of all Syria and Egypt were leagued against him. He had scarcely returned to Ptolemais, when the Sultan of Damascus besieged it with his army, demanding the sum of fifty thousand pieces of gold as its ransom. The want of provisions, however, obliged him for the present to retreat, and Louis was left to take the best measures for his defence against his future attacks.

While he was intent on repairing the fortifica-

---

* Joinville.

tions of the few cities which remained in the hands of the Christians, an unexpected misfortune greatly damped his hopes of success. The walls of Sidon were again nearly in a state of repair, when a tribe of Turcomans surprised the workmen, and, entering the town, put all the inhabitants to the sword. They then retreated to Paneas, whither Louis pursued them, and compelled them to retire with great loss. After this victory he hastened to Sidon, the roads leading to which were strown with the bodies of its unfortunate defenders. As they lay putrifying in the sun, the pious monarch desired the soldiers and some of the ecclesiastics to give them the rites of burial; but all shuddered at the idea of touching them; when Louis, leaping from his horse, took one of them up in his arms, and exclaimed, "Let us give a little dust to these martyrs of Christ!"

In order to complete the repairs necessary at Sidon, the King determined to remain there, and superintend the works himself; but before they were finished, intelligence arrived, which at once put a stop to his proceedings, and changed the whole current of his thoughts. The Legate of the Pope having announced that he had an event of importance to communicate, Louis led him into his chapel, where the prelate revealed to him the melancholy news of his mother's death. The King, as soon as he heard this intelligence, set up a cry of agony; but shortly after bursting into a flood of tears, he flung himself before the altar, and exclaimed, "I thank thee, O God, for having given me so good a mother: it was a manifestation of thy mercy; you now take her back as your own. You know that I loved her above all creatures; but let

thy will be done, O Lord! blessed be thy name
for ever and ever!" He then dismissed the Legate
and the Archbishop of Tyre, who had entered the
chapel with them, and remained alone with his
confessor, reciting the service of the dead, in which
employment he passed two days without seeing
any one but his chaplain.

A. D. 1254. Blanche was the sole support of
the government, and her death rendered it an im-
perative duty on Louis immediately to return
home.. Having consulted with his followers on
the subject, they were unanimous in advising his
departure; and the clergy, who, by the King's order, put up prayers in the church for divine direction, were equally urgent in giving the same counsel. Convinced by these persuasions, as well as
by his own conscience, that it was truly his duty
to bid farewell for the present to the Holy Land,
he embarked at Ptolemais in the month of April,
carrying with him his wife, his three children born
since his arrival in Palestine, and all his followers,
except one hundred knights, whom. he left to assist the faithful. During the voyage they were
several times in danger of shipwreck; but in the
hours of extreme danger, the King encouraged all
on board to trust in Providence, showing such
calmness, resignation, and devotion himself, that
he filled every heart with resolution, and a sense
of. holiness.. The fleet finally anchored. near
the Isles of Hieres, whence Louis pursued his
journey to Paris. Before entering the capital, he
offered up his thanksgiving at the altar of St Denis;
and the day following, a numerous assemblage of
prelates and barons escorted him into the city.

While Louis was employing himself in making

the circuit of his dominions, dispensing charities
and improving the laws, the Christians of Ptolemais were suffering greatly from the dissentions of
the different parties who possessedauthority in the
city. The Hospitallers and Templars, the Genoese and Pisans, waged continual war with
each other respecting their rights; and all ideas of
the public defence being forgotten in their private
disputes, the faithful were exposed as ready victims to the first assault of their enemies. But the
continual changes which took place in the government of Egypt, and the jealousy with which the Saracen princes watched the proceedings at Cairo,
preserved them from any immediate danger; and
the Moguls appearing about this time in Egypt
and Syria, they obtained the protection of that
powerful people. This alliance was speedily brok-
en by an attack of the Christians on some villages
subjected to the Tartars; and in defending themselves against their wrath, they increased it, by killing the son of the chief. The Moguls now began
to ravage the country, and were every day expected at Ptolemais; but an army of Egyptians arrived there before them; and peace being concluded
between the Christians and Mamelukes, the combined forces gained a decisive victory over the
Tartars, and drove them out of Syria.

A. D. 1265. This victory was no sooner obtained than the Egyptians exercised the greatest
cruelty against their allies. The Sultan, who endeavoured to restrain his soldiers from their violation of the truce, lost his life in the attempt, being
assassinated by the famous Bibars Bondocdar, who
was immediately proclaimed his successor. It was
not long before the worst fears of the Christians

were realized.   Collecting a vast army, Bibars entered Palestine, and proceeded to Nazareth. Terrified at his menaces, the faithful desired to make peace ; but he despised their overtures, set fire to the principal church, and, pursuing his desolating course across the country, arranged his forces round the walls of Ptolemais. Failing, however, to surprise that city as he had expected, he successively laid siege to, and took Cæsarea and Arsouff; after which he returned to his capital, and had the satisfaction to receive ambassadors from France, Spain, and other countries, soliciting a peace for the Christians which he proudly refused to grant.

A. D. 1267.   Having recruited his forces, the Sultan resumed the war, and ravaged the country about Tyre, Tripoli, and Ptolemais, and then laid siege to the fortress of Sepher, situated about fifteen leagues from Ptolemais, and belonging to the Templars. After an obstinate contest, he succeeded in reducing it. The garrison were assured of their lives and liberty if they surrendered; but the Moslem broke his promise the moment they were in his power; and those who would not renounce their religion, were either killed or loaded with chains. The King of Armenia next felt the power of this formidable chief ; and to secure success, he imposed a tithe upon his subjects to furnish the expenses of the war. Ptolemais again saw him encamped under its walls ; but he suddenly removed his forces to Joppa, which he took, as also the fortress of Carac and other places. Shortly after this, he conquered Antioch, and resigned it to be pillaged by his soldiers ; a full account of which event, with all the barbarities perpetrated on the occasion, he vauntingly sent to the unfortunate prince of that city.

The troubles which had agitated Europe for so long a period, and kept not only the princes but the Pope from taking any measures in favour of Syria, were for a short time diminished by the accession of Charles of Anjou to the kingdom of Naples and Sicily. As the Pope had thus effected one of his favourite projects, he was now at liberty to consider the condition of his afflicted children in the East, and he began to employ the usual methods for arousing the devotion of the faithful. The Latin empire of Constantinople no longer existed. Baldwin was a wanderer in Europe, and Michael Palæologus was seated securely on his throne. The new Emperor, on taking possession of Baldwin's inheritance, had written to the Pope to deprecate his anger, and the latter now urged him to fulfil his assurances of obedience. Little success, however, attended the Pontiff's efforts, and there were still signs of trouble in Naples and Sicily, from Charles's rival Conradin.

A. D. 1268. But while the whole of Europe was thus engaged on objects of temporal interests, and its princes were preparing themselves for prosecuting their private views, one monarch yet remained faithful to what was esteemed the duty of a Christian King. Louis had never laid aside the sign of the cross, and the threats of Bibars reawakened all his zeal for the Holy Land. Keeping his intentions unknown to any one but the Pope, he summoned a parliament which met in the hall of the Louvre, and as soon as the members were assembled, he entered, bearing the crown of thorns supposed to have been worn by our Saviour. The declaration of his intention produced great sorrow, both in the council and throughout the nation; but he was equally resolved as on the former occasion; and his example drew many of the most distinguished men of the court to engage in the undertaking. He next employed himself in levying the money necessary for the expedition, and large sums were collected by way of imposts. The Pope aided him in this affair with a powerful hand; and obliged the clergy, notwithstanding their clamours, to pay a tithe of their income for four years.

In England the intelligence of the new crusade produced the most active excitement; and Prince Edward, eldest son of Henry III., together with a large body of English and Scottish knights, received the cross. The Kings of Portugal and Arragon also enrolled themselves in the number of the crusaders, and several of the bravest chevaliers of Spain. The King of Naples and Sicily was, in the meantime, making extensive preparations for the expedition; but he was suddenly interrupted in his design by the approach of Conradin, with a large army. Charles, however, utterly defeated his rival, and having taken him prisoner, put him to death, thereby incurring the just reproaches of all Europe.

A. D. 1270. As the time fixed for his departure arrived, Louis doubled his zeal and activity in examining the affairs of the kingdom, and in framing such laws as might secure its tranquillity, and the proper administration of justice. His brother, the Count of Poictiers, employed himself in a similar manner, and guarded the liberties of his subjects with a wisdom and affection which would do credit to the most enlightened monarch... To

remove the doubts of the noblemen who intended
to accompany him, as to their means of paying the
expenses of the expedition, the King promised
them a sum proportioned to their wants and station; and Prince Edward, not being able to raise
the money he required, received a grant from Louis
of seventy thousand livres. These preliminaries
having been settled, Louis gave himself up to devotion; and after the solemn services of religion,
he left his palace with naked feet, and clad as a
simple pilgrim. In the wood of Vincennes he
took an affectionate leave of his queen, and then
proceeded to Aigues-Mortes, where he intended to
embark; his three sons, and his daughter the Queen
of Navarre, having accompanied him. Here he was
obliged to wait some days, before the Genoese fleet
and the rest of the crusaders arrived at the place
of rendezvous; but on the 4th of July the armament set sail; and it was now for the first time made
generally known, that the expedition was destined
for the African kingdom of Tunis, instead of the
Holy Land. The King of Sicily is generally supposed to have originally employed his efforts to
give this direction to the crusade, as its success
would free him from a near and dangerous enemy;
but Louis himself was enthusiastic in his hopes of
converting the sovereign of Tunis to Christianity;
and it is not unlikely that the brothers were equally
determined by these strong and opposite motives.

The approach of the fleet filled the Africans
with despair; and all who were in the open country, and even the sailors from the ships in the port,
fled into Tunis. The next day the army disembarked, in the face of a numerous force drawn out
to oppose it, but which retreated without waiting

an attack. Formal possession was then taken of the country; and the towers which defended the city, and stood on the site of ancient Carthage, fell into the hands of the invaders. The King of Tunis sent messengers to reproach Louis with his conduct in invading his territory, and threatened to return immediately at the head of an hundred thousand men. The situation of the army was, in fact, notwithstanding its superior valour, exposed to great danger from the numbers which the enemy could bring into the field, and from the union which he had made with the Sultan Bibars. But it was not evils of this kind which were destined to defeat the designs of Louis. The troops had not been long encamped before the sickly nature of the climate began to be heavily felt. Fatigue and famine added to the deadly influence of the atmosphere, and a pestilence shortly raged throughout the army. So many died every day, that it was impossible to bury them before the bodies putrified. The plague thus supplied its own nourishment, and many of the knights and principal men of the expedition were hourly sinking under the disease. The Duke of Nevers, especially beloved by Louis, from his having been born to him at Damietta at the time he was taken prisoner, fell a sacrifice to the contagion just as it seized upon the King himself. The Legate died at the same period, and the army exhibited a miserable spectacle of disease and want.

But all other feelings of anxiety were destroyed, as every day announced the increasing malady of Louis. The fever, indeed, was rapidly consuming him; and all hope of his recovery was soon lost. The excellent monarch, knowing that his end approached, occupied himself by turns with giving his last orders respecting his kingdom, and in the calm and solemn exercise of devotion. At length he desired the presence of his son Philip, whom he addressed in the most pathetic manner respecting the duties which, on ascending the throne, he would owe to his subjects; and on all the virtues and holy dispositions which he ought to possess, both as a man and a Christian. The young prince heard the last instruction of his father with deep emotion; and Louis having finished addressing him, took farewell of his daughter, with similar affection and anxiety for her future happiness. The ambassadors of the Greek Emperor being admitted, he exhibited a great desire that the church at Constantinople might be united with that of Rome. After this interview, he saw no one but his confessor. As death drew nearer, the fervour of his devotion increased; and on August 25th, at three in the afternoon, he expired.

Amid the profound grief and consternation which prevailed through the camp, the instant it was known that the King was dead, Charles of Anjou disembarked with all the pomp of martial parade. But the signals which announced his landing were unanswered; and, rushing to the tent of his father, he found him stretched on a bed of ashes. After the first emotion of sorrow was over, Philip sent messengers to France to confirm his father's ministers in office, and to express his desire of, in all things, following his example. The King of Sicily then assumed the command of the forces, but the African monarch sued for peace; and it was granted him, on the condition of his paying two hundred and ten thousand ounces of gold, giving the Christians a track of ground for forming a settlement, and releasing all the prisoners taken in battle. He also agreed to pay the King of Sicily the arrears of tribute formerly due to him, and to double the sum for the future. The Sultan of Cairo expressed his indignation at this compromise of the Moslem cause. The same sentiments were expressed on the side of the Christians; and Edward, who reached Africa at this juncture, refused to bear any part in the council of the chiefs. It was at last decided by the crusaders, that they would winter in Sicily, and then proceed to Palestine; but this resolution was altered into one which fixed the renewal of the expedition for that time four years; and the army then re-embarked for Europe. The King of Navarre and his wife died on their journey; the young Queen of France shared the same fate; and Philip entered his dominions, accompanied by the dead bodies of his father, his brother, and his wife. The Count of Poictiers and his wife were shortly added to the number of the royal family who had died on the journey; and more noblemen and knights than we can name, expired in the same manner, from the effects of the African pestilence.

A. D. 1271. The affliction caused by the death of Louis was not confined to France or Europe. With him, the Christians of Palestine saw the last of that line of heroes who seemed to have been raised up for the defence of the Holy Land; and when he expired, the antient flame of devotion, which had been long flickering amid the ruined altar of Jerusalem, vanished into darkness. Of all the princes who had vowed to renew the crusade, Edward of England alone kept his promise; but the smallness of the force he had with him prevented his doing any service. Mustering, however, about seven thousand men, the prince, in conjunction with the Hospitallers and Templars, marched into Phœnicia, and thence to Nazareth, which they entered, and barbarously massacred the unfortunate Moslem inhabitants, thus retaliating the burning of the church by Bibars. After gaining this useless victory, Edward returned to Ptolemais, where he entered into a communication with the Emir of Joppa. But for some cause, the nature of which does not seem vary clearly ascertained, he incurred the enmity of one of the Assassins; and the dagger of the murderer had reached his heart, when his agility proved an overmatch for that of the assailant. It was on this occasion, as it is said, that his consort sucked the poison from his wound, and gained, by her affection, so fair a name in the annals of female devotion. Another version, however, is given of this story; and the prince is reported to have been cured by the skill of a physician. But whatever were the means by which he was healed, Edward thought it high time to depart; and he left Syria, without having effected any thing which deserves recording.

A. D. 1274. A gleam of light broke upon the Holy Land, on the election of Thibault, who had long dwelt in Syria, to the Pontificate. On ascending the chair of Saint Peter, he persuaded the King of France to send some troops and money in aid of the faithful; and the maritime cities of Italy rendered a similar assistance. But the measure most favourable to the cause, was his summoning a second council at Lyons, which was held with great solemnity, and was composed of more than a thousand bishops and archbishops; the ambassadors of the Emperors of Germany and Constantinople; of the Kings of France and Cyprus; of envoys from the chief of the Moguls, and the principal princes and barons of Europe. A crusade was determined upon in this council, and laws were passed for carrying it into execution; but its decrees were forgotten almost as soon as the meeting broke up.

Bibars, in the mean time, continued to pursue his conquests with restless and untiring ambition, and every day threatened to besiege Ptolemais, the first place of importance which the Christians now possessed. While he was meditating this measure, and preparing to renew an attack on Cyprus, which had hitherto failed, he was suddenly taken ill, and his death relieved the Christians from their present terror. Bibars seems to have been a man of extraordinary perseverance, courage, resolution and ferocity—qualities which, in a warrior, might pass for genius, or give to his actions the appearance of proceeding from a powerful intellect. But there is a decision and promptness of action which result from mere animal vigour, despising rest and impatient of delay, altogether different from the firmness and noble resolution in which the mind rules and informs. Bibars appears, therefore, to have been held up as a wonder with little reason, and only deserves one of the lowest places in the rolls of fame.

The late Sultan was succeeded by Kelaoun, a man equally determined in hostility to the Christians. His reign commenced by a splendid triumph over the Tartars, who, in conjunction with the Armenians and Georgians, had invaded his territories.. The Christians, who dreaded that this victory would increase his ferocity, as well as power, immediately desired to conclude a peace. Their appeal succeeded, and he turned his arms against the King of Armenia, whom he completely. humbled to his power. Employing also a policy of the most refined kind, he formed a connection with some of the European courts, among which was that of Spain, where he had emissaries who constantly exerted themselves to prevent any measures leading to a crusade. It is worthy of remark, that in the state of depression in which Palestine now lay, there were for some time three pretenders to the throne of Jerusalem, namely, the King of Cyprus, the King of Sicily, and Mary of Antioch, daughter of Isabella.

After the truce existing between the Sultan and the Christians had been repeatedly broken, renewed, and again broken, Kelaoun at length determined to make the grand attempt on Ptolemais. Before doing this, however, he had to render himself master of Tripoli, in the siege of which he was aided by the dissensions of the inhabitants, and their melancholy at the death of their Prince Bohemond, which had just occurred. The garrison held out for thirty-five days, and then surrendered. The carnage which followed was unrestrained, and seven thousand Christians were the victims of Moslem ferocity.

Nothing now remained to stop the Sultan's proceeding at once to Ptolemais. Thither, therefore, he led his army, but a truce was again signed, and once more stopped the progress of the siege. The delay, however, was almost momentary, and the legate of the Pope is accused of having been

the first to renew the danger by his proud refusal to explain some trifling cause of dispute.
Another account ascribes the breach of the treaty
to the murder of a Musulman by a citizen, who
was led by jealousy to the act. However this
may be, the Sultan prepared for the attack, and
the Christians sent letters to the Pope to implore
immediate aid. Far different were the succours
sent to such as would have been of any assistance
to the faithful in their present situation. Sixteen
hundred undisciplined men, only served to increase the confusion which reigned in the city;
and when they commenced their excursions into
the neighbouring territory, the wanton barbarities
committed inflamed Kelaoun with a furious desire
of revenge. The inhabitants, finding how little
aid they were to expect from the West, desired
again to ward off the expected blow by a truce.
They, therefore, sent deputies to the Sultan, offering to punish all who had been guilty of the
violences complained of. But Kelaoun's resolution was taken; the deputies returned without
having been able to bend him at all from his purpose; and at the advice of the Patriarch, preparations for the defence of the city were commenced
without delay. Fortunately the King of Cyprus
arrived at this juncture with five hundred chevaliers; and the garrison thus reinforced, amounted to nine hundred horse and eighteen thousand
foot. This force, divided into four parts, was put
under the command of the best warriors present;
and the government of the city was deputed to a
council of eight chiefs. Kelaoun died before he
could begin his favourite enterprise; but with his
last words he charged his son and successor, Chalil,

to pursue the design; and the young Sultan attended religiously to his injunctions. The force which Chalil drew out on the plains before Ptolemais, formed a line of some leagues, and extended from the sea to the mountains. More than three hundred machines for carrying on the assault were placed against the walls; and even the bravest warriors, among whom was the Grand Master of the Templars, despaired of being able to resist such an armament. That experienced chief proceeded, therefore, by the consent of his brethren, to the camp of the Sultan, and again offered, after exaggerating his means of defence, to conclude a truce. Chalil agreed to an arrangement, and the Grand Master returned, greatly comforted, to the city; but he had scarcely communicated the result of his mission to the chiefs, when the populace broke out into a violent tumult, and declared their determination to have war. The assault was almost immediately commenced, and all day and night the ramparts were assailed by the tremendous engines of the Moslems. For a few days the besieged repulsed their enemies with the most spirited bravery; they made several successful sallies, and showered their darts from the walls with such skill, that files of the enemy fell beneath them. But quarrels began to rise among the chiefs, and large numbers of the garrison every day deserted from their standards. At length, the Sultan determined on a general assault, and he advanced towards the walls with all his forces and three hundred camels, on each of which was placed the huge Syrian tambour. The roar of this wild music, the appearance of the army, said to have amounted to four hundred thou-

and men, most of them clad in splendid armour
that glittered in the rays of the sun, and the destructive machines ready prepared to batter the
walls—this magnificent but terrible spectacle filled
the Christians with terror. The assault, mainly
directed against the tower and gate of St Anthony,
was continued the whole day. As the darkness
fell, the enemy withdrew; and taking advantage
of the supension of the battle, the King of Cyprus, who commanded on that station, withdrew
from the town, and, getting on board a vessel, set
sail with all his followers.

When the Saracens renewed the assault the
next day, they found the ramparts, which had
been defended by the King of Cyprus, unmanned.
Taking advantage of this circumstance, they employed the whole strength of their enormous engines unopposed. At last, the ramparts crumbled beneath their incessant blows. A wide opening appeared in the walls; the besiegers rushed
thousands after thousands to the breach; and the
Christians received them on the points of their
swords and lances. For an instant the assailants
were kept at bay; but their numbers increasing,
they pressed forward in a huge mass, drove the little army of the faithful from their post, and passed
the barrier. At this moment of peril and dismay,
the Hospitallers and Templars alone preserved their
courage unabated. The Marechal of the former
exerting himself with indescribable energy, ran
through the streets rallying the fugitive Christians;
and then turning upon the enemy, drove them before them with irresistible fury. Thus freed from
immediate ruin, the citizens passed the night in
repairing the breach, and making other prepara-

tions for the following day. As soon as the morning dawned, the people were assembled in the palace of the Hospitallers, and the Patriarch of Jerusalem addressed them in terms calculated to inspire them with all the resolution which can be derived from despair. There now remained of the garrison only seven thousand men. No succours were any longer to be expected from the West; and the vessels they possessed were too few to convey them from the city. Thus left to brave the peril which menaced them or perish, numbers of the citizens, who had hitherto remained unarmed, prepared for the battle, and all present took an oath to die rather than desert their brethren. While a part stayed behind to fortify the streets by raising barriers at the doors of the houses, and heaping together large piles of stones, the rest awaited the approach of the enemy on the walls. The attack was made in the same quarter as the preceding day, and after a desperate conflict, a breach was again made. In the midst of the clamours which rose at the sight of the falling barriers, the Patriarch was heard exclaiming, " O God, surround us with a rampart man cannot destroy! Cover us with the shield of thy power!" The Saracens rushed in multitudes through the breach; the citizens, who had supported their entrance in hopeless anxiety, flew to oppose them; a bloody conflict raged through the streets; and the Christians, by prodigies of valour, again drove back the enemy.

May 18th, 1291. At length arrived the day which was to decide the fate of Ptolemais. The Moslems had more than once shrunk in terror from the might and despair of their approach, and ascribed the success of their resistance to supernatural aid. It was asserted, that, in each visible Christian there were in reality two warriors, and that when one of the Franks fell, his place was immediately supplied by another who came out of his mouth. While these superstitions damped the courage of his soldiers, the Sultan, himself was rendered doubtful, by the perseverance of the Christians, as to the final success of the siege; and it is reported, that he was only induced to continue it at the instance of the renegade Franks with whom his army abounded. On the morning of the day above mentioned, the assault was more general and destructive than any before made; but it was met with greater valour on the part of the besieged. Seven infidels fell before one Christian; and, had the two forces been in any way proportioned to each other, the astonishing bravery of the faithful must have prevailed. But the hordes of Mussulmans, which covered the plains from the sea to the mountains of Carmel and Caroube, seemed undiminished; and no efforts of the most desperate courage could bear up against the continued renewal of their attack. Seeing no hope of supporting the direct charge of the enemy, the Templars suddenly changed their position, and, with the Grand Master at their head, rode impetuously into the Saracen camp. They were met by thousands of foes. The Grand Master fell, pierced with an arrow, in the midst of his brave knights; the Grand Master of the Hospitallers was also dangerously wounded; and those, who survived, were obliged to retreat hastily into the city, deploring the loss of their bravest companions. No better success attended the warriors employed in defending the ramparts. Reduced to less than a thousand, they were at length driven from the gate and tower of St Anthony, and the infidels again rushed into the town, filling the streets with their cries of victory. But the valour of the true Christians was still undiminished. The enemy advanced not a step without being assailed by showers of stones from the houses, or by the weapons of those who determined not to outlive the calamity. William of Clermont is named as among the foremost of the few heroic men who fought to the last for the cause of Palestine. But neither his devotion, nor the desperation of the citizens, availed any longer. The streets, filled with multitudes of women and children, who mingled their shrieks with the shouts of the combatants, presented a frightful spectacle of confusion and slaughter; and, to render this awful hour still more dismal, a terrible storm arose, which covered the heavens with so dense a darkness, that the standards of neither party could be discerned; while the wind and thunder, and swelling of the sea, swallowed up every sound in the threatening roar of the elements.

The infidels were at last left unopposed, and the slaughter of the inhabitants was carried on without intermission. Many fled to the shore, in order to escape on board the vessels in the harbour; but the storm rendered this, for some time, impossible. When the ships came within reach of the fugitives, those who possessed any wealth gave large sums to be taken on board; and many women of rank offered their jewels, and promised to marry any of the mariners who would assist them to escape. The venerable Patriarch of Jerusalem, who had with difficulty been persuaded to leave

the shore, received such numbers of the wretched
citizens into his ship, that, before it cleared the
port, it sunk, and all perished.   Those in the city
who had eluded the swords of the enemy, were still
endeavouring to defend themselves in the palace of
the Templars, their last retreat.   They offered to
capitulate, and the Sultan agreed to spare their
lives ; but the soldiers whom he sent to take possession of the fortress, violated the women who had
sought refuge there.   The knights instantly resumed their arms, and put the ravishers to death.
The palace was then again attacked; but the
Christian warriors continued their defence, till the
principal tower of the fortress fell, and buried both
them, and all whom they defended, under its walls.

Thus ended this memorable siege.   In a few
days, Ptolemais was in ruins, and retained no appearance of the wealth and magnificence for which
it had been so long famous.   Tyre, Sidon, and the
other Christian cities on the coast, immediately
opened their gates to the Moslem ; and the kingdom of Jerusalem was no more !

In looking back on the sketch which has been
given of these wars, it is difficult to determine
which merits our principal attention ;—the causes
of their origin ; the means by which they were
supported ; or their effects on the progress of society.   The limits of this work prohibit the author from entering into the discussion of these subjects, or tracing the causes which led to the extinction of that grand, but erring spirit of enthu-

siasm, to which chivalry and the crusades owed their existence. At some future period, he may venture to offer his ideas upon the subject more at length. No period of history better deserves the attention of either the moralist or the scholar, than the middle ages; and in the events and institutions which have been described, we possess the truest indexes to their principal phenomena.

THE END.

PRINTD BY J. HUTCHISON,
FOR THE HEIRS OF D. WILLISON.

CPSIA information can be obtained
at www.ICGtesting.com
Printed in the USA
LVHW061841181218
600925LV00006BA/38/P